LIVING FOR THE
REVOLUTION

LIVING FOR THE
REVOLUTION

Black Feminist Organizations,

★ ★ ★ ★ ★ **1968–1980** ★ ★ ★ ★ ★

KIMBERLY SPRINGER

Duke University Press ★ *Durham and London* ★ 2005

© 2005 Duke University Press
All rights reserved
Printed in the Unites States
of America on acid-free paper ∞
Designed by Amy Ruth Buchanan
Typeset in Scala by Tseng
Information Systems, Inc.
Library of Congress Cataloging-in-
Publication Data appear on the
last printed page of this book.

An earlier version of chapter 2,
"The Interstitial Politics of Black
Feminist Organizations," was
published in Meridians: Feminism,
Race, Transnationalism (Vol. 1:
No. 1) and is copyrighted by and
published with permission from
Wesleyan University Press.

CONTENTS

ORGANIZATIONAL ABBREVIATIONS

BWA	Black Women's Alliance
BWLC	Black Women's Liberation Committee
BWOA	Black Women Organized for Action
Combahee	Combahee River Collective
CORE	Congress on Racial Equality
NAACP	National Association for the Advancement of Colored People
NABF	National Alliance of Black Feminists
NBFO	National Black Feminist Organization
NOW	National Organization for Women
SCLC	Southern Christian Leadership Conference
SNCC	Student Nonviolent Coordinating Committee
TWWA	Third World Women's Alliance

ACKNOWLEDGMENTS

Where to begin my heartfelt thanks for all the sustenance that went into completing *Living the Revolution*? Much love and appreciation to my parents, Sandra J. Springer and Fitzpatrick Springer, for all the encouragement, wisdom, hard lessons, jokes, and pep talks. Likewise, the extended Springer family always provided several laughs and hugs for this bookish kid. Adopted families the Mutongi-DeGooyers and the Kent-Weavers helped me persevere with love.

Undoubtedly, this book would not have come together without the sistah-friends, long time and new, who've had faith in me and this project: Meredith Raimondo, Vanessa Jackson, Angela Cotten, Kenda Mutongi, Cheryl Hicks, Miriam Petty, Andrea Heiss, Sarita See, Bill St. Amant, Jennifer Ruth, Liz Ceppi, Amy Greenstadt, Wendy Kaplan, Kimberly Wallace-Sanders, Calinda Lee, Michelle Wilkerson, Shola Kukoyi, Dennise Kowalczyk, Robyn Spencer, Dr. Goddess / Kimberly Ellis, Gwendolyn Pough, and the Belvedere Lounge Crew. Also, thanks to Rob Kahn, Matthew Papa, Ken Michaels, and Andrew Weaver for laughter in the time of politics and luxury accommodation for all the trips to the archives this project entailed.

Invaluable advice on this manuscript and role-modeling generosity of scholarship and spirit came from Patricia Schecter, Robin D. G. Kelley, anonymous reviewers for Duke University Press and *Meridians*, and *the best* dissertation committee—Beverly Guy-Sheftall, Regina Werum, and Mary Odem. I should be so lucky to pass along the guidance and cheer you've all bestowed upon me! Additionally, Regina Kunzel, John Howard, Mark Turner, and Benita Roth were all the professional and fun, dare I say, bomb-diggity that kept me going.

Sincerest thanks to the institutions and people that provided financial support and resources, without which this project might never have finally come to publication: the Woodrow Wilson National Fellowship Foundation Dissertation Grant in Women's Studies, the Williams College Mellon Fellowship in Women's Studies and African American Studies (especially Jana Sawicki, Laurie Heatherington, and Craig Wilder), the American Association for University Women's American Fellowship, and the 2002 Engendering Africana Studies Summer Institute sponsored by the Africana Studies and Research Center at Cornell University and the Ford Foundation, the Lesbian Herstory Archive, the Schlesinger Library, Northwestern University Special Collections, the University of Illinois at Chicago Midwest Women's Historical Collections, and the Chicago Historical Society.

Finally, my sincerest gratitude to the black feminist activists who agreed to be interviewed, sharing their time, memories, and energy. In particular, thank you to Brenda Eichelberger, Barbara Smith, Aileen Hernandez, and Francis Beal for the physical and mental archives you kept in the hopes that someday someone would come along and tell the story of your pioneering efforts for black feminist activism.

1 ☆ THE SOUL OF WOMEN'S LIB

We must begin to understand that a revolution entails not only the willingness to lay our lives on the firing line and get killed. In some ways, this is an easy commitment to make. To die for the revolution is a one-shot deal; to live for the revolution means taking on the more difficult commitment of changing our day-to-day life patterns.
—Francis Beal, "Double Jeopardy: To Be Black and Female," 1970

The sociopolitical conditions and social movements of the late 1960s gave rise to an unprecedented growth in black feminist consciousness. That black feminist consciousness is reflected in contemporary feminist theorizing. Anthologies, such as *The Black Woman* and *Home Girls: A Black Feminist Anthology*, gave voice to black feminists' alienation from the sexism, racism, and classism found in the civil rights movement, the women's movement, social policy, and popular culture.[1] Patricia Hill Collins's influential book *Black Feminist Thought* charts the historical, cultural, political, and societal factors shaping black feminist thought and theory since the first Africans arrived on the continent. However, we know little about the formal organizations that helped shape black feminist consciousness.[2] Few know that any formal black feminist organizations existed.

Black feminists' voices and visions fell between the cracks of the civil rights and women's movements, so they created formal organizations to speak on behalf of black women with an explicitly feminist consciousness. Within five organizations I studied—the Third World Women's Alliance (1968–1979), the National Black Feminist Organization (1973–1975), the National Alliance of Black Feminists (1976–1980), the Combahee River Collective (1975–1980), and Black Women Organized for Action (1973–

1980)—several thousand black women activists explicitly claimed feminism and defined a collective identity based on their race, gender, class, and sexual orientation claims. As one activist I interviewed remarked, black feminists conducted their "politics in the cracks."[3]

Politics in the cracks, or, hereafter, *interstitial politics*, conveys two meanings for black feminists and their organizations. First, Third World Women's Alliance (TWWA) member Linda Burnham notes, black feminists, not unlike activists in other social movements, fit their activism into their daily life schedules whenever possible, serving as full-time, unpaid staff for their organizations. Second, black feminists developed a collective identity and basis for organizing that reflected the intersecting nature of black womanhood. I maintain that black feminists are, historically, the first activists in the United States to theorize and act upon the intersections of race, gender, and class.

Just as black feminists crafted their collective identity and organizations from between the cracks of the civil rights and women's movements, studying these vital organizations has fallen between the cracks of these two movements in the scholarly literature. *Living for the Revolution* contributes a crucial, but ignored chapter to the historiography of the civil rights and women's movements. Black feminist organizations, with their roots firmly entrenched in the civil rights movement, provide a crucial link to the burgeoning contemporary women's movement. Black women, as leaders in civil rights movement organizations such as the Southern Christian Leadership Conference (SCLC), the Congress on Racial Equality (CORE), the National Association for the Advancement of Colored People (NAACP), and the Student Nonviolent Coordinating Committee (SNCC) played a pivotal role in demonstrating the leadership capabilities of black women, as well as the burden of oppression under which they functioned.

Research in the area of black women civil rights leaders flourished in the late 1980s and 1990s, laying the foundation for examining the continuity of black women's activism through slavery, suffrage, the black women's club movement for racial uplift, and labor movements.[4] African American history, in the process of unearthing a wealth of information about the leadership role of black women in the civil rights movement, makes little notice of how this leadership influenced black feminist activism in the 1970s, 1980s, and 1990s. Black feminists learned valuable skills and ideological beliefs from the civil rights movement and integrated these resources into their women's movement activism. They based their analyses and actions on the work of their activist foremothers, but they also took

that work a step further by adamantly laying claim to gender as a salient point of black women's identity.

Similar to the gaps in civil rights movement historiography, women's movement histories lack in-depth descriptions and analyses of black feminist organizations that contributed to the expansion of the movement's goals and objectives. Previous studies of the women's movement document black women civil rights leaders who served as role models for white feminist activists, but they neglect to mention how the same black women leaders also mentored black feminist activists, in practical and ideological ways.[5] In addition, black feminist activists, through their theorizing and organizations, broadened the scope of the women's movement by challenging Eurocentric and classist interpretations of women's issues. The literature on the women's movement and black feminist activism sometimes cursorily acknowledges the existence of select black feminist organizations—most often, the Combahee River Collective and the National Black Feminist Organization—but mainly as a reaction to racism in the women's movement.[6]

The elision of black feminist organizations from women's movement histories perpetuates what Chela Sandoval calls a "hegemonic feminism." This type of feminism obscures, Becky Thompson notes, "a class and race analysis, generally sees equality with men as the goal of feminism, and has an individual rights-based rather than justice-based vision for social change."[7] Thompson rightly asserts that since more histories of the contemporary women's movement are emerging at this point in time, it behooves scholars to "interrupt normative accounts before they begin to repeat themselves, each time sounding more like 'the truth' simply because of the repetition of the retelling."[8] *Living for the Revolution* is but one intervention in the normative account of hegemonic feminism, an attempt to reshape the retelling.

However, just as Thompson notes the generation of women's movement history, recent scholarship in black women's studies and sociology is turning its attention to black feminist organizations as a *parallel* development to the predominately white women's movement, rather than merely a reaction to racism.[9] Wini Breines takes issue with this model, asserting that the political articulation of black feminism came more than five years after the development of the white women's liberation movement.[10] I still maintain that there was parallel development and believe that Breines's assertions of a nonsynchronous model of movement development depend on conflation of the development of ideology, organizations, and movements.

If we separate these three distinct aspects, we could more confidently assert that black feminist *organizations* developed later than white feminist organizations, but black and white feminist ideologies developed on parallel tracks. By recasting black feminist organizing in this light, we gain a sharper picture of the development of black feminist theorizing on the matrix of domination,[11] as well as a better understanding of how black feminists articulated their agenda in concrete action.

This book corrects the omission of black feminism's long, mostly unrecognized history in the United States, particularly in women's and African American historical narratives, by documenting and analyzing the emergence, activities, and decline of black feminist organizations from 1968 to 1980. Specifically, I ask when, why, and how black women developed a collective identity as feminists, and how this identity influenced the structure of the Third World Women's Alliance, the National Black Feminist Organization, the Combahee River Collective, the National Alliance of Black Feminists, and Black Women Organized for Action.

Black feminists, through these organizations, enacted interstitial politics focused on articulating their race, gender, and class identities as interconnected. Emerging from the civil rights movement cycle of protest, but also at the same time as the predominately white women's movement, black feminists attempted to simultaneously define a collective identity and establish organizations that encompassed their rights as both blacks *and* women. In the process of this organizational and identity formation, black feminists found, sometimes in difficult ways, that black women held a plurality of visions for social change because of their differences from one another in sexual orientation, class, color, and educational achievement.

Given this heterogeneity among black women, it is important to draw distinctions between the black feminist *movement*, black feminist *organizations*, and black feminist *activists*. Meyer outlines four characteristics of social movements: (1) they make demands of the state or another authority; (2) they "challenge cultural codes and transform the lives of their participants"; (3) they use means in addition to, and other than, those offered by the political culture; and (4) they are part of a diverse field of organizations all pursuing the same goals.[12] The black feminist movement encompasses the political and cultural realms of black feminists' activism including organizations, prose, essays, fiction, scholarly studies, films, visual arts, and dance that are the voice of black feminism in the United States. The organizations examined here were but a small part of a black feminist movement that continues to this day.

Reactions to black women writers are illustrative of the hostile environment in which the black feminist movement *reemerged* in the late 1960s and early 1970s. For example, texts such as Toni Cade Bambara's *The Black Woman: An Anthology* (1970), Michele Wallace's *Black Macho and the Myth of the Superwoman* (1979), and Ntozake Shange's "For Colored Girls Who Have Considered Suicide / When the Rainbow is Enuf" (1976) provided black women with a very public, if controversial, forum to air grievances against sexism and racism. These texts were, and still are, powerful because they *publicly* listed the ways misogyny functioned in black communities, violating the edict against airing the black community's dirty laundry in the predominately white public arena. As a result, the mainstream and black press vilified black women writers, in particular, Wallace and Shange. However, these women are considered pioneers of the contemporary black feminist movement for daring to assert, if not ideologically feminist consciousness, a gender consciousness integral to the struggle for black liberation in the 1970s.

In the 1970s and 1980s, debates around these texts, and the rising number of black women fiction writers, such as Toni Morrison and Alice Walker, were often heated among black men and women. Black periodicals brought this debate to the public in popular magazines such as *Ebony* ("The War between the Sexes: Is It Manufactured or Real?") and *Encore* ("Women's Lib Has No Soul"). At least eight issues of the *Black Scholar*, including the 1973 "Black Women's Liberation" issue and the 1979 issue "The Black Sexism Debate," wrestled with two recurring issues about black women and feminism: the feminist movement as potentially divisive to the civil rights movement and the implication that gender oppression was a diversion from the primary goal of black liberation.

Black feminist organizations emerged in response to many of these debates. They are the structured, formal units that constitute the black feminist movement. These organizations held as their objective the eradication of racial and gender discrimination. However, as this book shows, black feminist organizations varied in their objectives. Some of them expanded their agendas to include the eradication of class and sexual orientation discrimination.[13]

Lastly, black feminist activists are those political actors who are the backbone of black feminist organizations and the movement. In the 1970s, these activists arrived at a particular black feminist collective identity at a specific point in time as the result of sociopolitical and personal experiences. Black feminist activists were the most important component of the

black feminist movement and its organizations because they used their political agency and emerging personal transformation in service to the larger cause of the movement.

This book uses a telescoping lens to convey the richness of a movement, interrogating its historical roots to arrive at the big picture of contemporary black feminist activism. The organizations analyzed here, as well as the activists I interviewed, are the driving force behind a movement that in some ways has yet to fully get off the ground, depending on how one measures a successful movement outcome. However, this book serves as but a piece of the effort to build a black feminist movement in the United States that pushes past its own boundaries of socially constructed identity.

Memory and Methods

From my location as a scholar and a next-generation black feminist, my research methodology for this study is influenced by feminist, sociological, and historical methodologies. Semistructured, oral history interviews, and organizational archival records constitute the crux of this particular interpretation of black feminist organizational history with attention to black feminist standpoint theory as elucidated by Patricia Hills Collins, but as critiqued by feminists cautioning against essentializing the experience of black women. Listening to black women's voices, as they experienced the social and political times, is integral to constructing an interpretation few have written about from a firsthand perspective. These voices can lead us to important information about race, class, gender, and sexuality theories forged in the fires of black women's oppression but survived through a legacy of activism. Yet, it became increasingly clear that neither black women as a group nor black feminism are monolithic. Hence, standpoint theory is tempered with vigilance for the pitfalls of claiming one, unified voice and asserting an authoritative position on the events I relate here based on the women I interviewed. Thus, while I valued each respondent's recollections, differing ideas about what constitutes black feminism emerged. I should also note that other perspectives, by other scholars and black feminist activists of the time who I did not interview, could create different interpretations of this period of black feminist organizing.

While I do believe in the feminist project of centering women's voices in my inquiry, I also hope to have maintained respectful critical distance from the oral histories conducted for this study. With such distance, issues of personal and collective memory were the most challenging aspect to con-

structing a narrative of 1970s black feminist organizations. Specifically, I encountered the challenge of how to construct an accurate interpretation based on oral history interviews that valued my respondents' memories, but sought a representative middle ground when recollections conflicted with other respondents' memories or with the archival record.

In *Autobiography as Activism*, Margo Perkins expresses the belief that the memoirs of Assata Shakur, Angela Davis, and Elaine Brown act as teleological narratives that not only share recollections but also create history.[14] Semistructured interviews were optimal for creating and re-creating this history. Specifically, Kathleen Blee and Verta Taylor find semistructured interviews most useful in studying "loosely organized, short-lived, or thinly documented social movements."[15] Oral histories with key informants from black feminist organizations provided both "thick description" of the organizations' functioning, but also insights into the identity formation process that are less apparent in organizational documents.

Living for the Revolution is a text that seeks to makes sense of black feminist organizations in light of current black feminist theory, as well as acts as one version of how I, and the black feminist activists I interviewed, see their role in black feminist history. Perkins also comments on the excitement and difficulty that come with writing about the 1960s and 1970s, a period that living activists might recall differently from the narratives that scholars construct from interviews and archival records. It is my hope that black feminists involved with these organizations will pen their memoirs about the time period and subsequent activism. In fact, I welcome challenges to the narrative I put forth as I offer but one interpretation of the events that shaped contemporary black feminist thought and activism.

Periodization: Rethinking the Wave Analogy

Oral history interviews and archival material served to complement and correct one another, but also these two forms of source material played an instrumental part in determining the period of study. The first organization in this study, the TWWA, emerged from the civil rights movement in 1968. All five organizations were defunct by 1980. Within a hegemonic feminist narrative of the women's movement, these black feminists organizations would fit squarely within the second wave of the women's movement. Typically, the first wave is the emergence of the suffrage movement in the late nineteenth century to women's constitutional enfranchisement in 1920, while the period from the late 1960s through the 1980s is designated the

second wave of feminist organizing.[16] Recent literature notes the rise of a younger generation of feminists, beginning with those born in the 1960s, as the third wave.

It is important to pause for a moment and note, though, the growing dissatisfaction that multiracial and class-based women's movement scholars have with the wave analogy. This dissatisfaction, or rethinking of the wave analogy, involves noting the absence or exclusion from consideration as feminist of certain women and certain forms of resistance. The wave analogy excludes the nineteenth- and twentieth-century feminist activism of women of color. Specific to this study, African American women's history scholars note the resistance of enslaved African American women as early feminist resistance.[17] Active resistance to male supremacy in the form of rape, forced reproduction, and the commodification of black women's bodies demonstrated feminist resistance to this specifically female-gendered oppression. In addition, African American women's activism alongside white women's, in the abolition and antilynching movements, predates that of the suffrage movement, thus making the case for feminist activism in the United States preceding traditional first wave definitions.

Recent scholarship acknowledges that slavery and lynching were race issues; however, violence against blacks also directly relates to questions of *gender*, specifically femininity, masculinity, sexual violence, and white men's protectionism toward white women.[18] For African American women's activism, the concepts of first and second waves are problematic, but from a different angle, Sharon Berger Gluck issues a similar challenge to the wave conceptualization, noting a heterosexist tendency that excludes lesbian feminist activism from discussions of feminist activism. For example, she cites the 1955 emergence of the Daughters of Bilitis as an intervention in the heterosexist, white feminist master narrative of the 1950s as a dormant period in women's movement history. Based on this example, and arguing for the plurality of U.S. feminism, Gluck poses the question "Whose feminism, whose history?"[19] Similar to Gluck's repositioning of lesbian feminist activists, I resituate African American women's feminist activism, establishing a continuum of participants' efforts from the arrival of black women on the continent to the present but also integrating black women in feminist history and theory, moving that experience from the margins of the narrative of the women's movement to its center.[20]

Black feminist organizations were rooted in the civil rights movement, and their dates of emergence coincided with the transition of the locus of

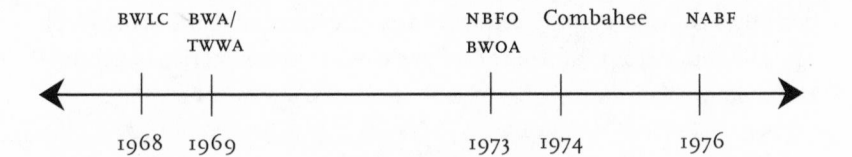

Figure 1. Emergence of Black Feminist Organizations

black activism from key integrationist civil rights organizations to black nationalist groups. As shown in figure 1, the first explicitly black feminist organization emerged as early as 1968 in the contemporary period of feminist activism. That year marks the emergence of the Third World Women's Alliance, which formed as the Black Women's Liberation Committee (BWLC) of the Student Nonviolent Coordinating Committee (SNCC), and also establishes a direct organizational connection to the civil rights movement.

These dates of emergence also marked a period of tremendous political upheaval and ideological struggles in the United States and abroad. Demands made by the civil rights movement and the escalation of the Vietnam War called for dramatic shifts in societal attitudes toward gender, sexuality, and race. In addition to situating black feminist organizations in relationship to the civil rights movement, an examination of black feminist organizations draws connections between black *and* white feminists as descendants of the civil rights movement. Both black and white feminists of the late 1960s developed their collective feminist consciousness based on formative experiences in the civil rights movement.

Secondary source materials, such as organizational newsletters and meeting minutes, corroborate dates of emergence for the five organizations, but exact dates of black feminist organizations' decline were more difficult to pinpoint. Black feminist organizations often disbanded without an official announcement. Best estimates, based on secondary source materials such as final organizational newsletters, link the decline of black feminist organizations to the rise of 1980s conservatism. Like many social movement organizations of the period, the black feminist organizational cycle began with the opening of political opportunities in the late 1960s and ended with the backlash against civil rights and women's rights gains during the Reagan presidency. Additionally, black feminists, as shown in chapter 6, often found their activism institutionalized in social services, governmental bodies, higher education institutions, and other organiza-

tions they could attempt to influence with antiracist and antisexist ideology. The period from 1968 to 1980 is the closest approximation of a formal and contemporary organizing cycle for the black feminist movement.

Theoretical Considerations

As with the methodology, the interdisciplinary theoretical framework for this study is rooted in sociology, history, and women's studies. The engagement of these disciplines explains the political, cultural, and historical contexts that gave rise to black feminist organizations. Specifically, social movement theories illustrate the organizational and individual processes that shaped how black women came to describe themselves as black feminists and to collectively act in organizations. Existing historical and sociological studies of the women's movement, the civil rights movement, and African American women's history provide the foundation for examining black feminist organizations. Nevertheless, these studies continually leave one central question: "How do black women and their race and gender interests fit into the historical narrative of black and women's liberation?" Analyzing the historical and sociological literature for signs of where black women predominated and where they were excluded is equally important because it helps to gain a more holistic perspective on the contours of black women's activism which were informed by race, gender, class, and sexual orientation identities.

The emergence of black feminist organizations is a central, yet largely ignored, part of women's and African American's social history. Working in this distinct field within historical analyses, social historians often examine events from the perspective of nonelites or those who were not ruling elites. This study contributes to social history because it examines how women organized who were generally perceived as neither belonging to the dominant racial elite nor the male elite. Moreover, black women were excluded from the women's movement's historical record. I focus on the activism of black women, once considered marginal because of the women's race and gender, but also for the form that activism took outside traditional definitions of politics.

Black feminist organizations offer case studies that bring together resource mobilization and collective identity theories, though they emphasize different aspects of social movement theory (organizational vs. social psychological). I maintain that like black women's multiple, intersecting identities, organizational structure and collective identity are linked. It is

possible to examine one aspect of a social movement without attention to the other; however, doing so creates an incomplete picture of social movement organizations and their members.

Although black feminist organizations are absent from social movement history and from the literature of social movement organization theory, they provide an insightful case study at the intersections of these two subdisciplinary fields. Specifically, black feminist organizations provide a bridge between resource mobilization and social constructionist perspectives as two competing, but not unrelated, schools of social movement organization theory. The interstitial politics formulated by black feminists stated that their socially constructed collective identity emerged from between that of "blacks" and "women." Yet, placing black feminist organizations into the historical record of social movement organizations highlights how this complex identity impacted the resources that black feminists mobilized (or failed to mobilize), influenced the formation of their organizations, and affected the maintenance of their organizations. In this way, black feminist organizations provide yet another example of the interstitial nature of black feminist politics as a practical and theoretical concept influencing black feminists' daily lives, organizations, and the black feminist movement overall.

Linking Identity and Resources in Social Movement Theory

Resource mobilization (RM) theory, which emerged in the academy as the 1960s yielded civil rights gains for African Americans and women. Countering theories of collective action as the work of unorganized, irrational individuals, RM theorists posited that people engaged in political action and social movement organizations through cost/benefit analyses. Resource mobilization theorists shifted the focus from social-psychological causes of collective action to the structural conditions that yielded social movement mobilization and cycles of protest.[21] Of particular interest to fleshing out the contours of interstitial politics are resource mobilization theories on the opening of political opportunity structures, leadership dynamics, and membership recruitment as facilitators of black feminist mobilization.

Recent social movement scholarship recognizes the need for bridging collective identity and political opportunity.[22] I offer the idea of interstitial politics as one way to connect political opportunity and identity specific to race and gender within social movements, but Raka Ray, in her

study of women's movements in India, offers another relational connecting point. Finding the political opportunity approach too utilitarian and exclusive of culture, she adopts Pierre Bourdieu's concept of fields and offers *protest fields* as a corrective to a narrow focus on organizational life span as solely resource dependent. Political cultures, Raka maintains, have accepted modes for participation, but within these cultures reside smaller, more localized, critical, oppositional "groups and networks that oppose those who have the power in the formal political arena and may or may not share the logic of politics in the larger political field, although they are constrained by it."[23] These smaller groups and networks are protest fields, and as such they contest the terrain of political engagement for a redistribution of power: "Thus an organization's actions are governed both by the distribution of power in a field and by the acceptable ways of transacting everyday business that marks the field."[24]

The opening of political opportunities signals to contenders in the polity that elites are vulnerable to challenges. Access to political participation, ruptures among elites, changes in "ruling alignments," and the creation of influential allegiances characterize these openings.[25] The civil rights movement's integrationist achievements in this new political climate persuaded feminists, black and white, that they could achieve similar gains for women through organizations in an era espousing equal rights. Also, by expanding the tactics used to demand change, the civil rights movement, much like the abolition movement before it, created new spaces and modes of social protest for feminists to emulate in their agitation for resources. Black feminist organizations inserted themselves into the cracks of the dominant political opportunity structure as well as into the fissures created by other social movements.

Activists in emerging social movements come to them most often through preexisting interpersonal networks. Friends, relatives, and fellow workers serve as the impetus for meeting attendance, rally participation, joining organizations, and other avenues of social movement involvement. As shown by women's movement theorists, these networks are especially useful for women traditionally confined to the private sphere of family life, but often unsure of the validity of their dissatisfaction. While black women outstripped white women in their rates of employment in the public sphere through the 1970s, their paid employment was often in the private sphere as domestic help, creating a type of "publicly private" isolation from other women. By banding with other like-minded women around issues of gen-

der and racial oppression in organizations, black feminists began to link their personal struggles to causes other than personal failings and racism.

Central to political actors' taking advantage of these openings of political opportunity structures and joining organizations is the translation of grievances into action. Much debate centers on pinpointing the exact moment in time when individuals realize that social conditions are not necessarily the product of personal failings, but rather the consequence of structural inequality. Doug McAdam effectively links preexisting networks and political opportunity openings through his examination of *cognitive liberation* as a crucial social-psychological process in organizing. Shifts in the political opportunity structure, McAdam explains, provide cognitive cues by demonstrating symbolically that challengers can extract concessions from dominant elites. Meanwhile, preexisting networks of like-minded activists provide the necessary stability for cognitive cues to trigger libratory thought and practice.[26] In his history of black radicalism in America, Robin D. G. Kelley incisively encapsulates what I found black feminists experienced in this time period: "The black radical imagination . . . is a collective imagination engaged in an actual movement for liberation. It is fundamentally a product of struggle, of victories and losses, crises and openings, and endless conversations circulating in a shared environment."[27] It is precisely through this process of a sparking black radical imagination and through cognitive cues, such as the passage of the 1964 Civil Rights Act, that black feminists experienced increasing degrees of cognitive liberation, or awareness, first around racial issues and then gender oppression.

Black feminists carried this cognitive liberation with them into the women's movement, but they also gained valuable leadership skills in the civil rights movement. Several women I interviewed named women leaders in CORE, SNCC, the SCLC, and the NAACP as influential role models who demonstrated black women's political savvy in civil rights organizations. Fannie Lou Hamer, Ella Baker, Septima Clark, and Ruby Doris Smith Robinson exemplified what Belinda Robnett conceptualizes as *bridge leadership*. Bridge leaders connect the will of the people to traditional leaders of the movement through their grassroots organizing skills that include relating to people based on commonalties.[28] Black women leaders, outside the qualifications for traditional public leadership (e.g., male, educated clergy), challenged the binaries inherent in social movement theory that assume that there are only leaders and followers. This bridge leadership modeling demonstrated for young black feminists that divisions between

leaders and participants, and elites and grassroots activists, were not necessarily permanent or natural. Similar to white feminist activists, black feminists employed different forms of leadership and organizational structure based on their experiences in the movement.

Overall, resource mobilization theory helps illuminate the organizational aspects and the environments from which black feminist organizations emerged. Black feminist organizations emerged, grew, and operated under similar political opportunity structures and similar recruitment methods, but they had varied leadership styles. As organizations within a black feminist *movement*, black feminist organizations reflected the heterogeneity of black women's activism and political perspectives.

New social movement theorist perspectives on collective identity formation begin to explain the plurality of organizing styles and ideological positions among black feminist organizations. Collective identity perspectives bring social psychology back into the literature by including identity-based movements as legitimate forms of social protest. Through framing, political actors link their values, beliefs, and interests with the goals, activities, and ideologies of social movement organizations.[29] Collective identity establishes a legitimate space for identity politics within an already established political culture.

Chela Sandoval's theorizing on oppositional consciousness brings, for this study, a critical addition to the collective identity perspective. She argues that oppositional consciousness is not an inherent trait of people of color, but that it "depends upon the ability to read the current situations of power and self-consciously choosing and adopting the ideological form best suited to push against its configurations."[30] I would draw analogies between Sandoval's oppositional consciousness, Collins's ideas on subjugated knowledge, and Gloria Anzaldúa's formulation of *la facultad* (the ability to see deeper realities or structures) and would even hearken back to W. E. B. DuBois's classic double-consciousness model.[31] All of these epistemological modes are survival skills. Black feminists *assumed* a similar, uniform oppositional consciousness as a site of commonalty among black women. However, as evidenced in the decline of these organizations, black feminist organizations were only at the beginning of this process of collective identity formation. Only later, with growing numbers of black women interested in their movement, would black feminists start to recognize the multidirectional flow of power and privilege *inside* as well as outside their organizations.

Organizations devise rhetoric and symbols to construct their political claims by using framing processes that take into account identity-based claims, as well as oppositional consciousness. The framing of these issues and claims influence recruitment into the organization, as well as how activists relate to the organization once they become members. Yet, David A. Snow and Robert Benford, in a reassessment of the finer distinctions between frames and ideology note that frames are dynamic, negotiated, and often contested processes.[32] Black women were in the process of shaping a black feminist ideology rooted in their specific race, gender, class, and sexual orientation interests as a group, but they also had to face how they differed from one another as individuals with differing backgrounds and political agendas. As these differences emerged, black feminist organizations experimented with different frames for their potency in attracting members and adherents to black feminist ideology. Black feminists found that their frames were socially constituted through dialogue within their organizations, as well as with adversaries.

Black feminist organizations offer a unique case study for examining the interaction between collective identity and resource mobilization. Black feminists took advantage of openings in the political opportunity structure, but they did not all do so in the same way. The organizations were but part of the protest field that included civil rights, women's, and black nationalist groups all vying for a redistribution of power that overturned white supremacist hierarchies. For these interstitially constituted political actors and organizations, gender, race, class, and sexual orientation all directly influenced the growth and sustenance of organizations. They were also influenced to varying degrees by the political culture in which they were embedded. Grounded in social movement organization theory, black feminist organizations add historical case studies of a cyclical movement process from emergence to decline.

The goal of this book is to explore the life cycle of black feminist organizations in the 1970s. These organizations were not merely a hybrid of civil rights and women's movement organizations, but sites for fostering a collective identity among activists distinct from that of those classic movements. Black feminists built organizations with distinct goals and strategies for eradicating racism and sexism. To that end, each chapter addresses one particular question about the life span of these organizations.

The rest of this chapter, briefly, situates 1970s black feminist organizations within the context of the historical legacy of black women's organiz-

ing. I also give insights into the historical and sociopolitical background that factionalized the civil rights movement and gave rise to black feminist organizations. What did black women's potential feminist identity mean for black men, antifeminist black women, white men, and white women during the social unrest of the late 1960s and early 1970s? Four sociopolitical factors influenced the emergence of black feminist organizations: (1) black women's activist roles in the civil rights movement, (2) their paradoxical marginalization and leadership in the women's movement, (3) representations of black women in popular culture, and (4) racist and sexist depictions of black women in social policy.

Emphasizing the role of organizational founders, chapter 2 explores the similarities and differences in black feminist organizations' emergence narratives. What were the sociopolitical conditions, intermovement dynamics, and intragroup dynamics among black women that prompted these particular women to form organizations? Francesca Polletta remarks that framing, as a movement tool, does not go far in explaining the precise moment when grievances translate into action and offers that we must employ storytelling to describe "the story of our becoming."[33] Nascent black feminists gained leadership skills from the civil rights and women's movements, but also revolutionary ways of thinking about racism and sexism. They also held grievances against discrimination in those movements that, until now, were assumed to have been the whole story of the beginning of contemporary black feminism. I engage Polletta's demand for narrative through black feminists' stories about how the individuals came to form their organizations. These emergence narratives contribute to organizational history and the genealogy of the first contemporary articulations of intersectional identities, that is, race, gender, and class as intersecting identities. These narratives tackle the how, and to a lesser degree the why, of black feminist organizations' emergence.

By the mid-1970s, the civil rights movement had experienced a backlash to the gains made in the late 1960s. Still the women's movement, buoyed by the *Roe v. Wade* decision, searched for a new anchor issue. This period also saw the expansion of the protest field, with the emergence of the environmental, gay rights, and antinuclear movements. What, though, enabled black feminist organizations in particular to experience a period of growth and increased mobilization during the mid-1970s? Chapter 3 focuses on the resource mobilization aspects of black feminist organizations. The leadership styles, membership structures, finances, and communication strategies of black feminist organizations reflect their racial,

gender, class, and ideological positions within the social protest community of the late 1960s and the 1970s. I analyze the hierarchical and collectivist structures black feminist organizations adopted to determine the costs and benefits of black women's political choices. Key to this chapter is the recognition that just because their members were women and feminists, not all black feminist organizations worked as collectives. In fact, black women's previous activist experiences influenced the structures they adopted and made significant differences in the longevity of black feminist organizations.

Black feminists sought to attain visibility and allies for a movement that encompassed race, gender, and class questions of social justice through their activities and myriad other traditional ways of organizing of the time period. In particular, chapter 4 asks and answers the question "How did black feminists define feminist issues and how did that definition shape their actions according to simultaneous race and gender considerations?" Specifically, the Third World Women's Alliance and Black Women Organized for Action's publishing efforts, the National Black Feminist Organization's Eastern Regional Conference, the National Alliance of Black Feminists' Alternative School, and the Combahee River Collective's series of Black Women's Network Retreats are explored as shaping feminist issues and the feminist agenda in the 1970s.

In recentering their experiences as black women, black feminists, ironically, created new margins. In this context, chapter 5 draws on the social constructionist literature in social movements to answer the question "How did black women come to define themselves as a category distinct from 'blacks' and 'women'?" The black feminist movement is known for its attention to race, class, and gender aspects of identity. However, I found that black feminist organizations placed varying emphases on these aspects of identity depending on the composition of their memberships. Black feminist organizations had to reconcile the heterogeneity of members' class and sexual orientation identities, which yielded significant diversity within the larger movement. Central to this process was consciousness-raising, a tool both the women's and civil rights movements used. Consciousness-raising empowered black women and illuminated classism and homophobia as sites of struggle *within* black feminist organizations. Although these schisms were not the only reason for the decline of black feminist organizations, they did play a role in other causal factors.

In chapter 6 I answer the persistent question "What happened to black feminist organizations?" Inter- and intraorganizational conflicts proved

problematic for the long-term survival of these organizations. Insufficient resources also precipitated the decline. Four out of five of the organizations did not have the resources to continue their recruitment and direct action activities that were central to acquiring and maintaining members. Directly related to insufficient resources was the burnout activists experienced as they attempted to capture the momentum of the civil rights and women's movement protest cycles by mobilizing large numbers of black women around feminist issues.

Julia Sudbury astutely cautions against romanticizing black women's history and emphasizes the importance of truth telling: "the desire to portray black women in a positive light leads potentially to silencing those aspects of back women's organizing which have been less than positive, or outright destructive. This idealization ultimately is of little benefit to black women because it dulls our ability to think critically about our actions. Ultimately, the liberatory narrative becomes a toll to silence doubt and dissent and this prevents us from learning lessons from mistakes or turning weaknesses into strengths."[34] In the interest of promoting stronger, if any, future black feminist organizations, we must acknowledge, in addition to the aforementioned classism and homophobia, internal factionalism in the form of ideological and leadership struggles that hindered the viability of black feminist organizations. Strategies for maintaining movement momentum were consistently disputed within black feminist organizations, causing intraorganizational disputes. Decisions about whether to form coalitions with white feminists and/or accept funding from predominately white organizations were major ideological disputes among black feminists. Direction of fund-raising and organization often fell to black feminist organizations' leaders, raising conflicts among black feminist activists over power, privilege, and the future of black feminism.

This book inserts a missing chapter in social movement history to convey the richness of an incipient black feminist movement in a social movement landscape and time period often whitewashed by historians. An unexpected lesson black feminists learned from their organizing experience was that all black women do not think alike. Diversity exists among black women in their physical appearances, which influence how they constructed their own personal identities. There are also unseen, but just as influential, aspects to black feminist identity that shape how black women approached feminist activism. Through historical and sociological analysis, this book constructs a narrative of a movement that shaped black feminist

theory and the women's movement, and that will shape African American history for decades to come.

Historical Legacies

Black feminist organizations did not emerge in a vacuum. Black women experienced growth in feminist consciousness at a particular moment in U.S. social activist history. Sociopolitical conditions occurred on the political, organizational, and individual levels, impacting black women's collective identification with feminism. Situating black feminist organizing in this historical context brings to the fore the costs black women paid in attempting to advance from their marginalized position in social movements and in U.S. society. At the same time, it is crucial to state that though it applies to how women of color who resist are addressed worldwide, it is a particularly Western conceit to label all resistive behavior of women "feminist." It is a fine line to tread between imperialist labeling and claiming space within feminism for women of color. This space is dependent on a definition of resistance that applies to gender, as well as race. In particular, I am thinking of Tera Hunter's definition of resistance in her study of Southern washerwomen's resistance to racism, sexism, and labor exploitation: "any act, individual or collective, symbolic or literal, intended by subordinates to deny claims, to refuse compliance with impositions made by the superordinates, or to advance claims of their own."[35] What follows is a brief historical assessment meant to place 1970s black feminist activism within a continuum of resistance strategies to gender and racial oppression.

Black women's resistance to gender oppression, while perhaps not labeled feminist at the outset, has been continuous since the arrival of enslaved Africans to the North American continent. Angela Davis's classic essay "Reflections on the Black Woman's Role in the Community of Slaves" and the second chapter of her book *Women, Race, and Class* pioneered analyses of black women in slavery that view them as political actors. If they were not political actors in the traditional sense of enfranchisement or electoral politics, enslaved black women certainly exercised political will in resisting forced reproduction and other forms of brutality that were unique to their position as blacks and women in the plantation economy. Moreover, Davis and emancipation narratives such as that of Harriet Jacobs attest to the lengths women went to in resisting white patriarchal, supremacist oppression directed at them, their children, and black men.[36]

Black women in the nineteenth century continued, postemancipation, to establish and assert a black women's identity that negotiated race and gender demands. They did this through rhetoric and black women's organizations that made demands: demands from black women to stand tall and proud despite racist and sexist oppression, demands for education for African Americans so that they could fully participate in the civic life of the country, and demands that black men accept accountability for themselves and the well-being of their families. They did this most effectively through national organizations, as documented by Deborah Gray White when she asserts that black women's prioritization of race or gender was cyclical. This is a key insight that helps explain why black women's activism is so often overlooked, particularly as it relates to gender issues. She notes, "Although it cannot be said that black women always chose race over other aspects of their identity, it can be said that race, along with gender and class were variables always factored into whatever national organizations did."[37] In this light, the work of two of the largest organizations, the National Association of Colored Women and the National Council of Negro Women, boldly asserted that they were race *and* gender workers. These organizations, and the women who led them, were early antecedents to contemporary black feminists in defining a black womanhood that was inclusive of a range of concerns in their own and in their communities' interests.

Black women continued the legacy of activism begun by pioneers, such as Ida Well-Barnett, Anna Julia Cooper, and Mary Church Terrell. Claudia Jones and Amy Jacques Garvey, for example, made linkages between black women's oppression and their status as workers in the U.S. economy. In what has been previously described as a period of abeyance in the feminist movement, in the 1950s, artists, academics, and grassroots organizers questioned the dominant mentality of home and hearth for women and how that played out for black women. After all, black women adeptly cared for their families under the involuntary servitude of slavery and since then were present in the workplace long before white American women. Margaret Wilkerson suggests playwright Lorraine Hansberry's feminist views, for example, in her plays *A Raisin in the Sun* (1959) and *The Sign in Sidney Brustein's Window* (1964) and prose writing. Although constrained by the pervasive containment ethos of the era, Hansberry grappled with women who were rebelling against their traditional roles.[38]

As inheritors of black women's political and social activism, from the mid-to-late 1960s, black women active in civil rights and women's organizations were keenly aware that these movements did not include the

simultaneous eradication of racism and sexism. Additionally, black women encountered structural obstacles upheld by racist and sexist theorizing in sociological and public policy literature that alleged a black matriarchy as responsible for the black community's ills. Last, black women faced discrimination in the cultural arena in the form of media stereotypes. The mammy or the hypersexual black woman icons received a face-lift in contemporary popular culture. All of these occurrences created sociopolitical conditions that ran counter to black women's racial consciousness and rising gender awareness.

Leadership opportunities and the ideology of the *beloved community* as experienced in the civil rights movement, provided black women with a repertoire of strategies that they later employed in feminist organizations.[39] Yet, the inability of the civil rights movement to extend its "rights" framework to include antisexist struggle alienated some black women. Similarly, black women active in the women's movement found that the movement's "sisterhood" framework did not take into account discrimination based on race and class. Overall, black feminists' gains from these two movements were mixed: they experienced discrimination rooted in racism and sexism, but gained the tools to overcome them in the formation of their own organizations.

Black Women Leaders and the Civil Rights Movement

Black women and men active in the civil rights movement were ambivalent about the role of black women in the movement and in the black community. White found that intercommunity tensions over black women's roles are historic, but the 1920s and efforts to create a definition of the "New Negro" put this ambivalence in high relief.[40] Then, and in the 1960s, women played key leadership roles in the civil rights struggle to end segregation and extend full citizenship rights to African Americans. However, women in both time periods challenged the movement leadership's chauvinism. Black women resisted demands that they conform to normative ideals of womanhood, or ladylike behavior—ideas initially constructed with black women as the opposite of ladylike in the first place.

In their assumption of bridge leadership roles, one-to-one interactions with male leaders, and consciousness-raising on the connections between race and gender, black women leaders contested sexism and normative models of womanhood. Through these actions, they questioned the limits of rights as a master frame for movement organizing and started a com-

plicated identity formation process. What rights did women have if black men insisted (and some black women concurred) that black women conform to a stereotype of proper womanhood—a stereotype that historically constructed black women as deviant?

The scholarly literature on black women civil rights leaders shows numerous challenges black women faced to their authority based on their racial and gender identities.[41] Black women students witnessed the obstacles adult women in the civil rights movement faced in asserting visible leadership in male-dominated, church-based movements. Indeed, though black women were effective organizers of direct action efforts, they encountered resistance from black men. Until recently, the historical record of the civil rights movement, while touting black women's participation, ignored their leadership.

For example, the publication of JoAnn Gibson Robinson's memoir *The Montgomery Bus Boycott and the Women Who Started It* tells us much about the Women's Political Council (wPC) that we did not know before the memoir's publication.[42] The wPC began mobilizing Montgomery's black population and preparing for a boycott long before December 1955, when Rosa Parks made her stand by refusing to yield her seat on the city's segregated buses. Robinson's account not only details her leadership and that of her co-organizers, including Parks as a longtime member of the NAACP, but also gives us a gendered view on the segregated South from inside and outside the black community. Equally important as race in staging the boycotts were concerns about respectability and moral fortitude, as these qualities pertained to the person who would jumpstart the boycott (Parks) and its participants (Montgomery's black population).

Robnett's conceptualization of the bridge leader has moved the field forward significantly in explaining gender implications for black women's leadership in the civil rights movement. Activists in the civil rights movement and historians consider leaders such as Ella Baker, Fannie Lou Hamer, Rosa Parks, and Septima Clark the "Mothers of the Movement." Such homage gives these leaders respect for their forceful, steady presence and their grassroots analysis of racism. For example, Ella Baker, as coordinator of the Southern Christian Leadership Conference (SCLC), worked behind the scenes with local constituents, while Dr. Martin Luther King Jr. represented the organization nationally. Although she was officially excluded from the decision-making process because of her gender and nonclergy status, Baker criticized King on strategic issues, such as the decision not to push forward with gains made from the Montgomery Bus Boycott.[43]

Disillusioned with the male and hierarchy-centered leadership of the SCLC, Baker spearheaded the organization of the Student Nonviolent Coordinating Committee (SNCC). She encouraged young people to model participatory democracy, an organizing philosophy that emphasized group decision making over leader-centered organizing.[44]

Sexism and authoritarianism were among the factors that prevented women from assuming public leadership roles in the civil rights movement.[45] Black women exercised power within the civil rights movement—power attributed them from their grassroots connections to local communities. Many women were respected as wise elders, but nonetheless they were still women whose gender prevented them from participating in the hierarchy of civil rights organizations and the movement. For example, in the program of speakers for the national 1963 March on Washington, not a single woman was invited to speak, though many women risked their lives alongside men in direct action against the state.[46]

The roots of black women's second-class citizenship are embedded in bourgeois notions of womanhood, femininity, and motherhood.[47] The rights framework of the civil rights movement involved integrationist efforts to assimilate into the dominant culture. An implicit, sometimes explicit, goal of the movement was the reassertion of the male breadwinner as head of household. This desire for African American men to represent the black community in the public sphere conflicted with the reality that black women were also competent organizers and had long been a part of the black community's public sphere. One must wonder too about the impact of black male attacks on black women's club work and character in the nineteenth century. White deduced that these attacks were as much about black women's activities in the public sphere, as about contestations over the meaning of black masculinity and femininity.[48]

Conflicts over women's leadership were often grounded in sociological theories of black men as weak and subject to black matriarchy.[49] Some leaders of the civil rights movement, in their active marginalization of black women, accepted pathologizing theories on the black community. Andrew Young, as SCLC chief aid to Dr. King, noted that men "had a hard time with domineering women in SCLC. . . . This is a generality, but a system of oppression tends to produce weak men and strong women."[50] Rationales for male leadership were posited as a counterbalance to black matriarchy, but would come to seem contradictory to women applying an equal rights framework to their position in society.

These gender tensions affected the role that younger women played in

organizations. In SNCC, for example, Diane Nash, Ruby Doris Smith Robinson, Francis Beal, Cynthia Washington, and Gwen Patton all played instrumental roles, organizing freedom rides, sit-ins, and communications. Zoharah Simmons (formerly Gwendolyn Robinson), at nineteen years old served as director of SNCC's Laurel Mississippi project and instituted an anti-sexual-harassment policy in response to intraorganizational violence against women.[51] These women, like their foremothers, took on leadership positions in student-run civil rights organizations and faced the challenges of leadership in mixed-sex organizations. Moreover, like men involved in the movement, they stood up to police violence. Yet, unlike older women involved in the civil rights movement, the first rumblings of the contemporary feminist movement influenced how younger women viewed their leadership potential.

One of the first eruptions of feminist consciousness in the civil rights movement occurred in the wake of a position paper delivered at SNCC's 1964 Waveland, Mississippi, personnel retreat. Casey Hayden and Mary King, two key white members in the organization cowrote "SNCC Position Paper (Women in the Movement)" and presented it in a workshop on the role of women. Hayden and King claimed that women in SNCC rarely made significant decisions in the organization and cited the existence of a sexual division of labor. The authors also called upon nineteenth-century suffragists' analogy of male supremacy over women as similar to white supremacy over blacks.[52]

The Hayden-King paper is often cited as the seed of feminist consciousness emerging from the civil rights movement.[53] Scholars interpreted reactions to the position paper differently.[54] Clayborne Carson maintained activists ignored the paper because of pressing racial issues. Sara Evans, on the other hand, believed that because of the paper, black and white women's perspectives momentarily converged around feminism but that they lacked the trust needed to come together for action.[55]

Differential positions in SNCC, in the leadership and the rank-and-file membership, account for this distrust. White women in SNCC, in deconstructing the sexual division of labor, failed to recognize the gender of black women. In effect, in King's and Hayden's analysis, black women's race *erased* them as women with some degree of power in the organization. Also, black women deemphasized their gender because they prioritized their racial identity in the struggle for black self-determination. Cynthia Washington, for example, did not recognize sexism in SNCC, because she and other black women in the organization held positions that,

while not senior positions, carried responsibilities often critical to surviving racist violence.[56] Diane Nash's leadership in Nashville's sit-ins and Washington's job as project director in Bolivar County, Mississippi, were instrumental positions in the operations of SNCC and recognized as such by black women *and* men in the organization. Evans and Carson do agree that some black women in SNCC occupied positions of responsibility, contrary to most white women's experiences in SNCC. Nevertheless, black and white women's differing positions in the organization created a barrier—however much a straw man—to constructing a common identity as women.

Margaret Sloan, chairwoman of the National Black Feminist Organization (NBFO), made the connection between sexism and the movement leadership at the early age of fourteen, when she participated in a Chicago rent strike. In a speech she gave to students at Carleton College in 1973, Sloan omitted the name of the organization because she believed that her experience could easily apply to any of several civil rights organizations:

> I can remember walking into that building and seeing women of different colors, in various either "prone" positions or servile situations. I saw white women in the kitchen making the lemonade, just eager. Just stirring! "Serve my brother." Wiping their sweat from the brow. You know those women? And those black women out in back playing with the kids in the little yard that was made into a little play area. And then you walk back up to the main conference room and there was a little coalition of black and white men mapping out the strategy for the demonstration that was going to take place the next day—doing the serious business. . . . And I found out that no matter how much we organized as women, no matter how many lead poisoning campaigns we organized and worked with on the Westside [of Chicago]; no matter how many tenant rent strikes we organized we weren't really that effective. It really didn't really matter so much how you organized during the day. It really mattered how well you performed at night. And who you attached yourself to. I was only fourteen. I didn't go too high in that particular organization [laughter]. But I learned a helluva lot.[57]

Sexual politics extended beyond stereotypes regarding women's leadership capabilities. For Sloan, and later observers of the movement, women's sexuality was a way to understand black women's access to political power. Sloan perceived definite sex roles in the civil rights movement and saw that some women's power derived from their connection to male leaders.[58] As she grew in her political activism and feminist consciousness, Sloan real-

ized that she would eventually need to seek out other like-minded black women for her organizing efforts.

In this analysis, we must also consider the culpability of black women in perpetuating sexism in the movement in the interest of supporting black men, even if that support came at a cost. Black male movement leaders often delegated leadership responsibilities to black women, and, hence, black women did not experience the same degree of sexism as white women. Charged with important responsibilities in the movement, black women leaders were hard-pressed to confront sexism within it while managing their duties as part of a cause whose primary goal was to challenge white supremacy. Black women in SNCC recognized male chauvinism in the organization, but they were reluctant to confront it because of the divide erected between racial and gender struggles.[59]

Despite male supremacy, a number of black women incorporated civil rights movement organizing skills and the movement's equal rights frame into new theorizing on the connection between oppressions. The transition from a monist politic grounded in an either/or paradigm (e.g., black or female) to recognizing multiple jeopardy was not made in one great leap.[60] Instead, by extending the rights frame to include the simultaneous fight against racial and gender oppression, black women questioned male supremacy and discussed the meaning of black womanhood. As black women began to do this gender work, black men were also turning to gender issues in the form of reassertions of masculinity through the black nationalist movement.

Black Women, the Black Cultural Nationalist Movement, and Gender

Men in black nationalist movements were more decisive than male civil rights movement leaders, and sometimes adamant, about their demands that black women support black men. Black cultural nationalist literature deemed childbearing and nation building the domain of the "Truly Revolutionary Black Woman."[61] The antiracist revolutionary struggle came first and was often the only item on the nationalist agenda. Black women were leaders in nationalist organizations and proved themselves capable of revolutionary leadership.[62] In the face of retrograde notions about black women's responsibilities, women in nationalist organizations, particularly the Black Panthers, spoke out for themselves as capable leaders *and* politically positioned against sexism. Still, by remaining in nationalist organi-

zations, they implicitly designated racism as the primary site of struggle. Black nationalist women did not ignore sexism; however, they did shun gender separatism.

Women in nationalist movements declared primary allegiance to ending racism out of the belief that issues of racial oppression were more pressing than gender discrimination. Following the tumult of the late 1960s and the continuing war in Vietnam, some black women felt that a revolution was imminent. We also cannot overlook the fact that *black people were dying*, whether from the violence of poverty or from Federal Bureau of Investigations (FBI) Counterintelligence Program (COINTELPRO) agents' bullets.[63] Many of the same issues black women face today in their communities (e.g., high unemployment, drug abuse, inadequate housing) were mounting problems in the late 1960s and 1970s. The majority of the black community, still riding high from victories wrought by the civil rights movement, compared their relatively low standard of living to that of white Americans. Based on these perceived inequities, African American women in the black nationalist movement held different priorities from those of white feminists. For example, institutions that some white, socialist feminists sought to dismantle, such as the nuclear family, black nationalist women hoped to strengthen for the stabilization of the black community.

Other nationalist women, particularly those in the Black Panther Party, felt they were on the right track in advocating a revolution, particularly within mixed-sex black organizations. What better way to confront sexism than working side by side with black men? In a pamphlet entitled "Black Panther Sisters Talk about Women's Liberation," unidentified Panther women observed that members assumed responsibilities based on their level of political awareness: "A lot of sisters have been writing more articles, they're attending more to the political aspects of the Party, they're speaking out in public more and we've even done outreach work in the community."[64] Remaining in mixed-sex organizations allowed black women to demonstrate that they were as capable and committed to revolution as black men.

The experiences of black women in the civil rights and cultural nationalist movements were but a few of the issues black women needed to consider in formulating positions on feminism. Individual black women recognized male chauvinism and the devaluation of women's leadership capabilities in the civil rights movement, but they hesitated to incorporate gender struggle into their ideals of participatory democracy or freedom. Through personal experience, black women activists clearly identi-

fied racist oppression as it impacted their racial concerns and the black community. However, racist discrimination in its violent manifestations (e.g., local police repression) against blacks seemed much more salient to black women than sexism that sometimes masqueraded as protection and honor.

Women in black nationalist organizations, many of them socialists, foresaw sexism's demise with the advent of a socialist revolution and the destruction of the U.S. class-based economic system. A central observation that black nationalist women contributed to black feminist theory, that is often unheeded, was women's culpability in perpetuating sexism by acting in traditionally gendered ways. Some black nationalist women, such as those interviewed for the newsletter the *Movement* and those in the Pan-African movement, believed that women needed to step up to the front lines of battle and not only challenge sexism when it was convenient for them. Like women in SNCC, Black Panther women espoused the delegation of responsibility according to ability and political consciousness. Falling back on traditional gender roles was neither revolutionary nor acceptable behavior for black freedom fighters of either gender.

Black Women and the Women's Movement

Conflicts surrounding racism within the women's movement are typically cited as the primary reasons why black women did *not* join organizations against sexism.[65] Black women's participation in this movement is often ignored or glossed over as insignificant in the popular periodicals of the era and secondary literature. However, recognizing differential recruitment patterns of black women or different paths into the movement—those who rejected and those who joined predominately white women's movement organizations—is critical to studying the emergence of black feminist organizations.

All black women experienced white racism, but they reacted to it differently when it came to relating, or not, to the women's movement. As a subset of hegemonic feminism, the concept of sisterhood, as proposed by the majority of white feminists, meant that all women were the same, regardless of economic or social differences.[66] Yet, this definition erased the discrimination that black women faced based on their racial differences from white women.[67] The result was an elision of women's differences in the interest of a common women's movement agenda. As a result, this ideal of sisterhood allowed many predominately white feminist organizations

and white women to avoid acknowledging their racial privilege. I use quali-fiers—*the majority, some, many*—because increasingly in today's studies of the 1970s women's movement, white feminists active in the movement at the time are confronting charges of racism and owning up to those charges, but also constructing interpretations of ignored antiracist initiatives and white women's groups that were actively antiracist at the time.[68]

The majority of black women in the United States did not participate in the women's movement, but they sympathized with the women's lib-eration movement at a higher percentage than did white women.[69] Black women had deep and compelling reasons for not joining the women's movement and shunning sisterhood with white women. Four concerns were (1) perceived increasing relational tensions between black women and men, (2) worries about black women's activist energies being diverted from the civil rights movement, (3) black and white women's distrust of one an-other, and (4) racist history and cultural stereotypes.[70] Each of these con-cerns influenced black women's mass nonparticipation in the contempo-rary women's movement.

Popular black periodicals of the time reveal that a primary consider-ation in whether black women joined the movement was how such gender activism would affect the relationship between black women and men. Part of this consideration was the popular press's refusal to recognize gender discrimination. *Jet* and *Ebony*, the leading publications, consistently recen-tered men's reactions to feminism and ignored the discrimination black women faced within the black community when reporting on the women's movement.[71] The black community's survival depended on the strength of relationships between black women and men, but the overemphasis on that relationship was itself diversionary. The "war between the sexes," the popular media dubbed it, overshadowed material issues of income dispari-ties, unemployment rates, and domestic violence in black homes that was statistically violence against women.

Black women's economic independence and interracial dating were at the heart of this war. This divergence from normative sex roles created ten-sions between black women and men that Toni Morrison attributed to the black man's "inability to deal with a competent and complete personality and her [the black woman's] refusal to be anything less than that."[72] In-volvement with the women's liberation movement, many blacks of both genders thought, would only make black women more independent and further aggravate tensions.

Black periodicals also stated that black women's participation in the

women's movement would disrupt the evolving renaissance in the ways black women and men were starting to view one another. An article in *Ebony* explained: "Now being wooed by the 'new' black man in both poetry and song, and knowing that her man has suffered at the hands of white racism, the black woman on the whole is in no mood to denounce him as a 'male chauvinist.' . . . *[B]lack women* are seeking a truce with *the black man* and are expending their energies in redefining their image"[73] Black women became collective agents in this new age of Black Pride. They had to remain vigilant of the feelings of the monolithic black man. The rhetoric of "Black Power" actively translated into the Black Pride aesthetic in music, art, and, most of all, the physical appearance of black people. "Black is Beautiful" reigned as the guiding principle for black women's and men's perceptions of one another. Black women's potential political allegiance with white women was viewed as disrupting the developing aesthetic of black beauty and breaking ranks with black men by seeming to value "white" politics over Black Power.

The new black aesthetic was, at best, an unstable truce in the war of the sexes, particularly when black men formed intimate emotional and physical relationships with white women. Historically, relationships between black males and white females were taboo, the very rumor of which resulted in a particular kind of gendered violence against black men: castration, lynching, or both. Despite this precedence of violence, in the late 1960s and early 1970s, black men took advantage of changes in sexual mores yielded by the sexual revolution and the counterculture: "But now, with all of the declarations of independence, one of the black man's ways of defining it is to broaden his spectrum of female choices, and one of the consequences of his new pride is the increased attraction white women feel for him," Morrison observed.[74] The black man's new sexual prerogative was, and still is, a source of jealousy and anger for many black women derived from centuries of humiliation and mislabeling. Adding fuel to that anger was the double standard applied to black women: the so-called renaissance in black love fell noticeably short when confronted with black women dating white men. Interracial dating gave black women, who were not immune to false competitions between women for male attention, little incentive to enter political alliances with white women, particularly under the banner of sisterhood.[75]

The sisterhood framework also failed to draw large numbers of black women into the women's movement because many black women already active in the civil rights movement worried that their participation in the

women's movement would divert gains from the civil rights movement to white women and usurp black women's activist energies. This concern about black women's resources became an issue of racial allegiance. Sloan, of the National Black Feminist Organization, voiced black women's frustrations when recognizing how discrimination impacted their lives on multiple fronts:

> There is always a problem with black women, I'm sure all minority women go through this, but the whole splitting up and parsing out loyalties is called a "priority game." And it gets crammed down black women's throats all the time in terms of what are you more: black or female. . . . It would be easy if the oppressor would separate out the week and say, "Well, from Monday to Wednesday we're going to screw her 'cause she's female and the rest of the week we're going to do it to her because she's black." . . . I think it's an insult. It's inhuman, it is cruel to expect a woman who is of a color to parse herself and split herself down the middle like that. It just does not work and it is impossible. It's like, "Separate yourself and deal with one issue at a time.[76]

This priority game was more divisive to the civil rights movement than black women's participation in the women's movement because it dismissed the special issues black women faced *as women* and neglected the totality of black women's oppression. In effect, it forced black women to prioritize where they would put their energies when both antiracism and antisexism were pressing battles to be waged simultaneously.

Community anxiety about the diversion of black women's resources also encompassed concerns that openings in the political field were not large enough to accommodate civil rights and women's demands. In an interview with *Ebony* magazine, one woman voiced the common derision that the women's movement was "just a bunch of bored white women with nothing to do—they're just trying to attract attention away from the black liberation movement."[77] African Americans often voiced this suspicion, but not without just cause. Take, for example, attempts of a Southern congressman to scuttle Title VII in 1964. This employment provision of the Civil Rights Bill was originally proposed in response to African American agitation to prohibit racial discrimination in the workplace. This particular congressman, who had a reputation for blocking progressive legislation, added anti–sex discrimination to the civil rights amendment in an attempt to derail it entirely.[78]

Although the amendment did pass, adding sex discrimination to it in

theory pitted African American men against white women in a contest for oppressed status that erased African American women, as both blacks and women, altogether. Studies in later years show that white women did, in fact, gain more from programs such as affirmative action than did any other minority group.[79] For blacks concerned with the loss of civil rights gains to a burgeoning women's movement, this political maneuvering served as evidence of the potential perils of a coalition between black and white women. In the eyes of most African Americans, black feminists would ultimately only betray black community political interests by helping white women gain a share of white men's power.

Black women's reluctance to join the women's movement's calls for sisterhood was also rooted in their interpersonal history with white women. From the initial economic and domestic exploitation of the slave/ mistress relationship to white women's position as the norm of female beauty, the relationship between black and white women was a contentious one that did not foster collaboration. Historically, womanhood and femininity were white women's exclusive domains; tradition defined them as delicate, ladylike, and in need of protection. As a result, since slavery de-feminized black women through the imposition of harsh "men's" labor, black womanhood was a nonexistent category. If white women were vulnerable to rape, black women, conversely, were sexually available. Black and white women's relationships were often historically and interpersonally adversarial. The majority of black women were not eager to join political organizations with their socially constructed opposite.

Despite this contentious history, some black women did join the women's movement. The most-often cited example of early black women's feminist activism is Sojourner Truth's work in the suffrage movement. Even though Nell Irvin Painter skillfully disputes the veracity of accounts of Truth's famous 1851 "Woman's Rights" speech, it is often used as an early example in which a black woman articulated the connections between race and gender oppression.[80]

Yet, Truth's involvement with the suffrage movement also illustrates the racism African American women experienced when they worked with white women. Participants in the women's suffrage movement engaged in contradictory behavior when they spoke out against slavery during abolition, but they later used white supremacy to justify the enfranchisement of white women.[81] White suffragists appealed to Southern white women, arguing that only white women's higher moral values could save the nation from damnation. Some black women in the late 1960s and 1970s re-

flected on this historical precedent and concluded that it was not in their best interest to join the predominately white women's movement. If white women held as their feminist heroes Elizabeth Cady Stanton and Susan B. Anthony, who espoused racist sentiments in the interest of white women's enfranchisement, would their feminist descendants also use their white privilege to advance their selective versions of sisterhood?

In spite of, and perhaps while preserving, these misgivings, black women did call themselves feminists. They played significant leadership roles in the mainstream and radical branches of the women's movement. As they did with the civil rights movement, black feminists transferred leadership skills and philosophies from the women's movement to black feminist organizations. Several African American women were guided by feminist principles while holding positions in governmental agencies and bureaucratic organizations, and they authored significant feminist texts. Pauli Murray, for instance, an attorney and ordained Episcopalian priest, was long at the vanguard of progressive movements as a member of President Kennedy's Commission on the Status of Women and while serving on the executive board of the American Civil Liberties Union.[82] Murray advocated for an independent women's movement organization and helped establish the National Organization for Women (NOW) in 1966, though she had left by 1967, citing issues of undemocratic decision making and a limited scope in its membership and coalitions.[83] Similarly, Aileen Hernandez served as one of the first commissioners for the Equal Employment Opportunity Commission (EEOC) in 1966. She later succeeded Betty Friedan as NOW president in 1970. Although she viewed her participation in NOW through a racial and gender lens, she later established Black Women Organized for Action (BWOA), an organization dedicated to building feminist leadership among black women.

Other examples of early black feminist activism included the work of Margaret Sloan, Cellestine Ware, and Florynce Kennedy. Sloan, a founder of the National Black Feminist Organization, toured with Gloria Steinem in the spring of 1973, lecturing on black women's connections to the women's movement. Sloan was also a founding editor of *Ms.* magazine, the most prominent national feminist publication of the 1970s. Also active in the New York feminist movement community, Cellestine Ware, author of *Woman Power*, was a founding member of New York Radical Women. Florynce Kennedy was involved with the founding of the NBFO and wrote the fiery women's movement text *Abortion Rap*.[84] She is best known for inspiring many feminists, black and white, with her motto "Kick ass and

take names." These are but a few examples of black women who joined the women's movement as founders of predominately white feminist organizations. Their writings on black women and feminism make us aware of their presence, but we can only guess about the numbers of black women grappling with feminism who did not have a public forum for their thoughts, despite assumptions about their antifeminist stance.

Inez Smith Reid tested this assumption in a study that assessed the nationalist militancy or feminist sentiments of black women.[85] Seeking black women's opinions on the women's movement, she asked informants' opinions of Aileen Hernandez's position in NOW. Smith Reid observed no consensus of opinion and emphasized respondents' polarization: "A couple of women felt that she [Hernandez] was rendering a valuable service to the female and black female community. Two or three others, feeling she was totally on the wrong track, suggested that she ought to abandon her work with women's liberation. Instead of continuing with women's lib, they contended she should take on a project, which would allow her talents to be used solely for the black community."[86] Although respondents were split in their opinion of Hernandez's women's movement participation, neither side saw women's and black liberation issues as complementary. Those who thought Hernandez provided a valuable service assumed that "female" meant "white women." They saw the interests of black and white women as distinct and separate. Hernandez's detractors refused to acknowledge the discrimination black women faced on the basis of gender and subsumed black women's identity under the racial category *black*.

Similarly, many white feminists, though a large number desired a united sisterhood, either ignored black women's gender or assumed black women were not interested in women's issues. Black women interested in feminism were even suspect, as demonstrated at the 1968 Sandy Springs Conference, one of two regional meetings radical socialist feminists held to discuss launching an autonomous women's movement. In the transcript of this conference, unidentified white feminists debate (among themselves) whether, if approached, black women activists would participate in the radical feminist movement.[87] There were glimmers of consciousness about racism, but for the most part, the transcript is riddled with misguided ideas about black women and feminism.

The transcript is informative because it lends insights into the motivations behind white feminists' racism in the early days of the contemporary women's movement. In the course of their conversation, it is evident that the women participating in this discussion did not trust black

women's allegiance to feminism. A standard, empathetic perspective on black women's lack of participation was, and still is, that black women were too busy coping with daily survival issues to join the movement. While this may be true for many black women, this reasoning does not apply to *all* black women. It excludes those who were interested in feminism and available to put time and energy into the movement—whether in addition to existing obligations or in spite of them.

Also informative is the candid revelation of white feminists' anxiety about organizing with black women. Several issues arose, including white feminists' fears that black women would make white women feel guilty about race and class privilege, thereby derailing efforts to develop the radical feminist movement.[88] Acknowledging that black women faced a different kind of oppression, white feminists worried that these differences and white guilt would obstruct the development of a unified radical feminist agenda, or "muddy up the waters."[89] We must also acknowledge the mixed messages white antiracist activists received in the transition from the civil rights movement's "black and white together" message to the Black Power movement's self-determination. Breines recalls the conundrum: "They [white women] were antiracist activists until they were no longer welcome in the black freedom movement, a point that white women mention often and resentfully. They were instructed not to work among African Americans and then criticized for not doing so."[90]

Derived from this morass of distrust, the women in the Sandy Springs discussion also voiced a contradictory concern. At one moment they were concerned that black nationalist women would not be truly dedicated to feminism. Yet, later in the discussion, these white women accused any black woman involved in feminism of being an "Uncle Tom," echoing sentiments voiced by black nationalist *men*.[91] Never once was it considered that not all black women, if politically involved, were black nationalists. Such a perspective may be due to white socialist feminists' work with groups such as the Black Panthers and only connecting with black men in leadership positions. The ironies abound in the complexity of identity, coalition, and sexual politics.

Black feminists faced the black community's accusations of inauthentic blackness because of their gender concerns. The Sandy Springs transcript reveals that black women also needed to beware of white feminists who considered them "the worst kind" of black women because of their alleged betrayal of blackness.[92] Both black nationalist and white feminist judgments on black women's racial authenticity assumed that a truly revo-

lutionary black woman prioritized her racial oppression over any gender considerations. Like black men, white feminists in this particular discussion refused to recognize the complexity of race and gender oppression. Instead, they chose to see black women as solely black, but not as women. As further insult, with their use of the racialized and derogatory Uncle Tom label, these particular white women labeled black feminists as duplicitous.

Still, those white feminists did not speak for all white feminists, and in spite of covert and overt racism, black women demanded inclusion in the contemporary women's movement. In responding to a racist agenda based on exclusive notions of sisterhood, some black feminists used prose and poetry as a mode of resistance from within the women's movement. For instance, poet Lorraine Bethel, an African American lesbian, wrote a scathing critique of the women's movement, specifically addressing the tokenization of black lesbian feminists by radical, white lesbian feminists. In her 1979 poem "What Chou Mean *We*, White Girl? Or, The Cullud Lesbian Feminist Declaration of Independence," Bethel raged against her imposed position as the educator of white feminists.[93] She struck at the core of sisterhood and its racist possibilities. On the one hand, white feminists asked for education about difference. Yet, when black feminists participated, they encountered white women who used limited cultural knowledge to enact a "Third Worldism" that simultaneously romanticized and condescended to third world people and their struggles.[94] Bethel, and other black feminists, gained little from these interactions that returned them to the role of political mammy for white women.

Bethel also laid bare the process of tokenization as white feminists approached the same black women, "selecting their victims" from a Rolodex "labeled feminists, black or lesbians" to "represent Third World women and lesbians on *their* feminist criticism panel."[95] Implicit in Bethel's account of women's movement dynamics is black women's exclusion from planning the direction of the movement based on some black women's angry and homophobic responses to feminism. White women made the movement their property, and black women were merely invited to participate on an already-established agenda. Bethel's poem showed that even black women's later experiences of racism in the women's movement were based on no real knowledge about black women and feminism. Two outcomes occurred. Either white feminists excluded black feminists from the women's movement out of guilt, or black feminists excluded themselves based on their exasperation with their role as token black feminists or black lesbian feminists.

Although some black women vehemently rejected the women's movement, other black women, in countering racism and ignorance about their identities as blacks *and* women, decided to struggle with white feminists, rather than against them. However, as black women are at the center of analysis in this book it is important to note that the women's movement sisterhood framework was and is too constrictive. Black women responded by forming their own organizations, but in doing so, there is one more hostile front they encountered: social policy and popular culture.

Black Matriarchy Theory and Social Policy

Segments of the black female population rejected the women's movement out of anger over racism, but others rejected it out of fear—fear that involvement with a movement labeled "lesbians" and "man-hating" would merely combine with other stereotypes of black women to condemn them. In *Fighting Words*, Collins examines public transcripts and how they confine black women politically. Public transcripts are "the public discourses or knowledges of academia, government bureaucracies, the press, the courts, and popular culture. Controlled by elite groups, this public discourse typically counts as legitimate knowledge and often is grounded in false universals."[96] Public transcripts on television, in films, and in public policy reports on the black community revived the mammy stereotype and gave it a contemporary look in the form of the black matriarch.

A common African American folk adage that "the only free people are white men and black women" accuses black women of collusion with white men during slavery and in the present to oppress black men.[97] In this racialized version of the Genesis narrative, black women betrayed black men, who were then cast out of the Eden that is the "Garden of Patriarchal Power." Daniel Patrick Moynihan, then a Harvard sociologist, brought this tale of betrayal to currency in 1965 with the publication of "The Negro Family: The Case for National Action." Sheila Radford-Hill marks this as the moment at which black women's traditional roles as reservoirs of the community's public morality and racial dignity were publicly attacked.[98]

Moynihan argued that the state of the black community was "pathological" because slavery imposed sex role reversal on black men and women.[99] Slavery emasculated black men and, thus, deprived them of their status as protector of their families and heads of household. In fact, Moynihan continued, an increasing number of black families are at a disadvantage because they are female-headed and defy the definition of the traditional

nuclear family. Moynihan alleged that black women were matriarchs because they "fail to fulfill their traditional 'womanly' duties" and were guilty of emasculating black men.[100]

The black matriarchy theory served as evidence of black women's collusion with the white power structure. As a result of this collusion, government policies punished black women for their nonnormative enactment of womanhood.[101] Sex-segregated employment and the 1965 report "The Negro Family: The Case for National Action" created a hostile environment for black women by making it appear that black women were already liberated. This idea, circulated in the black community and perpetuated by social policy, kept some black women from joining the women's movement. Black woman's alleged liberated status also helped some blacks downplay the necessity of forming independent black feminist organizations.

Several aspects of the Moynihan report are rooted in patriarchal and racist ideologies of the family and womanhood. Moynihan ignored persistent racial discrimination as a factor in black male unemployment rates. Black women did not usurp black men's jobs, because black women occupied gendered positions in the sex-segregated job market.[102] Instead, black men faced job competition from U.S.-born and white ethnic immigrant men. Yet, the Moynihan report only fueled black men's claims that black women took jobs from black men. Such an assumption ignores the persistence of a "woman's wage," a wage not meant to support one woman's most basic needs, let alone those of an entire family.[103] The so-called black matriarchies were far from financially stable without black men's second income.

Black scholars, cultural critics, and feminists of all races challenged Moynihan's assumption that the nuclear family was the only viable form of family, discounting the survival of African Americans through extended family and fictive kin as they evolved in slavery.[104] Moynihan, and most U.S. citizens, assumed that the patriarchal nuclear family, as depicted on 1950s-era television shows, was the only viable family structure. However, the increased labor force participation of white women, their decreased dependence on marriage for financial security, and climbing divorce rates meant that the viability of the nuclear family was a dubious construct even for white Americans.[105] Moynihan's report was based on an increasingly unstable model which proposed that black Americans, if they followed the model of white male-headed nuclear families, could halt the decline of the black family. The reassertion of patriarchy, Moynihan implied, would cure black America of its pathology.

Several essays by black feminist writers and professionals refuted the myth of the matriarchy. Analyzing statistics on education and employment, critics of Moynihan examined his theory of matriarchy through the lens of race and gender and found it lacking.[106] They contested, for example, the use of black women's educational attainment levels and their lower unemployment rates compared to those of black men as evidence of black women allegedly having greater freedom than black men. Black women's meager advancements in education did not mean greater freedom for black women, their collusion with white patriarchy, or the intentional emasculation of black men. For example, in 1968, black women barely outpaced black men by two percentage points in completion of four years of college. Data from the U.S. Census show that in 1966, 3.7 percent of black women completed four years of college, compared to 3.9 percent of black men. By 1968, 4.8 percent of black women completed college compared to 3.7 percent of black men.[107] In addition, black women were situated at the bottom of the economic ladder, compared to whites and black men.[108] Black women were trapped in low-paying, sex-segregated positions that did not reflect freedom, equality, or a triumph over black men, as defined by the theory of the matriarchy.

Within the gendered job market, black women dominated positions that did not stray far from society's image of black women as nurturing or maternal.[109] Furthermore, teaching, nursing, clerical positions, and domestic work paid less compared to work for men in construction, bricklaying, or roadwork.[110] Often racist hiring practices squeezed black men out of these positions, contributing to their high unemployment rate. Far from collaborating with white men to keep black men unemployed, many black women unwillingly carried the burden of supporting many, not all, black families on one, low-wage income.

Black women, ensuring the survival of their families in the white patriarchy, were unfairly labeled matriarchs. Social policy used black women's slightly higher educational attainment and lower unemployment rates as a wedge between black men and women. Forced to support black families in an economy built on exploitation, black women were vilified for the few successes they achieved. In this light, claims that black women were as free as white men were unfounded. The only way in which black women were free was as exploited labor in a job market that demanded their subservience and "innate" nurturing qualities. In service to capitalism, black women earned low wages for maintaining racist and sexist stereotypes of the Mammy.

Cultural Stereotypes of the Matriarch

Stereotypes of black women in social policy, film, and television reinforced the matrix of domination through an endless supply of cultural images that, according to K. Sue Jewell, "attribute their depressed socioeconomic status to individual and cultural deficiencies."[111] Mass media expanded the image of the mammy to include the theory of the matriarchy by incorporating it into their productions for black audiences. Black feminists witnessed continual media misrepresentations of black women. Popular culture also reinforced negative ideas about black women, as domineering, verbally abusive, and antimale.

Edward Mapp distinguished the line between the mammy and the matriarch as determined by whether the black woman in question took care of a white family or a black one.[112] As evidence, he juxtaposed the maternal role of Claudia McNeil in *A Raisin in the Sun* (1961) with Hattie McDaniel's earlier performance as Mammy in *Gone With the Wind* (1939) to demonstrate the black woman's shifting role in the realm of popular culture. With black film's commercial success in the 1970s, black women were still caretakers, but now they cared for and gave unsolicited advice to black characters. For black women, cultural stereotypes presented a no-win situation of mammy or matriarch, with no position in between.

In addition to this shift from mammy to matriarch, 1970s "blaxploitation" (black exploitation) films introduced the image of the Superwoman who cared for the black community. Producers and writers of blaxploitation films deployed sexist and racist ideas about African American women in hollow tribute to their power. Already defined in opposition to white womanhood as hypersexual, African American women's sexuality in these films was a source of power. In many ways, blaxploitation films served as further rhetoric for black nationalist movements. For example, SNCC's Black Women's Liberation Committee recalls that men, in debates over sexism in nationalist movements, asked black women to seduce uninitiated men into the movement.[113] During the height of black nationalist rhetoric, in film such as *Sweetback's Baadasssss Song* (1971) and *Shaft* (1971), black male heroes illustrated the establishment of a new black male patriarchy in line with masculinist Black Power rhetoric. Black women, whether as love interests or prostitutes, were merely a means of survival or a convenient conduit through which black male heroes proved their sexual prowess.[114]

When black women were the heroines, sexuality was merely another part of their arsenal. In films such as *Cleopatra Jones* (1973), *Coffy* (1973),

and *Foxy Brown* (1974), the heterosexist male gaze was always present, negating any pretensions of female agency. Athletic and active in cleavage-revealing costumes, blaxploitation heroines were ultimately unable to defend themselves when overpowered by villains, necessitating their rescue by black male lovers.[115]

Misogynist portrayals of black women were a reaction to the rise of the women's movement and fears of gender coalitions between black and white women.[116] These portrayals were, Mark Reid contends, equally attractive to women who were caught in feminist liberation and traditional subservient roles, as well as to antifeminist men.[117] For instance, in *Cleopatra Jones*, Tamara Dobson was a CIA agent determined to keep a white, lesbian drug czar from infecting the black community's children with drugs. As part of the subtext, in this and other Cleopatra Jones films, the black heroine is victorious in her battles with other women—the antithesis of feminist sisterhood.[118] Blaxploitation films degraded the strength of black women for the benefit of male titillation and upheld the myth that all white feminists were lesbians intent on turning black women into man haters.[119]

Blaxploitation films' messages also carried over into television, in such shows as the sitcom *That's My Mama* (1974–1975). The sitcom featured Clifton Davis as Clifton Curtis, a single man who inherits his father's barbershop. His mother, Eloise Curtis (portrayed by film and stage actress Theresa Merritt), makes constant demands for him to live his life the way *she* sees fit. Merritt fit the stereotype of the domineering mammy, but the one difference between this show and its predecessors was that for once, a black woman was allowed to play the mammy to her *own* family and not a white one. The National Black Feminist Organization went public with its disdain for stereotypes of black women and *That's My Mama*, holding press conferences in three cities: Atlanta, Detroit, and Washington, D.C. Covered by the *Atlanta Journal* and the city's black newspaper, the *Atlanta Daily World*, the NBFO denounced the airing of the show and the entire "television industry for being 'more motivated by profit than social responsibility.'"[120] Although it is difficult to ascertain what impact the NBFO action had on the program's eventual cancellation, it is evident in comparing coverage of the show in the mainstream *Atlanta Journal* and the black community's *Atlanta Daily World* that the latter understood the NBFO's action as on behalf of black women and the entire black community.[121]

Mindful that the 1970s were the beginning of television's era of "relevance programming," some television producers actually attempted to respond to the social upheaval of the late 1960s and began representing

marginalized groups.[122] Perhaps the best-known producer doing this work at the time was Norman Lear and his independent production company Tandem/TAT. Lear's productions, which included *All in the Family* (1971–1979), *The Jeffersons* (1975–1985), *Maude* (1972–1978), and *Sanford and Son* (1972–1977), ignited discussions of how, in the wake of civil unrest, to best represent issues of race and racism.[123] These shows dealt with issues at macro- and microlevels of U.S. society, ranging from racism, sexism, feminism, political corruption in Nixon's White House, the Vietnam War, and gasoline shortages. A Lear production that came to the attention of black feminists was perhaps the most popular black sitcom of the time, *Good Times*.

Featured on *Good Times* during its five seasons, from 1974 to 1979, the Evan's family persevered through the travails of poverty in a Chicago housing project. The show was heralded as one of the first television portrayals of black nuclear family life. Nevertheless, black feminist organizations, such as the National Black Feminist Organization and Black Women Organized for Action, orchestrated direct action against what they perceived as unrealistic and matriarchal representations of black women on the show, as well as against messages of black women's antifeminism. Already in the show that launched *Good Times*, Florida's antipathy for feminism was established. Marthe Lentz analyzes how in the television show *Maude*, and in particular in the episode "Maude Meets Florida," black and white women are pitted against one another against the backdrop of domestic and political space. Throughout the episode, Maude, a feminist for whom Florida works as domestic help, badgers Florida about liberating herself. Labeled a "preliberation Southern black," Florida spends the entirety of the episode resisting Maude's feminism (prompting Florida to call herself a "housekeeper" rather than a "maid" and demanding she use the front door and not the back because of the racial overtones). The episode ends with Maude's assertion that Florida is "too dumb" for feminist liberation. Lentz concludes that "blackness and feminism become quite explicitly opposed: blackness occupies a privileged relation to materiality, while feminism is branded as ridiculously ideological in its absorption with issues of language and representation."[124]

Florida's contentious relationship to feminism carried over to *Good Times*. In the show's second 1974 season, a standard perspective on black women's relationship to feminism was featured in the *Good Times* episode "Florida Flips." In this episode, housework and the demands of her family overwhelm Florida. In a moment of frustration, she slaps her youngest son,

Michael (who later becomes the show's black nationalist voice). Her neighbor and best friend, Willona, realizes that Florida is on the brink of a breakdown and decides Florida needs to attend a "Women's Awareness" meeting. The depicted meeting is rife with stereotypes about feminism, the kind of black women who would be attracted to such a meeting, and black male/female relationships, and Florida leaves skeptical about women's liberation. Once home, though, she encounters her husband, James, who echoes a sentiment heard at the Women's Awareness meeting: "the only place for the black woman is in the kitchen and the bedroom." It is then that Florida realizes for her fulfillment she needs more than her home, children, and husband.

Black Women Organized for Action organizer Aileen Hernandez wrote Tandem producer Norman Lear soon after "Florida Flips" aired. In her letter she praises Lear's company for its representations of racial and ethnic minorities in its productions but also warns that her organization monitors these representations "with a critical eye."[125] Because of this critical eye, Hernandez requests a meeting between Tandem and Black Women Organized for Action's Media Committee to discuss "past and projected segments of the show."[126] Valerie Jo Bradley, a BWOA member, recalls, "Norman Lear responded back and invited us to see the operation, meet with the writers. He even asked us to identify black women writers who could bring that sensitivity. He agreed that perhaps he had not paid much attention. So, as a result, Thelma's role expanded and Florida got a job. . . . Now I don't know if we did that single handedly, but we certainly did stay on it and Norman Lear did respond."[127] There is no archival documentation beyond Hernandez's letter that follows up on the BWOA-Tandem dialogue. However, Florida's understanding of feminism and position as reflective of black women's reality did improve in several subsequent episodes including "Getting Up the Rent," "Florida Goes to School," and "Florida the Woman." In these episodes Florida pokes fun at the black matriarchy theory ("Don't all the magazines say *our* women are supposed to be the head of the house?") and even asserts feminist consciousness ("women's lib don't mean we want to stop being women. It just means we want our chance in this world, too").

These small victories are but examples of black women's attempts to claim the feminist movement and put its tenets to work in their favor. In television and film, black women were most often represented as matriarchal figures that lived to serve their families and the black community. The other alternative roles for black women were as prostitutes or smart,

talking sapphires—yet another stereotype applied to black women. All these roles fell short of depicting the reality of black women's lives and influenced how U.S. society viewed black women.

* * *

Analyzed together, discrimination in organizations and institutions, and social experiences served as the social and political culture into which black feminists' collective identity and organizing emerged. Black feminist organizations formed in reaction to limits on black women's roles in the civil rights movement and to the rise of black masculinist rhetoric. These movements placed the role of gender in black women's lives on the back burner of their agendas. Likewise, black women formed separate organizations from white feminists because of the limited sisterhood frame, as defined by the women's movement and racism within it. Black feminist organizations also emerged in reaction to the theory of the black matriarchy as it circulated in social policy and popular culture.

The next chapter turns to organizational emergence within the cycle of protest of the late 1960s. These organizations expanded on the repertoire of strategies gained from the civil rights and women's movements, but they found that ultimately the black woman's concerns fell outside of "rights" and "sisterhood" frameworks respectively. Instead, black women enacted interstitial politics between race and gender but cognizant of both. Black feminist organizations formed in response to attacks against black women that demonized and scapegoated them as solely responsible for the ills of black communities. Indeed, black women were ready to become what one writer called the "legitimate instrument by which the women's movement and black movement can forge a power wedge for accomplishing significant change . . . that will benefit both groups."[128]

2 ☆ NO LONGER DIVIDED AGAINST OURSELVES

Common to all black feminist organizations' emergence was conscious-ness raising. In New York, San Francisco, Chicago, and Boston, black women held their initial meetings to create a change in their thinking about "what it means to be Black, woman and feminist."[1] These particular black women initiated what Snow and Benford would call "the not infre-quent remedial, reconstitutive work that is required when members of any ideological or thought community encounter glaring disjunction between their beliefs and experiences or events in the world."[2] Far from contem-plating formal organizations, black women reached out to one another to confirm that they were not alone in seeing disparities between the rheto-ric of the civil rights movement and the treatment of women within that same movement. Demita Frazier, a Combahee River Collective founder, recalls black women with allegiances to black and women's rights, "feeling divided against ourselves."[3] More than seeking grand plans for organiza-tions, black women simply wanted to know that they were not alone in see-ing the applicability of women's liberation for black women. Although they did not know it yet, they were part of a historical continuum and growing contingency of contemporary black feminists.

While black women did hold leadership positions in the civil rights movement, and in some instances wielded more power relative to their white counterparts, black feminists still noticed a disjuncture between democratic action and practice. Francis Beal of the Third World Women's Alliance (TWWA) recalls how this disjuncture manifested itself in SNCC:

> I mean, we used to stay up half the night talking about freedom, libera-tion, freedom, you know, all these ideas and it was natural—that in a sense

freedom was in the air. And all this talk—it's like Sojourner [Truth] says, "What's all this talk about 'Freedom'?" In a sense that happened to us, "what's all this talkin' about freedom?" . . . And then when people, internally, would do things that were not democratic there was a disjuncture between some of these broad philosophical ideas and some of the practice. . . . And it became obvious in some ways that the—well, the movement talked about freedom and liberation as it related to you as blacks, [but] it still accepted a lot of the premises when it came to women in terms of how life should be. . . . And this was very jarring and it was a disjuncture also because . . . women actually did step forward and play certain roles, leadership roles . . . and then, when people began talking about men should do this and do that and women should do that, we said, "Now, wait a minute. This sounds familiar" [laughter].[4]

Black women also perceived signs that social change was possible from their own experiences of desegregation. The basic groundwork for black women's interstitial politics was laid in the fissures created by contradictions in rhetoric and action—rhetoric of freedom juxtaposed with concrete sexist behaviors black women witnessed and sometimes experienced. As mentioned in chapter 1, Margaret Sloan, as a youth member of CORE and cofounder of the National Black Feminist Organization (NBFO), observed women performing tasks such as cooking and child care, while exclusively men planned strategy for Chicago's rent strikes and demonstrations in the 1960s. Cognitive liberation for black feminists involved equal parts inspiration and disillusionment as they saw real changes happening, but debated whether the civil rights movement could accommodate black women's growing gender awareness.

This chapter documents and interrogates the emergence narratives of the Third World Women's Alliance, the National Black Feminist Organization, the National Alliance of Black Feminists (NABF), the Combahee River Collective, and Black Women Organized for Action (BWOA). The organizations were composed of black women with similar ideas about ending racism and sexism, but they also had different ideas about what it meant to identify as black feminists. Each narrative documents preexisting organizational links and key members who helped shape them at the outset.

The Third World Women's Alliance

The disjuncture between movement ideals and practice, along with her growing awareness of sterilization abuse among women of color, prompted Beal, a former NAACP youth leader and member of SNCC's International Affairs Commission, to present a paper at a 1968 SNCC personnel meeting in New York. As part of this paper, Beal recommended that SNCC form a black women's caucus to explore the impact of sexism on the organization's constituency in addition to racism. This was a previously neglected aspect of SNCC's organizing, though one could argue that SNCC tackled race and gender as it related to masculinity and femininity and as they related to asserting human dignity.

Few SNCC members opposed the formation of the caucus, because the organization was in its final years of decline.[5] SNCC's destabilization due to the loss of popular financial support, failing Northern antipoverty campaigns, and increased militancy created an opening for the women who formed the Black Women's Liberation Caucus (BWLC). The few black men who did openly oppose the formation of the caucus did so on the grounds that it smacked of women's liberation and that it was a "white women's thing" designed to divide the race. These accusations were not new to the members of the BWLC who read popular periodicals and were in contact with black nationalist discussions and, therefore, not a deterrent to their explorations of feminism.

By 1969, the BWLC split from SNCC to expand its membership base outside the confines of the main organization. In particular, the new organization, the Black Women's Alliance (BWA) wanted to expand its membership base to include "women from other organizations, welfare mothers, community workers, and campus radicals."[6] Although it was following the political flow of the rapidly destabilized SNCC toward incorporating the poor into its work, the BWA felt an independent black women's organization could more effectively address the needs of black women than a mixed-sex organization such as SNCC and that it could do so without marginalizing gender.

The BWA's goals were threefold. First, similar to other black feminist organizations that emerged in later years, the BWA emerged to dispel the myth of the black matriarchy. The organization's second goal was to re-evaluate the oppression of black women in slavery. By countering "the widespread concept that by some miracle, the oppression of slavery for the black woman was not as degrading, not as horrifying, not as barbaric as it

had been for the black man," the BWA argued that in a society where black men were oppressed by their race, black women were "further enslaved by . . . sex."[7] The BWA's third goal, to redefine the role of black woman in revolutionary struggle, responded to the sexism of black nationalist rhetoric. This rhetoric, while elevating black women to a pedestal as "African Queens," called for their subservience to black men. In recounting the history of the organization, the TWWA collective illuminates the contradictions in nationalist rhetoric: "Now we noticed another thing. And that is, with the rise of nationalism and the rejection of white middle class norms and values, that this rejection of whiteness . . . took a different turn when it came to the Black woman. That is, Black men began defining the role of Black women in the movement. They stated that our role was a supportive one, others stated that we must become breeders and provide an army; still others stated that we had Kotex or pussy power."[8]

Beal recalls that former SNCC members in the BWA viewed genuflection to male power as contradictory and absurd. As black women did not bow to the violence of Alabama State Troopers in the South, why did black nationalist men think the women would submit to patriarchy on anyone's terms, be it in black organizations or in the bedroom?[9] The BWA recognized the contradictions in redefining blackness based on sexist ideas about family and sex roles, and called instead for "a true revolutionary movement [that] must enhance the status of women,"[10] highlighting the contradictions in calling for a revolution of white-dominated society, while attempting to model the white, patriarchal nuclear family.

At about the time the BWA incorporated anti-imperialism into its agenda, a few women active in the Puerto Rican independence movement and the Puerto Rican Socialist Party approached the BWA about joining the organization. Their request led BWA members to debate the dynamics of oppressive power relationships beyond the black/white paradigm. There were two positions on whether the BWA should permit members of non-African descent to join. Some women felt that the position of black women in the United States was so historically unique that the BWA should focus exclusively on them. These members felt that the work of the BWA would be diluted if it allowed nonblack women to become members, so instead they favored working in coalition with other revolutionary groups on specific issues.[11] The second position, as Beal explains, held that "the complexities of intersecting oppressions [were] more resilient than the distinctions of the particular social groups and . . . that there was no other group for these women to be involved in—that we should be open to our Puerto Rican sis-

ters to join with us."[12] This position, favoring a multicultural alliance that broadened the organization's agenda, held sway in the group.

The group formally established solidarity with Asian, Chicana, Native American, and Puerto Rican women based on anti-imperialist ideology and formally changed its name from the Black Women's Alliance to the Third World Women's Alliance. The TWWA felt that such an ideology illustrated its members' belief that women of color's similarities transcended their differences and organizing would be much more effective and unified in solidarity across race.[13] The TWWA linked differences of culture, race, and ethnicity to the fight against common exploitation by capitalism, stereotypes, and drug and alcohol abuse in communities of color.

Equally important to the multiracial expansion of the TWWA was the organization's geographic spread to the West Coast. Cheryl Perry, founder of the West Coast chapter, became a member of the TWWA through a preexisting network of friends in New York City who were connected with the Venceremos Brigade. In 1970 the Cuban government had set a goal to harvest 10 million tons of sugarcane to demonstrate that the Cuban Revolution could succeed despite American imperialist policies. The Venceremos Brigade, a U.S.-based group, organized to take young Americans to Cuba to help with the harvest and expose them to socialism in practice. The brigade had two goals: (1) to break the U.S.-imposed blockade against Cuba and (2) "to express the solidarity of progressive American youth, black, brown, and white, with the Cuban Revolution by participating in the harvest."[14] The following year, 1971, Perry went to Cuba with the fourth Venceremos Brigade and, upon her return, decided to relocate to the West Coast to be closer to the brigade's headquarters. The East Coast branch of the TWWA consisted mainly of black and Puerto Rican women, and the New York members agreed that a West Coast branch could help them expand their membership base, particularly to Asian–Pacific Islander women and Chicanas.[15]

Replicating her own recruitment into the organization, Perry recruited West Coast Venceremos Brigade participants into the TWWA, as well as members from other organizations, such as the Committee to Free Angela Davis. Also, in 1972, a number of black women who met at other women-oriented political events, particularly abortion rights rallies, formed an organization called Black Sisters United. Linda Burnham, for example, was a CORE activist since high school and a member in Black Sisters United who joined the TWWA at Perry's suggestion.[16] The West Coast TWWA operated under the same anti-imperialist, antisexist, antiracist philosophy as

the East Coast branch, with Perry acting as its liaison. The activities of the two branches were consistent only in their adherence to the same ideological philosophy.[17] Perry was the main organizer on the West Coast and, therefore, shaped the activities of that branch, which included health information fairs for communities of color. The East Coast branch, on the other hand, focused more on articulating the connections between feminism and anti-imperialism through the publication of the TWWA's newspaper *Triple Jeopardy*.

Federal Bureau of Investigation (FBI) Counterintelligence Program (COINTELPRO) records indicate that the TWWA was under investigation from December 1970 to March 1974. This investigation included at least six sources supplying the FBI with the TWWA's publication *Triple Jeopardy*, infiltration of the organization's meetings, reports on the activities of key TWWA members, and photographs of TWWA members for inclusion in the agency's Extremist Photograph Album.[18] The TWWA is the only organization in this study for which a Freedom of Information Act request yielded documentation. This indicates the strong threat the federal government believed the TWWA posed, particularly in connection with what the government called "the revolutionary Student Nonviolent Coordinating Committee." Indeed, SNCC and the TWWA were revolutionary in the thought and actions they proposed, but in the parlance of the FBI, *revolutionary* was a catchall phrase for dangerous and worthy of the FBI's most-wanted list.

The National Black Feminist Organization

In the late 1960s, many black women did not fully understand the meaning of feminism for themselves and initially downplayed how important it was that black women gather to talk. In a 1974 report to *Ms.* magazine on the founding of the National Black Feminist Organization, Margaret Sloan, the organization's only president, describes how a three-hour discussion unexpectedly continued on well into the night: "We listened. We laughed. We interrupted each other, not out of disrespect, but out of that immediate identification with those words and feeling that we had each said and felt . . . many times alone. We had all felt guilty and crazy about our beliefs. And yet, all the things that have divided black women from each other in the past, kept us from getting to that room sooner, seemed not to be important."[19] Using their interpersonal connections to other activists and acquaintances, black feminists across the country gathered in groups to examine what feminism had to offer black women. Yet, they also critically

questioned whether their involvement in feminist activism would benefit or harm the overall black liberation struggle. In the process of these discussions, black women shared their experiences as racially gendered and impoverished people, and they discovered their commonalities.

Similar to Beal's attention to sterilization abuse as a reproductive rights issue for black women, Sloan and members of the NBFO gathering noted sexist rhetoric that the recent Supreme Court decision in Roe v. Wade had sparked. Noting black nationalist denouncements of the proabortion decision as genocide and the women's movement's singular focus on abortion as the only reproductive rights issue prompted black women in New York to consider feminism as a viable political option. Fifteen of the thirty black feminists from the initial meeting organized a press conference on 15 August 1973.[20]

Initially held to announce plans for a regional black feminist conference, Eleanor Holmes Norton, then New York City Human Rights Commissioner, and Sloan tackled head on myths about black women and feminism. Pointing out that black men could not achieve liberation without black women, Sloan addressed the misconception that feminism divided the race. She and Norton also countered accusations of selling out or betraying the race with the assertion that black women's entrance into the women's movement would inject an antiracist politic and shift the focus from solely gender oppression.[21] Having addressed several points of contention, Sloan and Norton announced the plans for the Eastern Regional Conference four months later and declared the formation of the National Black Feminist Organization a historic moment in black and women's history.

Sloan, in retrospect, admits that the announcement of a national organization was a spur-of-the-moment decision from the previous night's meeting.[22] The women in attendance thought they would be taken more seriously if they claimed a nationwide presence with chapters in major U.S. cities such as San Francisco, Cleveland, and Chicago. This would later prove to be a tactical error because of the deluge of calls they received: more than four hundred women called the following day wanting to join the (nonexistent) local chapters mentioned at the press conference.[23] While the New York women did have black feminist contacts in these cities, they did not have the infrastructure to support the influx of new members.

Still, this response to the NBFO's national announcement, along with the overwhelmingly positive response Sloan received from black women during her two-year speaking tour with Gloria Steinem, convinced her that

the time was right for a national organization. Noting coverage by the *New York Times* and the German newspaper *Das Spiegel*, but the lack of coverage by the black press, Alice Walker later voiced the disappointment of many black feminists that black women's interests were clearly marginalized in the black community, but excitement that so many women expressed interest in the NBFO.[24] Several indicators spoke to the number of black women feeling marginalized by the black and women's movements. One sign that black women were ready to add their voices to the women's movement was the over two hundred women, ranging in age from eighteen to fifty-five, who attended the NBFO's first public meeting. Deborah Singletary and Eugenia Wilshire, NBFO members, both recall an immediate, positive reaction to the call for the meeting:

> *Singletary:* I'm not even sure I even thought about feminism before or thought about myself as a feminist, but when I heard that black feminists were convening, then I knew that that was where I belonged and I went to that first meeting.
>
> *Wilshire:* I didn't even know how long the organization had existed or not, but [the flyer] just said there was a meeting in a church and it was black feminists and it gave the time and it was in my neighborhood and I said, "That's for me." So I went.[25]

These comments and the meeting's large attendance numbers evidence that other black women recognized the moment was right for their voices and organizational skills to be put to work in black feminist organizations. Contrary to news and magazine reports, these women did not hesitate to join the women's movement—especially when they could define it for themselves. Other signs of this definition included the influx of women at the Eastern Regional Conference to discuss issues such as feminism, civil rights, and black male/female relationships, as well as a special section of letters to the editor in the May 1974 issue of *Ms.* heralding the Eastern Regional Conference as a turning point in black women's organizing.[26]

Not only did the NBFO proceed through openings created by the civil rights and women's movements, the organization also held open the door for other black feminist organizations, specifically, the National Alliance of Black Feminists and the Combahee River Collective. In a trickle-down effect, the NBFO's initiative in organizing but lack of formal infrastructure created tensions that yielded new black feminist organizations that did not agree with the direction of the NBFO. For the NABF, the NBFO provided the organizational opening and ideological impetus for the emergence of

a black feminist organization in Chicago. For black feminists in Boston, the NBFO held open the door to black feminist organizing, but the national organization did not adequately address class and sexual orientation in its mandate. Hence, the Combahee River Collective emerged as a challenger to the NBFO's elite position as the organization with, at the time, the most widespread attention and influence over large numbers of black feminists.

The National Alliance of Black Feminists

The NBFO, though located in New York, jump-started the consciousness-raising efforts of Chicago-area black feminists. Black feminists were already active in Chicago but following the formation of the NBFO, black feminist organizing in Chicago went into high gear. Over the course of a year, from June 1974 to September 1975, black feminists in Chicago conducted consciousness-raising sessions under the banner of the NBFO.

The NABF began as the Chicago chapter of the NBFO, meeting on 19 June 1974 at the YWCA in the main business district of Chicago: the Loop. The organization convened without the oversight of the NBFO national office, which led to organizational inconsistencies between the national office and the Chicago chapter. Still, as had occurred with the spur-of-the-moment founding of the NBFO, organizer Brenda Eichelberger took advantage of the momentum of the movement. Had Eichelberger waited until the NBFO's New York City–based leaders sent a representative to oversee the formation of the Chicago chapter, there might not have been a local chapter. Chicago-area black feminists were impatient to add Midwestern black women's voices to the clamor for gendered social justice.

Eichelberger had waited a long time for a group of women to address the pressing issues she had long felt existed around sexism and racism. The daughter of a stay-at-home mother and a postal worker father, Eichelberger grew up acutely aware of racist and sexist disparities. Her father, whom she characterizes as highly educated with a degree in Romance languages, found himself shut out, due to racism, of employment where he could use his degree but insistent on his children's educational strivings. Her father and mother did, however, allow her younger brother more freedoms than Eichelberger was allowed, piquing her interest in gender disparities. Such formative moments were but a few that brought Eichelberger to her leadership role in Chicago's black feminist community.

Eichelberger served as temporary chair of the Chicago NBFO chapter until it dissolved in October 1975. Along with Linda Johnston, Eichelberger

planned the agenda for the first meeting, which included discussing "the needs of the black woman in the Chicago area and determin[ing] the foci for the Chicago Chapter and the best methods for implementation."[27] Eichelberger and Johnston came to the meeting with topics for discussion that included employment, health care, sexuality, drug abuse, alcoholism, incarcerated women, ex-offenders, child care, rape, and consciousness-raising.[28]

The Chicago women quickly formed committees to oversee the daily functioning of the chapter, including an office space committee to find an inexpensive but accessible place for their meetings. The location of the meetings was important because the Chicago women felt the need to assert a feminist presence on Chicago's predominately black South Side, but they wanted to remain accessible to potential members throughout the city. They also needed to counter stereotypes that feminism was a middle-class movement; meeting in a location considered "bourgeois" would send the wrong message to the potential constituents. By July, the members decided to donate money toward the rental of office space at the Blue Gargoyle, a community center for the University Church of Disciples of Christ.

The Chicago chapter also established steering, fund-raising, membership, consciousness-raising, rape crisis intervention, periodicals, school, and social committees. Through these committees, and social interactions within them, the Chicago NBFO cultivated a social movement culture that attended to the "spirit of comradeship and sisterhood" in the organization.[29] For example, the social committee provided refreshments for meetings, scheduled social outings, and acknowledged the life events of members such as births, deaths, and illnesses. Social movement organization theorists recognize these moments of informal fellowship as instrumental in membership maintenance and cohesion.[30] The Chicago NBFO members recognized the strain that political organizing could place on interpersonal relationships and the toll it could take on members' lives. Chicago NBFO leaders offered incentives of comradeship and sisterhood in exchange for the time, energy, money, and political commitment members put into the organization. This exchange was key to the organization's longevity.

After several meetings, the Chicago NBFO members, worried about the continued lack of communication from the national office, took steps to ensure the smooth functioning of their chapter by electing a steering committee. The steering committee then suspended general business meetings for a month to systematize operations, meeting weekly to create a structure for the general body meetings and devise an orientation structure for

new members. The steering committee also used this hiatus to resolve concerns about the lack of communication with the national office by making plans for one or two members to visit the national office. It hoped to receive guidance about organizational policy and activities.

Until this trip occurred and the Chicago chapter gained official chapter status, the chapter renamed itself Chicago Black Feminists. This name change allowed the women in Chicago some distance from a national body they knew little about, but it also allowed for organizational growth locally. The Chicago Black Feminists continued to hold meetings for the next year and reformulated committees based on the interests of active members. New committees focused on collegiate outreach, females and education, health fair coordination, the media, a rape crisis line, and women and religion. Each new committee was designed to expand the organization's agenda and membership base. Chicago Black Feminists also participated in a number of activities in the Chicago area, ranging from traditional electoral politics to the more radical rape crisis intervention. They also advocated on behalf of black women they felt were wrongly dismissed from powerful professional positions, such as Barbara Watson, the highest-ranking black woman in the Nixon and Ford presidential administrations, and Edwina Moore, a veteran black television news reporter in Chicago.

In January 1975, the NBFO's chapters in formation received a letter from the national office detailing reasons for the inadequate communication, including the lack of human and financial resources.[31] By September of the same year, the Chicago women decided that the need for black feminist action in their city was urgent. They could no longer wait for directives from the national body. Eichelberger, initiator of Chicago NBFO, instigated a split from the national body to form an organization that could speak to the needs of women in the Midwest.

For the next nine months, Chicago Black Feminists worked out their own organizational structure for a new group, the National Alliance of Black Feminists. The NABF filled in some of the gaps left by the NBFO, formulating a "Black Woman's Bill of Rights" that spoke to the objectives of the organization, and the organization designed standing committees to work on short- and long-range plans The NABF also broadened its support base by allowing black men and whites to join the organization as dues-paying affiliates as long as they supported the NABF's mission, which was attaining for black women full social, political, and economic equality.[32]

With this mission and a stronger organizational foundation, the NABF

did not split from the NBFO for ideological reasons as much as the Chicago women grew impatient as the NBFO cast about for a focus and a functioning infrastructure. Eichelberger, along with NABF leaders Brenda Porter and Janie Nelson, built on the ideas of the NBFO independently from the national organization because they were unwilling to lose the momentum of interest in black feminist organizing among women in Chicago and the surrounding area.

The Combahee River Collective

The story of how the Combahee River Collective's principal organizers became radicalized was not unlike that of other founders of black feminist organizations. Beverly and Barbara Smith, twin sisters raised by an aunt in Cleveland, Ohio, came to political consciousness during the civil rights movement. As high school students, Barbara and Beverly participated in the school desegregation struggle in 1964. Following high school graduation, the Smith sisters volunteered with CORE as telephone operators and canvassers in Cleveland's housing projects. Barbara credits Cleveland CORE's executive director, a woman and therefore a leadership anomaly at the time, with giving her an opportunity for active politicization that might not have happened under the leadership of a male director. As Smith continued on to graduate from Mount Holyoke and pursue graduate studies at the University of Pittsburgh, the civil rights movement took a turn toward black liberation politics. This articulation of a masculinist view of struggle and liberation motivated Smith's gravitation toward the women's movement. She explains:

> I went to a major antiwar mobilization in Washington, D.C., in the fall of 1969 [the National Moratorium]. . . . I thought it was the last demonstration I'd ever go to; one of the reasons being black people back at Pitt [University of Pittsburgh] had so many nasty things to say about the fact that I was involved in what they say as a "white" entity, namely, the antiwar movement. There were not that many black people involved at that time and if they were, they certainly—well, I mean students are as they are— some of these people were faculty who were making these kinds of comments—not directly to me—but it was a very hard time to be a politically active black woman, who did not want to be a pawn. . . . I actually imagined that I would never be politically active again because nationalism and patriarchal attitudes within black organizing was *so* strong—we're talking

early '70s now—was so strong I just thought there would be no place ever for me to be politically active the way I had been in my prior life. But, then, I got involved in the women's movement through black feminism, the National Black Feminist Organization in 1973, and then I've been able to be active ever since.[33]

Smith's comments echo those of the NBFO's Margaret Sloan and the NABF's Brenda Eichelberger. These women were often challenged on their commitment to black struggle and derided for their adherence to feminist principles. Smith's detractors refused to see the connections among racism, imperialism, and sexism. Instead, they chose to believe that being against the Vietnam War was not a "black issue" and that she was betraying her race by participating in coalition work.[34]

Barbara Smith's negative experience with patriarchal attitudes was a positive push toward feminist organizing, but she was dubious of the predominately white women's movement, based on her initial contacts with white feminists through graduate and political work:

[The Eastern Regional Conference] was really pivotal for me because, see, I could never see myself joining a white women's organization. I just couldn't even imagine that. The first time I heard about feminism I thought those women were *crazy*. I thought they were *perfectly crazy*. I could not even understand it. And my sister says the same thing because, see, my sister, being at the University of Chicago, she was at the place where some of the strongest feminists—early feminists in the country was growing up. Heather Booth, you know, and all the rest of them. . . . We both talked about how we thought these people were just crazy because we couldn't understand what white women had to complain about. . . . It [the Eastern Regional Conference] was a very positive experience for me, but there were days when it was like, "Oh, my goodness, I'm the only black woman/woman of color in this room." But I had never gone to a NOW meeting. I never did that. So having something called the National Black Feminist Organization made it possible for me to be a black feminist because I just couldn't imagine being involved in a white women's group.[35]

The Smith sisters articulated the ambivalence of many black women during the period who thought feminism was a crazy invention of privileged white women, but still engaged with the feminist movement to move beyond media- and nationalist-generated stereotypes.

In addition to these radicalizing political experiences, Barbara's sister,

Beverly, played a central role in the emergence of Combahee. While on staff at *Ms.* magazine when it was a fledgling publication, Beverly met Margaret Sloan, a founder of the NBFO. Serving as the network through which Barbara received her information, Beverly was in a central position to relay information about the NBFO's Eastern Regional Conference. The conference was called for the eastern region, but women came from all over the United States to network and connect with other black feminists. Barbara Smith, who by this time lived in Boston, recalls caucusing with women from the Boston area in a stairwell because there were so many other women present from different cities in search of meeting space.[36] When Barbara Smith returned to Boston with the names of other local women who had attended the Eastern Regional Conference, she posted signs for a local chapter meeting of the NBFO in Roxbury, Boston's largest black community.

In January 1974 about a dozen women attended the meeting, including Brenda Verner, a woman Barbara Smith cites as having vociferous views against a black feminism. Verner did attend the Eastern Regional Conference and later wrote a vitriolic article for *Encore* magazine on the proceedings.[37] Smith cites Verner's vehemence in her antifeminism as scary to a number of potential members, particularly those women who had not attended the meeting in New York:

> And, see, what was so horrible about it is that for those of us who had been at the NBFO conference, we had something that we could build from as far as having a model and experience in our head of "Yeah, you can do this. Yeah, four hundred people can be with you. Yeah, Shirley Chisholm can be there and Eleanor Holmes Norton and it can be like that." For those who had not been at the conference in New York, I think that what Brenda Verner did was much more frightening, and, as I said, some of those women never ever came back. They never came back.[38]

Tactics that undermined emerging black feminist consciousness, such as declaring black feminism antithetical to black liberation, dissuaded women who were already ambivalent about black feminist politics. Lacking the empowering experience of the Eastern Regional Conference, some potential members did not perceive the building momentum of a black feminist movement. Also, since black feminists' collective identity was in formation, it was susceptible to misinterpretation or distortion by antifeminist opponents. Some of these opponents may not have necessarily been against tackling sexism or gender discrimination in black communities as much as

they were against feminism, in particular. Regardless of antifeminist sentiments, though, interest in forming the Boston chapter remained high.

Barbara Smith's personal interest in the NBFO grew during a brief stay in Washington, D.C., from May to November 1974. During that period Smith met Henri Norris and Katherine Macklin, members of the Washington chapter who kept Smith informed about the development of black feminism in the area. Also, while she lived in Washington, Smith still received letters from black women expressing interest in joining the Boston NBFO chapter, including Demita Frazier. According to Smith, Frazier wrote to say that she was relocating to Boston from Chicago. She detailed her interest in Boston NBFO, as well as her own feminist activism in Chicago. Frazier's description of her work and her enthusiasm for starting an NBFO chapter prompted Smith to subsequently contacted Frazier as an ally in organizing the Boston chapter.

In 1975, after a brief time away from Boston, Smith connected with her sister, Beverly, and Demita Frazier to reconstitute the local NBFO chapter. The chapter initially met at the Cambridge Women's Center, placing it squarely within Boston's burgeoning feminist activist community. Established as the result of demands for accountability to the community from Harvard University, the women who organized the center used it to hold a range of classes popular with women's liberationists and as a meeting space.[39] The Boston NBFO chapter used the space to focus on consciousness-raising, and it was through this mode that it examined the incipient politics of the NBFO. As they recall in the *Combahee River Collective Statement*, and as Frazier notes in a later interview, the women attending that first meeting were exiles from other movements and experienced "the overwhelming feeling that . . . after years and years we had finally found each other."[40]

In addition to consciousness-raising, the women who attended the Boston gatherings explored the incipient politics of the NBFO based on their experiences at the Eastern Regional Conference and the few position statements the NBFO had issued since then. They determined that the organization was headed in a reformist direction that would do little for the poor and working classes, most of whom were black. Several socialist and Marxist members had a significant impact on the ideological development of Combahee. One woman, Sharon Bourke, was what Smith calls an "educated Marxist" with a wide breadth of political knowledge, as well as life experiences that were instructive to younger black feminists just coming into political consciousness:

She had been very involved in the Black liberation movement. She actually lived . . . in Atlanta. She was involved with the Institute for the Black World. . . . That was an important cultural and political formation during those years. She also was a trained Marxist and she was one of the most brilliant people I ever met. . . . So, it wasn't like somebody who was in their forties—like Sharon was when I was in my late twenties—it wasn't like she was lording it all over us and saying "You all don't know what you're doing." She was very self-effacing, and she just knew how to work politically with all different people. So it was really an incredibly positive experience.[41]

Bourke brought to the table a class-based analysis of black women's issues that diverged from the civil rights movement's frame of middle-class integration. Boston black feminists perceived this tendency in the NBFO, and it influenced their chapter's move away from the NBFO and toward socialist politics. The populated protest field that was Boston's radical socialist feminist milieu included white feminist groups such as Cell 16 and Bread & Roses, making the case that the Boston women were in a rich activist-intellectual environment.

The Boston chapter also experienced many of the same frustrations as the Chicago, Atlanta, and Washington, D.C., chapters, related to the national office's lack of communication and structure. But an even greater concern to the Boston women was that they felt their developing politics were more radical than those the NBFO had espoused to that point. While there may have been radical, socialist, or nationalist NBFO members, their views were not reaching the NBFO's national constituency. The Boston women were left to conclude that the NBFO was merely imitating a bourgeois approach to reformist, feminist politics: "I don't think that we thought it was fine for them to be going the way we were going, because we were dealing with race and class realities. I mean, no black woman is going to be served by a simple NOW agenda. You see what I'm saying? We wanted to integrate a race/class analysis with an antisexist analysis and practice. And we didn't just want to add on racism and class oppression like white women did. And so, I think that we felt a NOW-type approach was definitely not going to work for black women."[42]

The Boston women participated in a sophisticated form of consciousness raising that, much like the work of the Third World Women's Alliance, combined consciousness-raising with what was traditionally labeled as high-theory political education. Reflecting on the outcomes of the civil rights and women's movements, Boston NBFO members determined that

"You do need reform simultaneous with radical or revolutionary kinds of demands and initiatives. But the difference, of course . . . between a radical and a reformist is that reformists think that those reforms are enough. And they have much more faith in a system that has proven itself to be motionless and exploitative than people like the ones who eventually made up Boston Combahee."[43] Smith's observation echoed social movement theorists and historians of the women's movement who attest to the merits of radical and reformist demands as complementary.[44] The Boston women did not advocate the dissolution of the NBFO because of its reformist politics, but they did decide to split from the parent organization. Smith summarizes: "I don't think we were happy with NBFO. I remember being incredibly disappointed with them and being very skeptical and very—we tried to maintain good relationships because—I remember a huge amount of talk about 'Are we "Combahee"? Are we the National Black Feminist Organization calling ourselves Combahee or are we something entirely different? Are we completely independent?' I think, of course, we opted to be completely independent, but those were complicated questions because we certainly did not want to alienate or cut off contact with other black feminists."[45]

Rather than alienate themselves from the group by attempting to force ideological changes within it, the Boston women decided to split from the NBFO. Naming their group after a heroic military initiative led by Harriet Tubman in 1863 at the Combahee River in South Carolina, Frazier and the Smith sisters proceeded to craft a black feminist statement on their politics. Widely read and anthologized today as a definitive work on black socialist lesbian feminism, the *Combahee River Collective Statement* carries with it the legacy of the NBFO. In that way, activists' roots in and grievances against the civil rights movement brought them to the NBFO's Eastern Regional Conference, but the differences Combahee members had with the NBFO in structure and ideology caused them to split in search of a politics more coherent with their own ideas of black feminist collective identity and objectives.

Black Women Organized for Action

Black Women Organized for Action formed in the San Francisco Bay Area in response to a lack of representation of black women in women's issues on the local level. Although members had strong roots in the civil rights movement, they gained equally valuable skills in the women's movement. More so than any of the other organizations, the BWOA exhibits the clearest

link to the predominately white women's movement. Aileen Hernandez was one of several black women who played a key role in the feminist movement before the emergence of black feminist organizations.[46] Hernandez, appointed by President Lyndon B. Johnson to serve on the Equal Employment Opportunity Commission (EEOC) following the passage of the 1964 Civil Rights Act, was instrumental in the landmark case to end discriminatory practices against airline flight attendants. Disillusioned by the limited powers of the EEOC, Hernandez resigned and later joined NOW, feeling that NOW could more effectively push for social justice for women. In 1967 Hernandez served as NOW's western regional vice-president and, in 1970, succeeded Betty Friedan as the organization's president.[47]

Hernandez maintained that NOW's statement of purpose addressed black women's issues as feminist issues. In fact, Hernandez, and two other future BWOA members, Patsy Fulcher and Eleanor Spikes, were part of NOW's National Task Force on Minority Women and Women's Rights.[48] Despite their participation in NOW, these three women cofounded Black Women Organized for Action (BWOA) because they wanted to explicitly define and work on black women's concerns, as well as encourage black women's leadership.

By the early 1970s, in the aftermath of the height of the civil rights movement, blacks made significant inroads in electoral politics. In addition to grounding in the women's movement, the BWOA also had roots in a political organization that was originally established as a fund-raising auxiliary for black male politicians. Bay Area women formed Dames for Dellums to raise money for Ron Dellums, a black politician from Berkeley who opposed the Vietnam War, in his first run for congressional office in 1970.[49] Valerie Bradley, a BWOA member from 1973 to 1977, recalls that Dames for Dellums continued after the election in this auxiliary fund-raising role as Black Women Organized for Political Action (BWOPA). Bradley is critical of the BWOPA for remaining relegated to a helping role: "This group supposedly had the same goals that eventually BWOA had, but what I found was they seemed to exist primarily to hold fundraisers for male candidates, to reelect male incumbents and did not seem to really be encouraging women to get involved in a more active way in the political process—by running for office, anyway, doing the grunt work."[50] Members of BWOPA decided to form Black Women Organized for Action, a single-sex organization, to "work to develop a consciousness in black women that politics is a 365 days a year activity, in which we must all participate if we are to survive and progress."[51] From the beginning, the BWOA's role was defined as more than

supplementary to black men's political aspirations, though the organization did continue supporting black men in their bid for public office. In fact, political candidates, regardless of race, gender, or partisan affiliation, actively courted the BWOA's endorsement.

Fifteen women helped found Black Women Organized for Action on 10 January 1973 when they assembled to challenge the San Francisco Mayor's Committee on the Status of Women.[52] The committee conducted hearings on the status of the city's women without hearing any testimony from black women. As Eleanor Spikes, a BWOA founding member told *Essence* magazine, "We decided that it was high time to test the Bay Area's long-standing image of grand liberalism."[53] The BWOA, through written and verbal testimony to the mayor's committee, successfully addressed the needs and interests of black women in the area, creating an identity for themselves in the public arena as black *and* feminist.

Empowered by this action, the BWOA's founders set about building an organization designed to voice the concerns of black women, but also to cultivate black women's leadership in addressing those needs. The BWOA "decided to educate, develop and motivate black women to function at all levels in the community—identifying issues, devising strategies for solving problems, finding and encouraging women to run for office and seek appointments to boards and commissions."[54] This emphasis on leadership development was one area that made the BWOA unique from its organizational compatriots of the time.

* * *

Black feminists came out of civil rights and women's movement organizations with a growing awareness of their particular place in the U.S. economic system. Aware of the ways that these movements ignored the intersections of racism and sexism, black feminists formed their own organizations to address their needs. Yet, black feminists also began to discover, as they struggled to structure their organizations, that there were also significant differences between black women. Black feminists, though united through a collective racial and gender identity, discovered cleavages based on their inattention to class and sexual orientation as shapers of the parameters of black women's oppression.

The collective identity black feminists formed as a group occurred in the process of organizational emergence. Moreover, as analyzed in the next chapter, the organizational leadership styles and structures of black feminist organizations mirrored members' belief that the race and gender ele-

ments of their collective identity should be an integral part of how black women approached leadership within feminist organizations. Black feminists' previous activist experiences, however, inspired varied organizational structures. Similar to the structures in predominately white feminist organizations, organizational structure included formal bureaucratic and non-hierarchical, collectivist. Neither structure was ideal. The heterogeneity of black feminists' individual political perspectives would yield dissention, but that dissention would in turn expand the boundaries of black feminist politics and the base of the black feminist movement.

3 ☆ BARBECUE AND BAKE SALES
WON'T FUND A MOVEMENT

Commonalties and differences among black feminist organizations reflect the heterogeneity of black feminists' political views. Jo Freeman maintains that the styles of organizing used by women's movement organizations were heavily dependent on members' political education and experiences in the civil rights and New Left movements.[1] Such an analysis, applied to black feminists' organizational structure, provides a link between resource mobilization and collective identity formation. As black feminists' understanding of multiple jeopardy and their collective identity grew, they found that their organizations also needed to reflect their political education, understanding of the intersection of race and gender, and personal experiences.

This recognition contributes to rethinking a number of ideological assumptions Becky Thompson believes are made because militant feminists are omitted from the historical record. A key assumption that this study of black feminist organizations refutes is the idea that women are "naturally inclined" toward collaborative, less hierarchical organizational structures.[2] This chapter illustrates the interplay between socially constructed identities and how identity shaped black feminist organizations' approaches to structure, membership definitions, and access to resources. Table 1 outlines these factors and compares them by organization.

Organizational Structure

Leaders of black feminist organizations faced the tasks of mobilizing participants and framing issues in ways that linked participants to the organization. Archival records on black feminist organizations reveal that orga-

Table 1. Black Feminist Organizations: A Comparative Chart

	TWWA	NBFO	NABF	Combahee	BWOA
Organization influences	NAACP; SNCC	CORE; Women's Action Alliance	NBFO	CORE; Antiwar movement; NBFO	NOW; Government civil rights agencies
Date of emergence	East Coast: 1968; West Coast: 1971	1973	1976	1974	1973
Number of core members	12	9	6	3	12
Estimated number of members[a]	200	2,000	133	40	400
Leadership structure	Collectivist	Bureaucratic (1973–1975); Collectivist (1975)	Bureaucratic	Collectivist	Collectivist
Date of decline	East Coast: 1977; West Coast: 1980	1975	1980	1980	1980

[a] Membership numbers are based on newspaper reports, meeting minutes, and organizational self-reporting. The NABF was the only organization with a membership roster available for quantification.

nizational structure often mirrored the founders' previous civil rights or women's movement experiences. Founders who emerged from civil rights organizations, such as the NAACP, executed hierarchical forms of organization, whereas women's movement activists formed nonhierarchical organizations.

Of the five organizations in this study, the NBFO and NABF were hierarchical organizations that had formal officers, written bylaws, and a division between intellectual and administrative work. Conversely, the TWWA, Com-

bahee, and BWOA were collectivist organizations that rejected hierarchy and sought more egalitarian modes of decision making. Many founders of black feminist organizations gained organizing experience in hierarchical, civil rights organizations as youths, but decentralized, student-led organizations (e.g., SNCC and CORE) radicalized them. Two equally daunting tasks, the formation of collective identity and creating organizational infrastructure, shifted to accommodate one another, as black feminists discovered that not all black women held the same political beliefs. Some black feminist organizations even underwent dramatic shifts in their organizational structure as they attempted to distribute power among their members according to their evolving understanding of interstitial politics and how these politics shaped power dynamics *within* their organizations.

Hierarchical Black Feminist Organizations

The NBFO and its spin-off, the NABF, were both hierarchical organizations with formal officers and bylaws to guide the daily functioning of the organizations. As founders of both organizations soon learned, within rapidly expanding hierarchical organizations, the burden of responsibility usually fell to those selected (by election or default) to lead. It was then up to this leader to delegate responsibilities, motivate others to complete assigned tasks, and align the organization's frame into agreement with potential recruits and existing members' growing consciousness. For NBFO leaders, these tasks proved difficult because of the organization's rapid membership growth and the struggle to define a black feminist collective identity. Comparably, the NABF, as an offshoot of the NBFO, learned from its predecessor's mistakes. Early in the NABF's emergence, its leaders defined the leadership structure and established the vision of the organization before formally announcing its existence.

Figure 2 shows three transformations the NBFO experienced as it tried to create a structure amenable to its feminist constituency. As related in the organization's emergence narrative (chapter 2), the NBFO's establishment was announced prematurely and the founding members did not anticipate the overwhelming demand for a national black feminist network and the subsequent complications in organizing it. An array of black women, all with differing definitions of black feminist activism, joined the organization, and the NBFO's leadership was unprepared to effectively meet those demands.[3] The NBFO's founding members faced the tasks of simultaneously defining the organization's agenda, orienting women in other

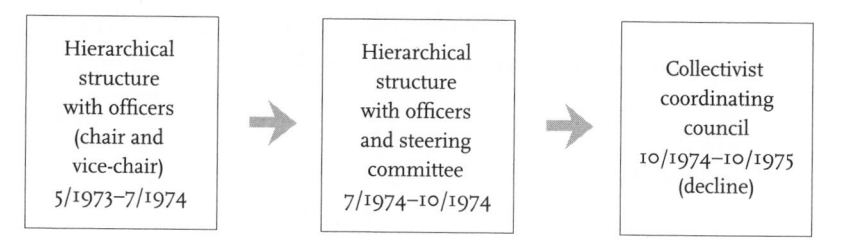

| Hierarchical structure with officers (chair and vice-chair) 5/1973–7/1974 | → | Hierarchical structure with officers and steering committee 7/1974–10/1974 | → | Collectivist coordinating council 10/1974–10/1975 (decline) |

Figure 2. Phases of the NBFO's Leadership Structure

cities who wanted to form chapters, and effectively delegating the work of running the national office in New York City. A hierarchical structure was, in effect, the fastest way to organize given the unique circumstances of the NBFO's formation.

Resulting complications included domination of the organization by the initial members, lack of long-range planning, burnout, growth with no plan, no clear lines of accountability, poor or nonexistent office systems, and extremely long meetings that were not conducive to action and member retention.[4] The NBFO did not have an established leadership base at the time of its press conference nor had it mapped out a clear direction for the future of the organization.

From May 1973 until July 1974, Sloan and Jane Galvin-Lewis served as the NBFO's chair and vice-chair, respectively, and oversaw the daily operations. Sloan, through her work at *Ms.*, and Galvin-Lewis, as a staff member of the Women's Action Alliance, were familiar with hierarchical organizing through their involvement with the civil rights and women's rights branch of the movement.[5] This was the model they initially saw as effective in taking advantage of openings in a political culture that yielded to the demands of civil rights and women's movement organizations with similar structures. When an array of black women, all with differing definitions of black feminist activism, joined the organization, the NBFO's leadership was unprepared to effectively meet those demands.[6] Both Sloan and Galvin-Lewis possessed the skills to run a national organization, but they were overwhelmed with the scale of the task. In hindsight, both women have voiced the desire for more time to have developed the organizational structure of the NBFO.[7]

Nine other members, including several founders of the NBFO, recognized the precarious position of the leadership. In response, they formed a policy committee and proposed issuing a policy statement to give the organization a structural foundation. Combining hierarchical structure with

the feminist desire for collaboration, the policy committee amended the structure of the NBFO to include a steering committee.[8] The policy statement also implemented a system of checks and balances between the steering committee and the officers: any actions, programs, or policies initiated by the steering committee or the officers were approved by the other entity.[9] The policy paper also proposed integrating an advisory board into the organization to involve people who were well connected but unavailable to participate in the NBFO regularly. The hope was that the NBFO would benefit from connections with important black women who were also linked to potential financial resources.

Although the policy committee proposed this new structure, it was not implemented soon enough. The volume of work proved to be overwhelming and, citing burnout and personal issues, Sloan resigned as chair of the NBFO in July 1974.[10] By the next month, the women left on the steering committee increased their meetings from once a month to once a week and established a coordinating council to plan the organization's future.

The evolution of the organization from a bureaucratic, formalized structure to a collectively run coordinating committee reflected the desire of the leadership and the general body for a truly participatory, democratic organization. The founders wanted membership input on policy and structural issues, but they did not have channels for receiving that input from chapters or members outside of New York City. The NBFO's shift from a leader-centered structure to a multiple-member coordinating council was an effort to solicit that input and allowed the organization to hold off activist burnout by drawing on the resources of more than a few members. This new delegation of tasks established accountability, and the new coordinating council benefited from the groundwork established by Galvin-Lewis and Sloan, who dealt with constant challenges to black feminists' race/gender analysis early in the organization's existence.

Until the organization's next executive board election in October, a temporary coordinating council worked to define the focus toward attracting potential recruits and regaining membership trust. The coordinating council hoped to jump-start the NBFO in New York City with a number of committees and services such as a clothing exchange, "a rap line" for social service referrals and advice, and regular child care for the NBFO's monthly meetings. Most important, the coordinating council planned to produce a monthly newsletter to keep national dues-paying members better informed about the operations of the NBFO.

The monthly newsletter was the only initiative accomplished, and its

content primarily focused on establishing a new, democratically elected seven-person coordinating council. The general body agreed to this leadership structure. Galvin-Lewis recalls that the temporary coordinating council moved closer to feminist ideals of cooperative leadership, but she and Deborah Singletary, both coordinating committee members, also remember the pitfalls of egalitarianism:

> *Galvin-Lewis:* We divided the work, we ran the meetings, we did the agendas, we did the press *with* the various committees. See, that was the whole point of having a coordinating council instead of president, vice-president, treasurer—all that kind of thing was to spread the decisions over the group.
>
> *Interviewer:* And so did that work better than having the officers?
>
> *Galvin-Lewis:* No. Not in my opinion.
>
> *Singletary:* I never realized that the coordinating council was the problem. Did we have in-fighting on the coordinating—?
>
> *Galvin-Lewis:* Not at all.
>
> *Singletary:* I don't remember the coordinating council being the problem. I felt the problem was our own egalitarian way of being. That we wanted to avoid the more patriarchal concept of "What we say is right." We wanted to hear from other people. I think that's the part that didn't work.
>
> *Galvin-Lewis:* Yeah. That's what I meant: that the coordinating council was the format that we used to get to that goal. That's what I meant. . . . We slipped from president, vice-president. But the coordinating council itself remained solid 'til the end, and we worked beautifully together, I think, and it was a great—that was the one good thing. The relationships . . . were the good things that came of the coordinating council. That's the whole idea—that it was born to spread out the leadership was, in my opinion, a mistake.[11]

In her comments, Galvin-Lewis makes a distinction between a small core group working together collectively and attempted egalitarianism among *all* organizational members. A pitfall of egalitarianism, or structurelessness, is that factionalism can more easily erupt between members with differing political agendas and ideologies claiming a stake in the organizational structure. Unfortunately, as detailed in the final chapter of this book, the NBFO was never in an organizationally or ideologically stable position, and certain factions took advantage of its egalitarianism, thus leading to the defection of chapters.

The NABF, as the Chicago chapter of the NBFO, was not privy to details of the disorganization in New York, but from the lack of communication with the national office its members assumed all was not well. After communicating with other NBFO chapter leaders in Atlanta, Washington, D.C., and Detroit about problems with the national office, the Chicago chapter decided to split and form its own organization. In the process, Brenda Eichelberger and other members took a six-month hiatus to plan the structure of the organization.

The result of the NABF's hiatus was a three-tiered organizational structure that included a board of directors.[12] In theory, this highly bureaucratized structure delegated responsibility and accountability to several members of the NABF. In reality, the NABF had difficulties keeping these unpaid positions filled, and, thus, the majority of the work fell to Eichelberger and Gayle Porter. Eichelberger, the executive director for the duration of the organization's existence, was responsible for representing the NABF publicly and for fund-raising. Porter served as chairperson, overseeing the daily operations of the organization, such as internal finances and communications.

A steering committee, composed of each active NABF committee's chair, as well as an advisory board of consultants, helped guide the NABF. The advisory board consisted of invited prominent black women from universities, labor organizations, media associations, and social service organizations and kept the organization informed about the needs of the community.[13] The board also helped obtain resources for the organization through solicitation of funds or serving as an oversight body for possible grants.[14]

These consultants provided the expertise NABF needed for many of their activities. For example, when the NABF held a community health fair, a physician from the advisory board conducted a workshop on health issues affecting black communities. Or the NABF might ask an accountant to discuss financial planning with individual members or to advise the steering committee on the organization's finances.[15] In essence, the NABF drew upon the talents of black women in the Chicago community to supplement its activities. Women who were not NABF members still helped the organization fulfill its political obligations to its membership and the broader black community.

The NABF, in its work over four years, adopted an effective hierarchical leadership structure, and, as much as possible, responsibilities were diffused among a number of its members. Compared to the leaders of the NBFO, which existed for two years, NABF leaders realized that the survival

of the organization depended on using its primary resource—its members —without overtaxing them. Although organized hierarchically, the NABF served as an incipient model for the type of feminist organizations Jo Freeman proposed: a structure that best facilitated the completion of tasks to move the organization forward from introspection to direct action.[16]

Yet, contrary to Freeman's hopes for this form of organization, all members of the NABF did not feel empowered to make decisions. The NABF was not unlike other women's movement groups in which friendship networks, while effective recruitment channels, could also create an elite within an organization. Some members were jealous of the amount of attention Eichelberger received in the media, and others thought she was dictatorial in defining the terms of black feminism in the Chicago area.[17] The NABF, with Eichelberger as its leader, did not manage to avoid the star system, and, in turn, participation from members was not as high as it might have been. Members felt no obligation to put resources into the group once they accomplished their personal objectives, which ranged from a better understanding of how feminism could help their lives to encouragement in their career goals.[18]

Collectivist Black Feminist Organizations

The Third World Women's Alliance (TWWA), the Combahee River Collective, and Black Women Organized for Action (BWOA), like most women's liberation organizations of the time, all functioned as collectives. These three organizations had smaller aspirations than the NBFO and the NABF, who wanted to attract members and influence racial and gender politics nationally, but also build their local support base. There were significant differences in how the TWWA, Combahee, and BWOA enacted collectivist politics, but these organizations were successful in combining models from the civil rights and women's movements into their organizing principles at the local level.

The Third World Women's Alliance, as a direct descendant of SNCC was, in Beal's words, "ultra-democratic."[19] The organization operated under the inherited philosophy of participatory democracy that encouraged members to work in all facets of the organization, including decision making. The East Coast branch of the TWWA had a steering committee, but membership on the committee was open to all members and all decisions were brought to the general body. The West Coast branch did not have a steering committee and, instead, was centralized under the leadership of Cheryl

Perry, contrary to the stated goals of democratic centralism. Other members of the West Coast TWWA eventually challenged Perry's leadership when they wanted to take the organization in a different direction, which included collectivist politics.

The Combahee River Collective did not have an articulated definition of collectivity, and decision making was informal. Similar to Honor Ford-Smith's contemporary experience in a Jamaican women's collective, Sistren, there were discrepancies in how members defined collectivity that masked power differentials between black feminists within Combahee in the 1970s.[20] Freeman points out that though groups claiming structurelessness believe all members have equal power, "structurelessness becomes a way of masking power, and within the women's movement it is usually most strongly advocated by those who are the most powerful (whether they are conscious of their power or not)."[21] In a 1975 memo to Combahee members, Barbara Smith explicitly linked structures of black feminist organizations to the survival of the movement: "Major elements of our [black feminist] movement seem bent upon parodying the hierarchy and power-mongering of 'mainstream' organizations. The only way black feminism can survive is as a radical movement whose goal is the overturning of patriarchy, the complete questioning of things as they are. In our internal structure we should strive for collectivity and reject the tokenism and careerism that has undermined other movements."[22] In her avocation of collectivity, Smith aspired for Combahee to observe lessons from other civil rights and women's movement organizations and made an effort to organize nonhierarchically. Members of Combahee did work together on a broad range of issues, but interpersonal dynamics, availability, and the needs of the movement were key considerations when attempting collectivity and an informal organization structure.

Smith was aware that her position as a leader in Combahee gave her a different perspective on the organization's collectivity than others who felt they were outside of leadership positions. Smith's understanding of the leadership of the organization was based on a distinction between collective decision making and the role of the leader. She defines leadership as "really based upon someone who did the work and who had the capacity in their lives to fit in doing the work. . . . It wasn't a male model of leadership."[23]

Barbara Smith, Demita Frazier, and Beverly Smith are remembered as the central leaders in their organization based on their joint authorship of the *Combahee River Collective Statement*. These women were not selected leaders, but their availability and commitment allowed them to invest more

time in the organization. Members of Combahee were undergraduates, pursuing advanced degrees, working full-time jobs, engaged in other political causes outside of their involvement with Combahee, or a combination of these activities. Without establishing a subjective hierarchy of who were the most committed members, it becomes more difficult to measure availability to the organization. How individual members prioritized their obligations to Combahee, to their families, and to their political ideals played a significant role in the development of an elite within Combahee.

Two other Combahee members, Margo Okazawa-Rey and Mercedes Tompkins, disagree with the view of the organization as collectively run. Tompkins and Okazawa-Rey, housemates in a collectively owned house, learned of Combahee through word of mouth and joined in the winter of 1975. Okazawa-Rey, a social worker, participated in consciousness-raising with a branch of the homophile organization Daughters of Bilitis, but later joined Combahee to meet with other black, lesbian feminists. Tompkins, at twenty-one, was not politically active with any particular group when she joined Combahee because she was only beginning to define her lesbian identity.

In contrast to Smith's view of Combahee's collectivity, Tompkins and Okazawa-Rey both experienced hierarchy within the group, and they contest the use of the term *collective* when applied to Combahee. Tompkins notes that Combahee's members discussed issues as a group, but she also acknowledges her position as outside of an "underground network" within the group: "Before things came to the group, things got filtered. So most of the requests for information or participation, or anything that was . . . on the docket for Combahee, went through Barbara Smith."[24] Tompkins perceived herself as outside of the elite leadership core because she "pushed the envelope around the whole issue of class and educational elitism."[25] I also maintain again that submerged friendship networks, while good for recruitment, had adverse affects on democratic decision making in collective women's movement organizations. Friendship loyalties often made the organizational decision-making processes difficult in black feminist organizations regardless of structure.

Okazawa-Rey concurs with Tompkins's perspective on the failure of collectivity in the organization, believing certain core members held disproportionate power within Combahee: "I think 'collective' was probably a misnomer. I think the ideal was to have it a collective, but because it was really loose—first of all, for a collective to be a collective there needs to be . . . clear ideas about decision-making that are consensus and all that. . . . So, in a way,

it was kind of hierarchical. . . . It was tricky. It was a tension there."[26] Barbara Smith, for one, was a driving force behind Combahee, and it is possible that her talents as a writer put her in a privileged position in a movement that valued connecting the personal to the political through the written word and verbal acuity in academic circles, as well as in a thriving underground feminist press. By the late 1970s, the women's movement began to make disciplinary inroads into academia as women's studies, creating another space for Smith's work as a feminist theorist and literary critic and fore-grounding her role in the articulation of contemporary black feminism. As Smith accurately assesses, in social movements "people who write get far more visibility than those who don't."[27] This is particularly true when we consider the civil rights movement, where women performing in the pri-vate sphere were not recognized as leaders, unlike men who represented the movement in public. In the same way, until more scholars reconstruct narratives of the black feminist movement, and until more black feminist movement participants record their memoirs, well-known personalities of the movement will continue to predominate in the historical record.

Black Women Organized for Action was also collectively run, but this organization began with a well-articulated vision in which members who share the work also share the power and the glory.[28] The organization was structured so that leadership, work, and community involvement were shared among members willing to participate. Instead of having hierar-chical officers or assuming a leaderless structure, the BWOA operated with three coordinators for a three-month tenure. Coordinators convened, orga-nized, and facilitated meetings, as well as served as spokespersons for the group in the media and in direct action.[29]

This structure was consistent with the organization's mission to develop leadership among as many different black women as possible. In addition to completing the work of the organization, Aileen Hernandez found that the rotating coordinator structure recognized the varied political positions of black women:

> The way we were structured we gave whoever happened to be the coordi-nators for that quarterly period full authority to do what they wanted. We had some very distinctly different approaches when we had coordinators because some of the coordinators were very heavily involved in the Black Power movement at that point in time. Some of them were very much in-volved in the Democratic Party. . . . We almost never had an ideological difference, because we had agreed that one of the things we wanted to do

was link African American women from whatever perspective they were in. And when people sort of said, "Well, that's crazy because some people will do wild things," we said, "Well, how much trouble can you make in three months?" What we said essentially was "Get the ideas out there. We don't run from any idea." It certainly made a difference in some cases as to who was participating in a particular event, but it was never an ideological difference in terms of how the organization functioned.[30]

Potential problems with this structure included inconsistency in information dissemination or poorly facilitated meetings, but nonetheless the BWOA managed to operate effectively for seven years.[31] By honoring the diversity of black women's political interests, the BWOA appealed to many different women, inside and outside the organization. Members were free to choose the activities in which they participated, and they were not obligated to subscribe to a BWOA-dictated political perspective. The imperative for the BWOA was for black women to be involved in political organizing in any way they chose. Hernandez also notes some members participated throughout the duration of the organization because, they "were philosophically committed to bridging all of the different points of view in the African American community."[32] The survival of black communities, in the BWOA's opinion, did not depend on one solution, but on the conscious, consistent political awareness of the community's members.

Another reason for the success of the coordinator structure was the number of women who also held memberships and leadership roles in other civil rights, women's, and black nationalist organizations in the Bay Area. The BWOA provided a forum for women to further develop their leadership skills or experiment with styles that were not permitted in mixed-sex organizations. Valerie Bradley, for example, relates the coordinator experience of BWOA member Flora Gilford during a three-month period:

> Flora had been, you know, had raised her children and worked at the Veteran's Administration as a director of purchasing. . . . But she said that she really felt intimidated about being in a leadership position or whatever until she got in BWOA and got so involved. She was a coordinator at one point. And it gave her a lot of experiences. I mean, Flora is just a dynamo now. She does all kinds of things now. And she did then. I saw her grow. You know, I saw a lot of women grow who might not have done something had they not been encouraged in an organization like BWOA.[33]

In addition to fostering leadership, the rotating structure thwarted the media's tendency to create a star spokesperson. This avoidance of star representatives also prevented the BWOA from becoming dominated by any one faction or personality.

Black feminist organizations serve as an exemplary case study for resource mobilization theories on leadership styles because they offer several models for analysis. Leaders of organizations, particularly nascent ones with tenuous financial status and memberships bases, often face the dual dilemmas of keeping their organizations running smoothly while dealing with interpersonal dynamics. For example, Sloan, Eichelberger, and Smith were all leaders with written and verbal talents that thrust them into the spotlight in their communities as cogent voices on black feminism. Of the three women, two were leaders of hierarchical black feminist organizations, but one led a collective. Were they intentionally controlling the direction and focus of emerging black feminist organizations? Or were they enacting leadership skills and styles that while they may have seemed dictatorial, sustained their organizations through crucial times of emergence in a newly articulated feminist movement? None of these women were purged from the black feminist movement, but eventually they left the organizations they helped establish because of interpersonal conflicts related to the star system, as perpetuated by the media and a public in search of a spokesperson. Regardless of organizational structure—hierarchical or collective—leaders in the women's movement faced the dual tension of successfully disseminating information about black feminism, but also the pitfall of perpetuating hierarchies among black women.

With the East Coast TWWA and BWOA, two organizations with articulated definitions of collectivity, the media was thwarted in creating star spokespersons because all members of the organizations spoke for the organizations. For the TWWA and the BWOA, their principles of participatory democracy and sharing the power and the glory, respectively, grounded the organizations in group-centered leadership. Particularly, useful from the TWWA and BWOA models is the strategy of consistently orienting new members to these leadership principles by creating an agreement between the organization and its members that decision making was communal, framing leadership as a responsibility instead of a right.

Black feminist organizations worked toward modeling a feminist philosophy of leadership with varying degrees of success. Organizations that began with collective structures, and an articulation of the meaning of

those structures, fared the best in avoiding factionalism and developing black feminist leadership among their members. Those organizations with hierarchical structures found that their leaders grew weary of carrying the load of mobilizing and trying to unify a plurality of black women's perspective on black feminism.

Nationalist and Feminist Identities as Criteria for Membership

Assuming that black feminists were homogenous in political thought, the criteria for membership in their organizations would seem simple: black womanhood. But to assert that *all* black women were potential recruits for black feminist organizations assumes too much; it erases differences in class, color, sexual orientation, and physical ability. Black feminists came to their organizations through traditional recruitment channels, but members also had to reconcile assumed points of commonality.

Ironically, though white feminist and black political communities challenged black feminists on their racial and gender authenticity, respectively, black feminists faced similar questions in recruitment: what does *black* mean for membership in a black feminist organization? What does *feminist* mean for black women? As women joined black feminist organizations during the emergence of the women's movement, they deliberated, for strategic reasons, whether to label their organizations feminist. Black feminists faced issues of racial and gender allegiance in the formation of black feminist collective identity, but decisions about who counted as black and whether to claim feminism influenced aspects of organizational recruitment.

The NBFO, NABF, BWOA, and TWWA based organizational membership on racial categories, but some defined these categories more explicitly than others. For the TWWA, a descendant of black feminist organizing in SNCC, members' shift from black to third world meant specifying the racial and/or ethnic identity of "third world" women. Based on members political interests in anti-imperialism, the TWWA defined *third world* as African, Puerto Rican, Native American, Chicana, and Asian descent.[34] Prompted by international revolutionary struggles and the Vietnam War, minorities in the United States made connections between their marginalized positions domestically and U.S. imperialism abroad. Minorities, and women in particular, experienced a cognitive shift from thinking of themselves as *minorities* to considering themselves part of sizable African, Latin, and Asian diaspo-

ras. To label themselves *third world*, establish a multicultural alliance, and offer solidarity to domestic and foreign nationalist struggles were revolutionary acts.

The NBFO and BWOA also took militant stances in identifying themselves as black, a politically intentional and charged label in the 1970s. Both organizations allowed recruits to self-identify as black, denoting racial awareness and nationhood. The NBFO specified African descent as a criterion for membership in its organizational literature. Sloan required third world women of non-African descent to self-identify according to black nationalist definitions: "We have many black Puerto Ricans who have told us that they can't identify with third world groups because there are Asians and white Puerto Ricans that oppress them as black Puerto Ricans. So they want to be in touch with their black roots. So we say welcome—but we will not put other priorities above those of black women."[35] Unlike the TWWA, the NBFO was dedicated to the concerns of, specifically, black women. If mixed-race women joined the NBFO, they had to deprioritize their non-African nationalist concerns. Black feminists' disdain for the prioritizing of racial and gender identity reinscribed the priority game for other women of color that Margaret Sloan had spoken against earlier in the NBFO's formation. Such a requirement safeguarded against the dilution of a black feminist agenda and expanded the NBFO's membership base, but this requirement did not recognize the connections of a black feminist agenda to imperialism and third world women.

The BWOA was an organization for black women, but it did not restrict definitions of blackness to African descent. In fact, this organization advocated an unprecedented openness in allowing members to self-identify. The BWOA's membership credo was that the organization was open to "old sisters, young sisters, skinny sisters, fat sisters . . . the poor and the not so poor . . . you and me . . . from blue black to high yellow. A bouquet of BLACK WOMEN—action oriented, composed of feminists and non-feminists concerned with the political and economic development of a total black community."[36]

The BWOA's use of a continuum to define blackness was a conscious effort to avoid color discrimination as it played out in black communities. The founders of the BWOA undoubtedly reflected on color discrimination in the early days of African American sororities and color consciousness among African American elite. In response, the "Black is Beautiful" aesthetic unwittingly created a new paradigm of black beauty. The BWOA subverted discrimination within black communities based on color, physi-

cal appearance, or class by welcoming *all* black women into the organization. The organization focused on activism, rather than social constructs of beauty or social class.

Black identity complicated membership criteria in these organizations, as did feminism as a basic tenet of black feminist organizing. Black feminists spent a great deal of time fending off external attacks because of their allegiance to gender oppression, so they attempted to intercept this discussion internally. For black women to repeatedly revisit the argument of whether to associate with feminism while trying to establish their organizations was detrimental to harnessing the momentum of the movement. For this reason, the NBFO stated that a member was "any black woman of African descent who accepts feminism as the organizing priority for the NBFO and who participates in the program."[37]

Similarly, the members of NABF assumed that anyone who joined their organization would adhere to feminist principles. But in the organization's early days as an NBFO chapter, the founders and potential recruits had a heated discussion on the pros and cons of requiring feminist identity as a criterion of membership. Those against using feminist in the organization's name predicted that they would spend too much time defending their name against those who thought feminists were antimale. Proponents of feminism maintained that feminism was profemale, not antimale, and worth asserting from the outset.[38]

For both sides of the debate, the discussion provided an opportunity for consciousness-raising because it offered potential recruits the opportunity to analyze feminism and its application to their lives in dialogue with women of varying degrees of gender consciousness. Of all the organizations, the BWOA's avoidance of the label feminism while practicing feminism was indicative of future developments in black feminist organizing. The BWOA avoided using the term *feminist* in its name to recruit feminist and nonfeminist women to the organization, but its goals of struggling against racism and sexism were explicit. Black women, who reportedly sympathized with the women's liberation movement, joined black feminist organizations and as a result constructed their collective identity through the process of activism, reflecting the interconnectedness of recruitment and identity formation.

Recruitment and Membership

John Lofland observes that determining the membership size of social movement organizations is methodologically difficult given the dual dilemma that social movement researchers and organization members often develop different indicators of membership.[39] Within resource mobilization theory, membership size is considered important because it serves as an indicator of successful mobilizing. In terms of documenting social movement organizations, numbers serve as an indicator of organizational strength for theorists in selecting organizations for study. Black feminist organizations, with relatively small membership numbers, eluded study for precisely this reason. Nevertheless, there are ample reasons for inserting black feminist organizations as case studies into the membership aspect of social movement theory inquiry.

Interviews with black feminist organization members, secondary sources, and organizational records help outline recruitment strategies and provide estimates of membership numbers.[40] Black feminist organizations membership numbers are an indicator of black women's interest in participating in the feminist movement. Existing membership numbers influenced potential recruits' assessments of the cost and benefits of participating, as well as whether black feminist organizations entered the women's movement narrative based on their membership numbers. It is also important historically to document the relatively low number of core participants, which calls attention to causes for the activists' later burnout.

Social movement organizations often minimize or inflate their own magnitude depending on their immediate goals.[41] For example, a 1970 *New York Times* article featured the TWWA and set its East Coast membership numbers at two hundred, though in reality there were only about twelve core members. When organizations inflated their numbers, they also hoped to show potential activists the possibilities of social change with large groups of people.

In another example, when a journalist asked for the NBFO's membership numbers at the first news conference, the founders claimed membership in the hundreds.[42] Sloan later wrote about this interaction: "Fifteen of us national," she scoffed, "how beautifully black and arrogant. They will probably try to kill us."[43] As a matter of strategy, the founders recognized that the media would more likely take their stated goals seriously if they claimed to represent an organization, rather than merely a group of women who met one Saturday night to discuss black women's issues.

One reason black feminists inflated their membership numbers was to convey to potential members that they would not be alone were they to join the black feminist movement. While media representations of feminists groups as a bra burning and hysterical radical fringe could dissuade potential members, large membership numbers could draw more members to the feminist cause. The NBFO's strategy of inflating its numbers also won the organization national press coverage. This exposure helped them succeed in drawing large numbers of black women to the organization. For black feminist organizations, espousing large membership numbers also lent validity to their grievances, but this inflation also added premature pressure to the organization's leaders to act like a large-scale organization, rather than the nascent groups that some of them were.

Membership numbers were not an accurate indicator of black feminist organizations' strength or influence in feminist and black communities. In hindsight, black feminists were not as concerned with the number of women who actually joined their organizations as they were with the number of women they reached with their writings, activities, consciousness-raising sessions, and networking.

Black women joined black feminist organizations based on prior contact with someone already involved. In fact, the majority of the black feminists interviewed for this study joined their respective organizations because a friend or relative told them about a meeting or a direct action. Face-to-face interactions with organization members, interpersonal connections with friends, and social movement networks all facilitated involvement. These close ties as recruitment venues easily increased membership but also posed interpersonal problems: tensions in friendships or intimate partnerships threatened to carry over into organizational matters and cause ideological ruptures.

Two members of the National Black Feminist Organization mention joining their organization through mediated channels, specifically an ad in a local black newspaper.[44] Undoubtedly, other black feminists joined through public channels such as announcements in women's movement periodicals. In *Ms.*, for example, the magazine's editors ran a rare listing of black women's organizations nationally with contact information and brief descriptions of the organizations' work, while the feminist newspaper *off our backs* featured preconference advertising and extensive coverage of the NBFO's Eastern Regional Conference.[45]

Coverage in nonmainstream media outlets was a resource available to black women with preexisting communications networks to the women's

movement, but these women were also fortunate to be in geographical proximity to New York City, a hot spot of the movement. Related to this geographical proximity was structural proximity, meaning the setting in which movements and potential participants can come into contact.[46] For black feminist organizations, rallies and other women's movement events provided the structural proximity needed to recruit participants. Recall from the TWWA's emergence narrative (chapter 2), Cheryl Perry's recruitment into the TWWA through the Venceremos Brigade on the East Coast and her recruitment of other members on the West Coast from women's and black liberation organizations.[47]

Television or news media coverage of black feminist organizations was far more rare, and was thus less useful than submerged networks were for recruitment. However, correspondence from potential national recruits to the Chicago NBFO and the NABF reflects the potential for the media dissemination of black feminist philosophy in the form of television. Several hundred women wrote these two organizations for membership information following the broadcast of a 1974 episode of the *Phil Donahue* show featuring a discussion on black feminism and another episode featuring a discussion of black female/male relationships.[48] Unfortunately for black feminist organizations with national ambitions, their infrastructure did not exist to support widespread media coverage to reach black women nationally.

Black feminists used mostly private and a few public channels to recruit members who agreed with their newly formed visions. Their identities as racial and gendered individuals put them in structural proximity to one another. Sometimes this proximity was the positive result of isolation at women's movement events or in organizations, as black feminists sought out one another in a crowd of white faces. At other times, friends with shared beliefs joined organizations and reinforced their connections as allies in the black feminist struggle.

Funding and Staffing Black Feminist Organizations

Black feminist organizations' resources were limited to members' material and nonmaterial contributions. As with most grassroots activist initiatives, financial statements for the NBFO, NABF, and BWOA revealed struggles to remain financially stable. Finances were a major concern — and even more so for the NBFO and the NABF because both attempted to create national chapters, requiring more funds to facilitate outreach and respond to women nationally. Combahee, the BWOA, and TWWA managed to cover their costs

with in-kind donations and dues. Black feminists found that their position as blacks, women, and working class influenced their ability to raise money and to contribute nonmaterial skills, the most important being time for organization building.

During the late 1960s and early 1970s, black feminists were not privy to grants from major foundations or to the largesse of elites who had sustained noninstitutionalized civil rights organizations in the past. Still, like other black organizations, black feminists wrestled with accountability and possibly co-optation in accepting funding from white feminist or mainstream black organizations. In the special cases of the TWWA and Combahee, it was unlikely that foundations, liberal feminist organizations, or black community institutions would contribute funds to organizations that adhered to socialist principles and called for a complete revolution of U.S. patriarchal, imperialist, and capitalist modes of oppression. But, for more reformist-oriented organizations such as the NBFO, NABF, and BWOA, foundations and elites remained potential sources of sustaining income.

Black feminist organizations obtained material resources through member dues, fund-raising events, and external sources. These three sources had underlying implications for black feminists. In the ethos of black self-determination, the organizations held fund-raisers that served as recruitment tools to entice potential members and supporters. These fund-raisers included theater benefits such as African American productions of *The Wiz*; forums for black political candidates; and speaking engagements that addressed black feminism at churches, university classes, and community groups.

The primary sources of income for black feminist organizations were dues that members paid on a sliding scale basis, ranging from $2 to $50. Expenses varied, but organizations asked their members to contribute what they could to pay for office space rental, photocopies for flyers and other publications, occasional financial support for political prisoner defense funds, cosponsorship of rallies, and other events.[49] All black feminist organizations confronted a similar dilemma in attempting to include black women of all economic positions versus the need for capital to further their social change agendas.

Lacking a steady contribution of dues, some black feminist organizations—particularly the NABF, the NBFO, and BWOA—approached mainstream sources for money and in-kind donations. The NBFO, for example, obtained a $500 grant from *Ms.* magazine and $5,000 from the Lucius and Eva Eastman Foundation to cover expenses for its Eastern Regional

Conference.[50] The NBFO was in a privileged position in relationship to other black feminist organizations because of preexisting ties to *Ms.* magazine and other women's movement organizations experienced in feminist fund-raising.

The grants from *Ms.* and the Eastman Foundation, however, resulted in tensions that questioned the commitment of black feminist organization leaders to black nationhood. Some black feminists interpreted grants from white supporters as outsider bids to control the NBFO and influence the agenda of the black feminist movement. Some black nationalist NBFO members wanted to remain independent of whites, especially *Ms.* They believed in a policy of self-determination and, subsequently, did not think the NBFO should accept free office space from Jane Galvin-Lewis's employer, the Women's Action Alliance; grants from white-led organizations; nor anything else from nonblack sources.[51] Adversaries of black feminists could also use white financial support as proof that black feminists "sold out" or were in collusion with the white power structure. Sloan, as the chair of the NBFO, directly confronted this dilemma of co-optation, pointing out that black social and political institutions showed no support for the organization. Realizing the implications of low membership returns on dues and the magnitude of the NBFO's ambitions, Sloan thought it foolish to turn down strings-free grants from political allies.[52]

In the case of the NABF, this assertion rang true, as the executive board members, particularly the executive director, personally paid for organizational expenses when member dues fell short. But, the NABF devised a unique system that effectively circumvented white allies' donations from influencing the organization's activities or mission. It developed three membership categories: members, individual affiliates, and organizational affiliates. Only black women could join as NABF members, but whites and black men were allowed to sign on as individual affiliates. Other organizations, such as academic departments, unions, and other women's organizations, signed on as organizational affiliates. In this arrangement of affiliates, constituents who believed in the NABF's goals could support the organizations financially without exerting inappropriate influence.

Overall, black feminist organizations had few material resources to rely on because their constituents, black women, had few material resources to give. Middle-class blacks with disposable income were already beholden to sororities, churches, and mainstream civil rights organizations whose goals may have supported traditional sex roles more in line with their personal aspirations. It was an ironic and unfortunate position for black femi-

nists: the very people who needed these organizations the most could not afford to sustain them. Black women did have nonmaterial goods, such as their time and skills, but they faced similar challenges in how their identity impacted the availability of those resources.

Members' contributions to their black feminist organizations took the form of office work, input at meetings, active participation on committees, service in speakers' bureaus, theorizing, and writing to spread the word about black feminism. Black feminist organizations also received in-kind donations that both helped sustain them and built coalitions with allies. The TWWA and NBFO, for instance, accepted donations of office space from a Manhattan church and the Women's Action Alliance, respectively. Combahee held its meetings at the Cambridge Women's Center and accepted in-kind donations of meeting space for their Black Women's Network Retreats. Black feminists and their allies operated from a grassroots position, bartering nonmaterial resources to support the social movement community of feminists, leftists, radicals, and black nationalists.

Dependence on nonmaterial resources also had it benefits and drawbacks. Black feminist organizations required members to contribute to the organizations in return for membership, but organizations also contended with black women's availability issues. Black women, as collectively discriminated-against beneficiaries, sometimes worked more often, for longer hours, and for less pay than their white counterparts. Structural impediments to black women's participation in the predominately white feminist movement also hindered black women's involvement in black feminist organizations. And, unlike white feminist organizations, black feminist organizations faced the problem of how to remain accessible to black women who could not participate in the organizations for the very reasons that black feminist organizations existed. In effect, black feminists did not know how to negotiate class differences between black women that determined the availability of women to participate in organizational growth. Rather than turning toward exclusivity rooted in class disparities—availability, disposable income, leisure time for organizing—many black feminist organizations opted to allow as many black women as possible to claim membership in their organizations. Such a policy resulted in inflated membership numbers for black feminist organizations, but few actual resources.

Since no one was paid for her work in maintaining the organizations, black feminists' benefits were their social and political interactions with one another. Black women also hoped that in the long run, by their par-

ticipation in these organizations, racist, sexist, heterosexist, and classist discrimination would be eradicated, allowing for material gains in society. In the meantime, through organizational membership, black feminists gained new ways of viewing themselves as capable organizers and leaders of a new movement.

Like the emergence narratives, the leadership structures of black feminist organizations reflect their position at the intersection of race, gender, and class. Although they struggled against discrimination on both fronts, black feminist organizations would have been markedly different had they argued for incorporating solely race *or* gender. Instead they developed a black feminist political viewpoint that would accommodate their racial *and* gender concerns. By coming together and discussing their experiences, black feminists realized that they could form organizations independent of black men and white women that would address their particular survival issues based on the intersecting nature of oppressions.

Black feminist organizational structures were based on civil rights and women's movement models, but these organizations developed innovations that considered how the matrix of domination influenced hierarchy. Attentive to the limits placed on women in other organizations, black feminists worked to have egalitarian organizations that considered the varying political perspectives of black women. Moreover, black feminists tried to incorporate a class analysis into devising their organizational structures so that as many black women as possible could participate in the organizing of a black feminist agenda despite economic or educational limits.

4 ☆ BLACK WOMEN'S ISSUES
AS FEMINIST ISSUES

Black women faced the dilemma of a hypervisibility based on stereotypes in the U.S. race and gender structure. As noted in chapter 1, derogatory images of black women as mammies, sapphires, and jezebels persisted from slavery through the emergence of black feminist organizations in the late 1960s. Black women were visible, but not on their own terms. Monolithic definitions of feminism and black nationalist assertions that feminism was an unviable ideology for black women reinforced black *feminist* invisibility. The task then, for black feminist organizations, was to engage in self-definition that countered stereotypes, to define feminism on their own terms, and to draw black women to their organizations.

Black feminists organizations reflected their interstitial politics between the black and women's liberation movements by addressing race and gender dimensions of social justice. These organizations participated in traditional forms of organizing, such as rallies, marches, and the underground press. However, they also orchestrated projects specific to their definitions of black feminist issues, including black feminist gatherings and alternative education that contextualized black women's lives as a complex interaction of identities. The challenge in organizing activities that spoke to black women was to illustrate the intersecting issues of race and gender. The Combahee River Collective's antiviolence work in Boston, in which it protested and worked in coalition with white feminists and local black organizers in a group called CRISIS to demand police accountability in investigating the murders of twelve black women, is documented as an example of black feminists' enactments of interstitial politics.[1]

Black feminists engaged in activities that put them at odds with some white feminist organizations and struggled to expand the definition of

what precisely constituted a "feminist issue." Work on behalf of political prisoners is a useful example of contention between mainstream white feminists and black feminists around legitimating certain issues as race or gender issues, but not both. Sensitized to the FBI Counterintelligence Program's (COINTELPRO) disinformation campaigns and brutal treatment of dissidents, black feminists knew firsthand the importance of applying black feminist critiques to black women prisoners, in particular.[2] For example, the NABF took an active role in the Cassandra Peten Defense Committee. Peten, a black woman from California, was serving a ten-year sentence for defending herself and murdering her abusive husband. Long before contemporary legal recognition of battered women's syndrome, the NABF, through fund-raising and advocacy, brought to light the connections between patriarchal violence and punishment based on racism and sexism. The organization used the Peten case as an example to highlight domestic violence issues in its members' geographic area. In another example of antiracist, feminist activism on the part of black feminists, the Third World Women's Alliance's Frances Beal observes that white feminists frequently questioned the TWWA's commitment to women's issues because many white feminists chose to define narrowly a feminist agenda as solely concerned with gender. At the 1969 New York City "Liberation Day" parade, Beal recalls that the TWWA participated in the parade in hopes of attracting more women of color to the organization. Members carried signs that read, "Free Angela" to highlight the case of Angela Davis, then underground and eluding law enforcement authorities. During the parade, a member of NOW allegedly ran up to TWWA members and told them, "Angela Davis has nothing to do with women's liberation." Beal replied, "It has nothing to do with the kind of liberation you're talking about . . . but it has everything to do with the kind of liberation we're talking about."[3] This interaction highlights the purpose of black feminist activity: the kind of liberation the TWWA alluded to was a liberation that encompassed the multiple aspects of black women's and women of color's identity. Through visible protest, and perhaps frequent clashes with white feminists, black feminist organizations pushed for an expansion of the lived meaning of liberation and women's issues. If women's liberation were truly to be about all women, white feminists would have to relinquish their proprietary hold on movement goals and organizing tactics.

Through increased visibility, public statements, and education, black feminist organizations empowered black women to critically engage with feminism as an ideology that could create social change in their lives and

the livelihood of black communities. Integral to these activities was a constant negotiation between separatism from and coalitions with white feminists and black liberation activists and organizations. Ultimately, most black feminist organization activities, such as neighborhood health fairs, impacted black communities at the grassroots level, but this does not diminish the importance of these activities in the struggle against social injustice.

In the remainder of this chapter, the activities of the five organizations studied demonstrate black feminist organizations' attempts to disseminate their particular views about black feminism, as well as recruit new members to their organizations and adherents to black feminism as a viable ideology. The Third World Women's Alliance and Black Women Organized for Action published an underground newspaper (*Triple Jeopardy*) and an organizational newsletter (*What It Is!*), respectively, that served as informational conduits for members and a recruiting tool for potential allies to black feminist ideology. The National Black Feminist Organization's Eastern Regional Conference, the National Alliance of Black Feminists' Alternative School, and the Combahee River Collective's Black Women's Network Retreats did much of the work of enhancing visibility by arming black women with answers to their questions and doubts about black feminism.

Organizational and Underground Publishing

Organizational newsletters and newspapers served a dual purpose for black feminist organizations and, as such, were a valuable tactical tool. First, some black feminist organizations discovered sooner than others that publications were critical to disseminating information to members and mobilizing them for action. Publications were also black feminist organizations' most successful recruiting tool because they allowed clear demarcation of the connections between race and gender oppression as they related to black communities.

Three of the five black feminist organizations published a newsletter or newspaper at one time or another during their existence. Combahee did not publish a regular newsletter, but its members, specifically Beverly and Barbara Smith, wrote about black women's responses to the *Combahee River Collective Statement*.[4] The other exception, the NABF, published a monthly calendar of events from 1976 to 1980. As such, it indicates the NABF's range of activities and served to mobilize members around organizational events, including feminist conferences, participation in the NABF consciousness-

raising sessions, and organizational committee work. The NBFO published three issues of its newsletter in January 1975 in an effort to connect its national office to chapters in formation. Although the newsletter delivered information about the organization's activities, feminist legislative initiatives, and upcoming national conferences, it came too late. The organization was already in decline, and the newsletter did not convince members that they were part of a salvageable endeavor.

The TWWA and BWOA publications offer the widest range of material available for analysis of black feminist organizations' activities. The TWWA's newspaper, *Triple Jeopardy*, published at least ten issues from 1971 to 1975. The BWOA's newsletter, *What It Is!*, was published monthly from 1973 to 1980 with rotating publication responsibilities among its members. Members of both organizations wrote in-depth articles about women's issues as they related to women of color and wrote about issues of interest to the wider communities. For both organizations, these publications allowed black women to gain experience in writing, interviewing, small press publishing, and other journalistic skills as part of their leadership development.

In addition to developing leadership skills among members, black feminists' publications reflect the evolution of feminist thought as parallel to white feminists, but also innovative in its incorporation of race and class into feminist analysis. The TWWA's *Triple Jeopardy*, while publishing feminist critiques of consumerism, beauty standards, and political aspects of women's health, also incorporated an anti-imperialist and antiracist analysis into its publication. Articles and poetry about women's roles in liberation struggles in Angola, Mozambique, Chile, Cuba, Puerto Rico, and Vietnam and analyses of women of color political prisoners in the U.S. were printed alongside critiques of domestic issues, such as Watergate and corporate welfare. For example, the first issue of *Triple Jeopardy* contained extensive coverage of prisoners' rights issues. It published a list of demands following the Attica prison uprising that included adequate food, water, and shelter for all inmates; an end to censoring reading material; and religious and political freedom.

The issue also covered the assassination of political writer and activist George Jackson at San Quentin Prison, drawing attention to discrepancies in official reports about his murder, and it published an appeal for funds by the TWWA Legal Committee in defense of TWWA member Kisha Shakur, who was ensnared in the machinations of the FBI, COINTELPRO-driven case against her husband, Dhoruba Bin Wahad, and accused of playing a role

in the murder of two police officers.[5] Accompanying the article was a letter from Shakur detailing her treatment, as well as that of immigrants detained in the jail. Coverage of political prisoners served to link the TWWA's concerns about the injudicious use of law enforcement and the growing imprisonment of female political activists.

Triple Jeopardy also covered a range of local and national issues that linked together the organization's anti-imperialist, antiracist, antisexist agendas. Frequent features tackled the day care issue. Although day care was an issue that predominately white feminist organizations covered, *Triple Jeopardy* linked the need for day care not only to women's work lives, but also to the intersection of city, state, and federal policies surrounding welfare as they impacted the well-being of communities of color.

The writers in *Triple Jeopardy* also wrote about cultural issues and their larger political significance. In an article titled "Feminine Stink Mystique," Beal dissects how the promotion of commercial feminine hygiene products merely distracts women of color from racism, unemployment, drafting third world men into imperialist aggression, and drug addiction.[6] A bilingual (Spanish/English) article covered a Puerto Rican women's workshop held at Hunter College that engaged the TWWA members in guerilla theater as a tactical tool to build interorganizational understanding and to invigorate the group's anticapitalist protests.[7] Workshop participants, for instance, developed a skit that dramatized what they thought poor women in a tea commercial would say were it accurate: "FIRST WOMAN: When you drink Tetley Tea, you are getting the finest tea leaves from my country, Indonesia. It is picked by workers who are exploited by Tetley, getting low wages and living in sub-human conditions." The skit goes on to dramatize similar exploitation in other countries, noting the draining of natural resources as the price of a cup of tea.[8] It was characteristic for *Triple Jeopardy* articles to connect the seemingly everyday, mundane aspects of women of color's lives to global implications.

As mentioned in chapter 2, the FBI's COINTELPRO initiative conducted extensive, often repetitive, summaries of *Triple Jeopardy*. In particular, it noted contacts with those considered enemies of the state: Angela Davis, Puerto Rican nationalist Lolita Lebrón, any and all contact with Vietnamese women, and sympathies or contact with Cuba

Triple Jeopardy's range of content reflected the TWWA's far-reaching goals and political principles.[9] The TWWA focused on bringing the organizations, its members, its recruits, and its potential allies into agreement on the

ideological and practical applications of its third world, socialist feminist perspective on a range of issues.

BWOA's *What It Is!*, on the other hand, provided fewer clues for analyzing mobilization strategies, but many more opportunities for seeing black women in action. *What It Is!*, a monthly newsletter distributed to all dues-paying members of the organization, offered services such as job announcements, health information, political endorsements, and financial advice. The newsletter also served as a morale builder among its members, heralding its members' achievements and reaffirming members' collective identity connections to the organization.

The editors of *What It Is!* reminded members of the importance of persistently asking, How do black women fit into this picture? For example, a BWOA editorial critiqued *Black Enterprise*, an African American financial magazine, for succumbing to capitalism and its polarizing effects on black communities. Several *Black Enterprise* articles ignored discrimination against black women in business in favor of extensive analysis of competition between (white) women and blacks (men).[10] The BWOA's newsletter also included political analysis, consistently examining the implications of the organization's political endorsements of candidates or ballot measures as they impacted black communities, and black women in particular.

Through their publications, black feminist organizations hoped to deliver on incentives promised to members. With limited resources, black feminists relied on their own abilities to disseminate information about their activities by calling upon members to take active leadership positions. Publishing newsletters, newspapers, and other publications about black women and feminism allowed black women to share leadership responsibilities and affirm their common identity as activists. As illustrated by the NABF's split from the NBFO, without active communication, members felt disconnected from the organizational bodies and questioned the strength of the black feminist movement.

Conferencing as a Site for Consciousness-Raising and Mobilization

The NBFO's Eastern Regional Conference (ERC) is a notable event in black feminist organizing history because it was the first time a large number of black women gathered to discuss feminism. There were, historically,

many black women's gatherings to address gender and race as they impacted black women's lives, but none did so within an explicitly feminist framework. The ERC is also a unique case study for the opportunity it offers to examine black and white feminists' reactions to this incipient move of defining a place for black women in the women's liberation movement. Specifically, white feminists' coverage of the event for the underground feminist newspaper *off our backs* (*oob*) and white and black feminists' letters to feminist publications in response to the conference provide a lens for gauging the NBFO's potential as a defining center of black feminist politics.

> Noting the 'enormous pressure' on black women not to join the women's liberation movement, a group of black women announced the formation of the National Black Feminist Organization this August. . . . Margaret Sloan, an Editor at *Ms.* Magazine and co-founder of the organization, said the majority of black women have rejected what they believe are negative stereotypes of women in the women's movement. However, she mentioned recent polls indicating black women's interest in feminist issues. . . . The group hopes to sponsor a black women's conference in New York this November.[11]

So noted the beginning of *oob*'s extensive coverage of the NBFO's Eastern Regional Conference. A small NBFO volunteer group strategized about how to gather enough black women to build on the group's founding discussion of black women's survival concerns. To that end, members organized a weekend-long conference at the end of 1973 in space donated by Cathedral of St. John the Divine in Manhattan, whose congregation was long known for a commitment to supporting progressive, grassroots social change.

Various sources report attendance as anywhere from 250 to 500 black women at the ERC.[12] The conference was originally intended to be limited to only those black women on the East Coast, mainly because the organizers did not believe, despite the phone calls to the contrary, that their initial press conference announcing their formation received widespread notice outside that geographic area. Women did come from elsewhere in New York and from Massachusetts, Pennsylvania, and Washington, D.C., but they also came from as far away as Illinois, California, Texas, and Mississippi. The *New York Times* ran a few column inches on the organization's formation and mentioned the conference, but it remains difficult to account for the subsequent three hundred to four hundred calls the following day, and the attendance of so many women at the ERC. It is likely that most black

women heard about the conference through word of mouth in the feminist network—not only from black women who considered attending, but also from white and black feminists who read about the conference in *off our backs* and spread the word to black women friends and fellow activists. Conference participation was limited to black women, but white female reporters were allowed to attend the keynote speeches. They could not, however, attend workshops or plenary sessions. Men were excluded from attendance completely, and black female reporters were asked not to report on the closed sessions, in order to allow black women to speak freely without intimidation from the press presence.

The conference offerings included about twenty workshops that focused on making the ethos of "the personal as political" relevant to black women's lives. Workshops included discussions of "black women and the struggle for child care, welfare, women's liberation, politics, the church, media, labor force, homosexuality, cultural arts, female sexuality, prisons, addiction and education."[13] Connecting gender and race were the explicit goals for the workshops, but organizers also hoped that women attending the conference would see the necessity for the organization's existence and contribute ideas for putting into practical action the NBFO's mission statement. The conference was one of only a few meetings since the group's inception about two months before, and, as such, the workshop discussions likely focused heavily on making concrete race and gender connections to the topics at hand.

In addition to the workshops, conference participants heard keynote speeches from Margaret Sloan, Florynce Kennedy, and Shirley Chisholm. In each instance, these women—all clearly advocates of feminism—did the work of setting the stage for formulating the parameters of and launching a black feminist movement. However, the work that they had done on the individual level and in their writing, convincing black women that feminism had applicability to the social, economic, and political dimensions of black womanhood, became the basis for much debate that lasted throughout the weekend. On the first night of the conference, Sloan addressed the risk involved in attending the ERC: "Some of you are here out of curiosity, some out of arrogance, and some out of frustration and loneliness. There are lots more of us who didn't make it because they were pressured not to come."[14] In acknowledging the risk, she validated women's conflicted feelings about attending the conference and all those who had written the NBFO after its press conference. However, this acknowledgement of dispa-

rate motivations also opened up a space for disagreement about the purpose of the organization.

An informal discussion emerged following Sloan's welcome, in which NBFO cofounders addressed conference participants' questions around black women and feminism. *Oob*'s white feminist reporters, perhaps out of the arrogance that Sloan spoke of, reinforced black women's invisibility by narrowing its reporting on the subject to feminism's impact on "women" and "blacks." Reporter Fran Pollner, for instance, stated that the black feminists' discussion "centered mainly around two issues: the racism of white women and an angry reluctance to be affiliated with the women's movement, and the absence of any emphasis on aligning with black men to fight the general oppression of black people."[15] Throughout the *off our backs* coverage, white reporters' feelings of alienation were repeatedly recentered, thus reinforcing black women's criticism of white feminists' apparent obsession with massaging their white guilt in lieu of simply listening and truly grappling with racism.

The black women in attendance at the opening discussion expressed an array of perspectives on why they had attended the ERC. Two women, both described as members of NOW, detailed their experiences of racism within that organization, ranging from being mistaken for one another ("they all look alike.") to having their ideas about feminist issues relegated to the margins of the movement.[16] Other women astutely noted lesbian-baiting and nationalist conspiracy theories as factors in the reluctance of many black women to attend the meeting. Yet one woman came to the defense of black men's potential as allies, using her own marriage as an example of feminism's positive impact on her relationship: "*He* has been educated . . . and he pushed me to this meeting. People think that all black feminists are single . . . but it [feminism] made my marriage better."[17] Such affirmations of feminism's libratory potential for black women, the lingering doubts, and perhaps disavowals of lesbianism by some heterosexual women would prove to be kindling for the remainder of the conference weekend's fiery discussions. Voicing these perspectives gave ERC participants the space to air their apprehension, but it also began to show them the plurality of black women's political thought.

It was important that black women were allowed a black feminist gathering as a space for openly debating their role in feminism, and it was a discussion that occurred repeatedly in different organizations. However, the purpose of the conference was to center the experiences of black women,

not to continually focus on white women's racism and countering accusations of male bashing or of lesbianism. Black women's letters to the editors of *Ms.* following the conference belie less of a focus on these two dynamics as reported in *oob* and more on the overwhelmingly positive experience of attending a conference of like-minded black women.[18] For some women, this was the first time they were thinking about feminist issues or coming out of the isolation of their respective communities to speak with other black women about gender issues. I quote extensively from their letters because it is imperative to document that process of self-definition—a highly valued tenet of black feminist theory—that evolved from ERC conference participation.

> The conference was both a promise and a warning for me. A promise because I now know for a fact that we have within us the strength (as we redefined "strength") to fight and free ourselves of our *self*-oppressions, break down our defenses against each other and get on with the larger battles. A warning because, as the sister said, "We are all damaged." It's a malignant damage that grows and spreads, within and without. I felt we broke through to a shared understanding of some of the ways in which we are oppressed by ourselves and by each other as well as by our society.
> —Suzanne Lipsky, Brookline, Massachusetts

> I realized at the NBFO conference that it had been much too long since I sat in a room full of black women and, unafraid of being made to feel peculiar, spoke about things that mattered to me. . . . I asked myself: Who will secure from neglect and slander those women who have kept our image as black women clean and strong for us? And at the conference, I met women who are eager to do this job.
> —Alice Walker, Jackson, Mississippi

> When my mother first asked me to go with her to the first Eastern Regional Conference on Black Feminism, I thought it would be a good chance for us to be together without my two brothers and my father. When the conference began and I realized what I was really taking part in it, I felt so excited I could hardly keep myself together. . . . My mother and I are probably the only black feminists in town. None of the young black women at my school are interested in really contributing to the liberation of black people. . . . They tell me feminism is dumb and stupid. It was a wonderful feeling to find so many together black women who think feminism is important. I felt warm and alive and part of something important and good. . . . I found

that it didn't make any difference to any of the women that I was 12 years old. Even in the two workshops I attended, all the sisters made me feel that I was wanted and that my ideas and thoughts counted.
—Halima Malika Taha, Ossining, New York

These letters strongly echo nineteenth-century black women who called upon black women to define who they wanted to be in spite of racist and sexist oppression. They also serve as a testament to the continuity of that thought and its importance in contemporary times. Other black women's letters told of previous experiences with activism that made them wary of attending the ERC, but they came anyway and were surprised at what they found:

The beautiful thing about it [the conference] was that we were able to see each other as women. Period. Not as Southern black women, or professional black women, or welfare mothers, or household workers, or college students or middle-class black women or poor black women or light- or dark-skinned black women or gay or straight black women. We were able to do what white feminists have failed to do: transcend class lines and eradicate labels. Because we cannot afford the luxury of splinter groups, we recognize that this one organization must address the needs of all black feminists.
—Ashaki Habiba Taha, Ossining, New York

For four years, as a black lesbian feminist, my experiences in relating and working have been with white women (feminists and lesbians) and one other black woman. At the NBFO conference, the workshop that was most beneficial for me was the one on the "Triple Oppression of the Black Lesbian." There were about 30 women who participated in the workshop. . . . Educating the black community about the oppression of black lesbians, helping the black community to understand that lesbians are people with needs, feelings, and rights, and developing a working relationship with our heterosexual sisters were set as priorities.
—Mary Faye Roe, Austin, Texas

I came to the NBFO conference filled with skepticism, after too many conclaves of black sisters where the subject was supposedly us, but which had ended sadly, for the sisters felt guilty to even be thinking about themselves as people, while other liberation struggles surged. Consequently, they were always destructive experiences. But this time was different. . . .

To have been a part of that moment when millions of crumpled dreams and aspirations sprang back to life will always be my proudest moment.
—Clarey Jones, Harrisburg, Pennsylvania

The letters to *Ms.* and the conference question-and-answer session brought together women who did not consider themselves activists and some who had already worked in activist groups. Both groups of letter writers had in common their heady idealism about the potential of the NBFO and black feminism. As the next chapter discusses, to assert that black women were above the identity differences that split predominately white feminist groups was premature. Still, with the rise of a black middle class in the 1970s, class status—educational or economic—was increasingly dividing the spaces in which black women could convene and discuss their common issues, making the euphoria of these letters understandable.

Differences in black women's views about whether to adopt feminism, despite the reflections of writers to *Ms.* magazine, remained contentious. In fact, coverage of the ERC in one black publication starkly demonstrated the uphill battle black feminists and the NBFO would face if they persisted in asserting a feminist presence in the black community. *Encore* magazine's April 1974 issue featured the cover story "Women's Lib Has No Soul." The cover depicts an African American woman in an African-print coat with a fur collar. Standing proud with an Afro and an outstretched rejecting hand, she appears to be staving off the advances of feminism. Feminism is represented by the cartoon character Olive Oyl, dressed in drag as her male suitor, Popeye, and offering the righteous black sister a can of, presumably, "feminist spinach." Cleverly signaling a black rejection of feminism as merely an attempt by white women to assume the role of white men in a bid for strength, the cover only scratched the surface of bias and virulent disdain for black feminism in *Encore*'s reporting on the ERC.

In an article entitled "Brenda Verner Examines 'Liberated' Sisters," Verner offered a scathing critique of the conference rooted in traditional notions of feminism as irrelevant to black women, revisionist history of black women's participation in the women's movement, and homophobia.[19] Before even reading the article, it is easy to intuit the conclusions Verner drew from the aforementioned cover, the choice of pull-quotes (those quotes used to draw attention to the article's more provocative points), and the accompanying illustrations. The pull quotes read, "Black men were not allowed at the conference," "The organization adopted all of the White Feminist approaches," and "Members of the NBFO sang White feminist songs

to each other." Of two accompanying illustrations, one represented feminists as strident, open-mouthed, halter-top-wearing, Afroed harpies—despite the wardrobe update, a not unfamiliar depiction in which women who
advocate women's rights are seen as too vocal.[20] Taken together, the illustrations and quotes had the import of giving very little credit that black
women could define their own position vis-à-vis feminism.

Feminism was always already defined as a "white thing," resulting in
a perspective from which the NBFO could not emerge as distinctive from
white women's organizing. While *off our backs* reporters perspectives centered on how Florynce Kennedy's speech offended them as white women
(despite the fact that Kennedy was one of the few black women to work
in coalition with white feminists on a regular basis), Verner's reportage
reasserted the feminism-as-irrelevant-to-black-women party line stating
"it seems as if Kennedy was involving herself in an 'in-family' quarrel."[21]
Verner likened Kennedy's speech to that given by Sojourner Truth in 1851
at a women's suffrage convention, portraying it as merely "the antebellum
image of African woman as protector of the master's house and his children—only now, she is helping to protect the interests of the master's *wife*."
Contrary to popular, if contested,[22] interpretations of Truth's speech as af-
firming the early connections she made between race and gender, Verner
argued for an interpretation of this and all other assertions of black feminism as merely imitative of white women, and ultimately serving only the
interests of white women in securing their place within a white supremacist patriarchy.

Verner catered to lesbian baiting in her descriptions of NBFO volunteers
working at the conference and the workshops: "One woman, approximately
six feet tall, wore a man's tan corduroy suit with a black turtle neck sweater
and carried one of several walkie-talkies that were to be used both inside
and outside the activity areas of the conference. A second woman wearing a full Afro, mustache, man's sweater, pants, and ankle boots, appeared
to be the official photographer."[23] While it may have been more expedi-
ent to simply say that there were lesbians present, Verner implied deviance
through her description of conference volunteers' sartorial choices as evidence of masculine traits and of black feminists' wanting to be men. The
women's height and facial hair were as central to Verner's imputation of lesbianism as her implication that these women were dispatched to keep the
"real" women safe with their use of walkie-talkies and masculine dress. If
the implication of Olive Oyl as Popeye was not clear from the cover, Verner
imputed further examples of the (alleged) nefarious mission of feminism

to convert black women to lesbianism and make them handmaidens of white supremacy.

Of the workshops, Verner observed that though she only glanced at the agenda, she "realized that the organization did not intend to sponsor any workshops directed toward open discussions of relationships between African-American men and women. No workshops were listed that were concerned with the Black family, Black Nationalism, or Pan-Africanism. Yet there were workshops entitled 'Black Women and the (White) Women's Rights Movement' and the 'Triple Oppression of the Black Lesbian.'" Asserting that, like their style of dress, black feminists merely mimicked white women in their approach to these issues, Verner consistently refused to recognize any agency on the part of conference participants in working through the strengths and weaknesses of a black feminist movement for themselves and that organizers lacked any civil rights or black nationalist activism in their histories. Highlighting *Ms.* magazine as the conference's primary financial benefactor—when, in fact, the magazine was one of two sponsors—Verner's article belied an investment in maintaining the idea that black feminists were unauthentically black and traitorous to black liberation.

Organizers within the NBFO were portrayed as older, reformist, dictatorial agents of white feminism, invested in their own predetermined agenda. Class and generation are how Verner explained that the NBFO's black feminists pushed a so-called white lesbian feminist agenda. Black feminists were, according to Verner, "older women who held higher degrees and who were established in higher-salaried positions," who "seemed all too willing to yield our cultural and political unity . . . for some vague, emulative form of White feminism."[24] In one exchange, Verner observed that a younger woman rightly questioned whether white women would subjugate black women as domestic servants while they went to Women's Lib meetings. Without commentary, Verner noted the response of "an NBFO member in her early fifties, wearing a mingled gray Afro," who "leaped to her feet, her eyes wild and her fist punching the air." According to Verner, this woman shouted, "Yes, I work for her! And love every minute of it! I'll work for her while she goes to all the meetings she wants! And let her pay me. White people told me I was pretty long before any Blacks did!"[25] Verner hopes this outburst, taken out of context and uncommented on, proved her point: black feminism is about black women following behind white women and picking up any scraps that they leave behind, be they in the home or the workplace.

National Black Feminist Organization leaders Margaret Sloan and Margo Jefferson crafted a reply to Verner's misdirected vitriol, calling her claims "horizontal hostility—allowing the powers that be to stroll away with the real political, economic, and cultural power still in tow."[26] Asserting that the principles outlined in the NBFO's mission statement "are hardly modern White-patented and marketed concepts imposed on passive and brainwashed Black women," Jefferson and Sloan disputed Verner's claims and those of the larger black community that black women were mindless dupes in a white feminist plot. They used black women's heterogeneity as a defense, but did not attack the homophobia evident in Verner's views: "The hundreds of women who attended wore men's pants, women's pants, dresses, skirts, combat boots, sling-back shoes, and a host of other clothes that most of us were too busy to notice."[27]

The NBFO and its members were only at the beginning of defending black feminism against recurring derision. Undoubtedly, black women came to the Eastern Regional Conference with doubts and skepticism, but many also left with significantly changed views on the potential for a black feminist agenda, organization, and movement and on their potential place in it.

Alternative Education

Educating black women about feminism and about themselves was a dual task that the NABF took on through consciousness-raising workshops and classes. Modeled after the Student Nonviolent Coordinating Committee's Freedom Schools, black feminists devised their own schools in black communities to teach black history and raise black consciousness about racism and oppression. The Third World Women's Alliance held "Liberation Schools" in New York that were open to people of color communities to examine the intersections of racism, imperialism, and sexism through interactive theater and discussion groups.

Taking this civil rights movement–based concept one step further, the NABF devised a plan for a freestanding alternative school. Eschewing separatist models, the Alternative School offered classes and workshops for members and nonmembers of the NABF, for women and for men of all races. The school also often offered workshops for black women only— usually those related to consciousness-raising and body issues. Members of the NABF served as the school's volunteer staff, performing tasks such

as registering students for classes, answering phones, preparing refreshments, and, most important, teaching the courses.

Already engaged in a popular education mandate, the NABF conducted consciousness-raising sessions from its inception as the Chicago chapter of the NBFO. After expanding its regular meeting space into a Black Women's Center, the NABF conducted bimonthly consciousness-raising sessions for its members and for interested community women.[28] Unique to the NABF, the organization also held sessions for black men, which expanded the connections between gender and racial oppression to masculinity's privileges and oppressive aspects for black men. Other workshops included sessions on black women's relationships to one another, the history of feminism and black women's role in it, relationships between black women and men, drug awareness workshops focusing on innovations in birth control, and political awareness workshops.

The decision to institutionalize these workshops as the Alternative School curriculum was based on increased workshop attendance, but also on a desire to figure out how black feminism applied to daily realities. Rather than conform its courses to dominant assumptions about the definition of feminist issues, the NABF went about constructing courses that were mindful of Chicago's black and women's communities, in particular black women's place at the nexus of those community interests. Courses on feminism, for example, provided a historical overview of the movement, but they inserted black women into the narrative through the use of historical texts and secondary sources, such as Gerda Lerner's book *Black Women in White America*.[29]

Also in demand at the time were assertiveness training courses. Based on the idea that school, churches, families, and other institutions socialized women, defined uniformly, to be passive and subordinate, the NABF offered beginning and advanced training designed to push women to define their needs and assert themselves with conviction, particularly in the workplace. That the NABF's Alternative School offered assertiveness training presented a paradox as to how the organization defined its mission in relationship to black women as individuals and as community members. On the one hand, black women were stereotyped as always already assertive as maintained in public policy and black nationalist accusations of a black matriarchy. The Moynihan report and certain black nationalist and civil rights leaders might have argued that black women needed "deassertiveness" training, that is, to learn how to be submissive or step back in the interest of black man-

hood. Thus, the NABF's assertiveness training fed into stereotypes about feminism and nationalist paranoia that feminism would take black women away from black struggle by making them more individualistic.

Conversely, if we consider the broader ramifications of this training and its possibilities for black women, assertiveness training could have proved to be more conducive to black women's potential as full members of the black community. While some black women were, and still are, raised to be independent and assertive in their work lives, in their community activist work black women time and again took a backseat to black male leadership. In this respect, assertiveness training had the potential to encourage black women to step to the forefront of black leadership. Also, given stereotypes of black women as loud, unruly Sapphires, assertiveness training offered alternative ways of negotiating stereotypes in the dominant culture. To some degree, though, this idea harkened back to nineteenth-century, bourgeois aspirations of fitting black women into a more "ladylike" mold, and it is questionable as to whether this would have been the desired outcome for many black women.

The Alternative School's activities were decidedly heterosexist in their orientation. Although there were courses that explored female sexuality, it is not apparent from course descriptions that these courses dealt with the range of black female sexuality. The language of the descriptions is often gender neutral ("Have you ever had an orgasm with a partner?"), and they do question the heterosexual paradigm ("Do you prefer sex with a man or a woman?"), but the courses appear to have been specifically geared toward heterosexual women's understanding of their bodies and those bodies in relationship to men. The female sexuality course, for example, worked in tandem with the Alternative School's course on black male/female relationships. Brenda Eichelberger and Janie Nelson, NABF founders, cite this course as one of their most popular.[30] It was open to black women and men and allowed an open forum to discuss the rumors, stereotypes, and myths that shaped gendered, intimate interactions in the United States. Although this course held the prospect of examining black male and female relationship on many levels, for example, mothers/sons, fathers/daughters, lovers, and so on, the discussion topic, at least on paper, was confined to black women and men as intimate partners. Dialogue on homosexuality remains sorely missing from the black community's discourse on gender, so it was a missed opportunity for the NABF's to expand on black feminism's impact on the entire black community. In the face of lesbian baiting, it is under-

standable, if not pardonable, that the NABF did not take advantage of this opportunity.

The popularity of the black male/female course translated into a marketable venue for the NABF to extend its black feminist philosophy to Chicago's black community. This course, as well as the course on feminism, parlayed into community forums held at local colleges. While it may have seemed counterproductive for black feminists to continually reiterate why they were feminists and how this movement related to black men and children, NABF members accepted this as part of its mission. This dedication is evident in the NABF's monthly calendars of events, published from May 1976 until September 1979. In addition to listing organizational meetings and consciousness-raising sessions, the calendars are replete with listings of talks on black feminism given by NABF members several times a month. While some people might have been hesitant to seek out the NABF's Black Women's Center or Alternative School, these same people could hear about black feminism at local colleges, such as Chicago's Malcolm X College, Southern Illinois University, and Chicago State University. Additionally, NABF members routinely sought time in local media outlets to reach marginalized communities. They participated in radio and television call-in programs, such as *Chicagoland and Its People* and *The Shirley Harris Show*, and they had their own weekly broadcast for fifteen minutes on a Chicago AM station. This exposure led to the NABF members leading assertiveness training and black feminism workshops for a range of groups, including Chicago-area U.S. Postal Service women, the U.S. Department of Energy, the Militant Forum, and the Black Voters of Illinois. Media opportunities and public appearances supplemented the NABF's Alternative School, which may have had limited appeal due to its explicit affiliation with feminism. The public speaking engagements also supplemented the NABF's coffers, as the entirety or a large share of honorariums went directly to running the organization.

The Alternative School's mission was to provide an alternative, black, and feminist education to all who sought it. Members and nonmembers of NABF alike discussed a range of issues based on the premise that feminism had another perspective to offer black women as individuals and members of the black community. Constantly being called on to elaborate on the connections of feminism to black women did not prevent NABF members from being active in the women's self-help movement, the reproductive rights struggle, welfare rights, and employment issues. In fact, through its nu-

merous activities, the NABF was one of the most prepared organizations in its ability to answer the question "What is black feminism?" and to expand upon that definition based on members' frequent interactions with the black community.

Spiritual, Ideological, and Educational Networking

The activities that black feminist organizations conducted were, in fact, strategies for disseminating black feminist ideology to black women. As we have seen, black feminists enacted a black feminist politic at different levels. The NBFO, as well as the NABF, held large-scale national conferences for black women interested in learning more about black women. They could then take this information and apply it to their own lives or modify it to fit their needs. However, though they now knew there were other women out there who held similar political views, some black women returned to isolated communities and families that might not necessarily be accepting of their newfound feminism. If the community were educated, as was the possibility with the NABF's Alternative School, the integration of black feminist ideas into community life may have been, if not simple, accessible to black women and men. Still, in addition to pursuing community and large-scale activities, black feminists continued to work at the individual level to define and effect black feminist change. In essence, they worked to make black feminism visible to the larger community, but also to make feminist activism an edifying space for black women.

The Combahee River Collective sought to carve out this space through a series of Black Women's Network Retreats, held sporadically from 1977 to 1980. Already organizing under the banner of the Combahee River Collective since 1974, Demita Frazier, Beverly Smith, and Barbara Smith invited a network of politically active women to "assess the state of our [black feminist] movement, to share information with each other about our political work and to talk about possibilities and issues for organizing black women."[31] The retreats were conceptualized as an opportunity for advancing what Combahee members saw as a burgeoning, nationwide movement. This belief is reflected in the preretreat surveys sent to potential participants.

The Combahee Black Women's Network Retreats were clearly about more than consciousness-raising. Participants in these retreats were presumably already engaged in consciousness-raising in their local communities, and the retreats, while hoped to be "politically stimulating and spiritu-

ally regenerating," were sites for movement building through examination of theory and activist practice.[32] The women invited to the first retreat were from New York and New England, and they were predominately writers, including Cheryl Clarke, Lorraine Bethel, Audre Lorde, and Linda Powell. The retreat organizers encouraged participants to bring written material, including their own creative works, relevant to black feminism. Such an invitation encompassed the idea that black women create theory in many forms—from position papers to magazine articles to prose and poetry —and that further consciousness-raising would grow from concentrated interaction.

The first retreat was held in South Hadley, Massachusetts, July 1977. Five session themes for the weekend were organized using feedback from the preretreat surveys. The first session focused on exploring participants' experiences with formal black feminist organizing. They came from a range of activist experiences, including reproductive rights, antiviolence, lesbian feminist, and health activism, so this session allowed the women present to seek out common experiences as black women organizing around feminism, as well as to begin to find places where their organizing concerns overlapped. Theory and analysis were the goals of the second session. The starting point for the discussion was *The Combahee River Collective Statement*, but participants also suggested developing a more specific black feminist economic analysis than the statement offered, deeper examination of violence in black communities, and exploring the meaning of lesbian separatism for black women. Combahee's statement briefly addressed each of these topics, but this retreat offered an opportunity for women from a wider variety of life experiences and activist backgrounds in addition to the statement's authors to add their insights to the document's analysis.

Saturday afternoon's sessions covered one of the same topics discussed at the NBFO's Eastern Regional Conference and in the NABF's Alternative School Feminism course: "Is there a black feminist movement?" This was a rhetorical question, posed by women who had already decided there was a movement, but that the movement was in its infancy. To nurture this movement, retreat participants noted the barriers they had faced in organizing (e.g., "anti-feminism, repression, ascribed class . . . heterosexism, racism, ageism, sexism"), and they strategized methods to overcome these barriers, including coalition building, collectivism as an organizing tool, and the potential for publishing to advance black feminist revolution. Importantly, the afternoon session also included space to explicitly explore

how sexism was racialized in issues such as sterilization abuse, health, and battering.

At the third retreat, several women participated in a workshop called "Visions of Black Lesbianism" that, as reflected in extensive notes on the session, examined lesbianism in a black context. One question they asked was "What events in black women's lives make lesbianism 'circumstantially impossible' for many of us?" Responses (e.g., poverty, self-hatred, community hostility, and how they combined racism, sexism, and heterosexism) all hinted toward solutions that would require black lesbians to be more open in declaring their sexuality to confront homophobia in the black community, in other women who were struggling to come out, and within themselves.

Workshop participants also delved more deeply into lesbianism through the concept of the *woman-identified woman*. Citing Toni Cade Bambara's novel *Gorilla, My Love*, and Toni Morrison's two earliest novels, *The Bluest Eye* and *Sula*, Cheryl Clarke—the note taker for the workshop—posed the question "Is it just the lack of sanction or is it mainly those remnants of self-hate that keep black women from loving one another whether the love is characterized by sex or not?" Changing the direction of the question allowed participants to move beyond sex as the defining characteristic of sexuality and explore what it meant to have intimate relationships with mothers, sisters, aunts, and sister-friends who were all interconnected through struggles against racism and sexism. A woman-identified perspective also allowed workshop participants the opportunity to discuss how heterosexism functioned for lesbian and straight women in all of their relationships, sexual and nonsexual.

The first three retreats focused on getting to know one another and coming to a common understanding of black feminism and its issues. As the retreat participants continued to meet, and bring other women into what they now called a Black Women's Network (as opposed to becoming members of the Combahee River Collective), some participants wanted to harness the energy of the retreat and parlay it into concrete activism in the name of the network. The options were varied. Members could continue with their own local political work and attend periodic network retreats to share information and organize insights. Or, they could organize under the rubric of the network and seek ways to sustain activity across long distances. In either case, members of the network and Combahee were sensitive to past organizing experiences. Linda Powell, an organizer, reminded the group, "We have all been part of groups that moved 'too far, too fast'

without a clear sense of direction. On the other hand, we've also seen promising women's organizations strangle on their own inactivity and inertia."[33] In particular, some women involved in the network had experienced the rapid growth of the NBFO and its subsequent floundering for direction. As a result, network members felt the need to define their purpose, whether it was strictly like-minded communion or joint political activities.

A couple points of strain arose among the retreat participants as they tried to find a productive outlet for their analysis and common interests. For one thing, it became apparent to network members that there were divisions between those who were Combahee, Boston-based members and those living in other parts of New England and the Mid-Atlantic region. Carroll Oliver, a New York City resident and network member, voiced frustration over the inability of the group to put together a simple newsletter to keep retreat participants informed between retreats:

> If we're going to merely get hung up in the passion and excitement of the retreats and then later say "fuck it," its [sic] one thing. But if we're trying to be about some serious work, political education, sharing in a collective process and feminist purpose its [sic] hard to understand exactly whats [sic] happening. The regional thing and the problem of distance are part of it I think but that is hardly an excuse since we're presumably about building a network. . . . [I]f we're not productive on a collective as well as personal level, all of our politics, analysis and theory are worthless.[34]

Oliver's comments reflect a downside of the retreats. While they were a rejuvenating source for women who were often isolated in their home communities, these same women had to return to those communities and carry out their activism in continued isolation unless they managed to bring other people into their network of black feminist allies. Clarke expresses this dilemma in her notes to the group on the third retreat: "I really looked forward to our Retreat, looked forward to talking about literature, politics, and each other's lives since our November retreat. My job has been getting on my nerves. I am not too popular with the black male upper level administration because of my style of assertion."[35] Perhaps women such as Oliver and Clarke returned more confident and with renewed energy for black feminism avocation in their activism, workplaces, and personal lives. Yet, as Oliver notes in her correspondence, these same women needed some type of sustained connection in those days of 1970s activism that predated electronic mail and the break up of telephone company monopolies that would result in low long-distance telephone costs.

Another point of contention that divided retreat and Combahee members was interpersonal politics. Barbara Smith noted in her correspondence to the group:

> I would like to do criticism/self-critique about the political discussion we had on Saturday morning about what it means to be out. The reason we decided to have that particular discussion had to do with a personal situation-conflict between me and another person in the group, which only the women from Boston were aware of. They have pointed out how uncomfortable they felt knowing this dimension of what was going on and it not being out on the table for everyone. I think it did put a strain on the discussion for which I apologize. Perhaps we can discuss this in New York on May 20 or in the summer.[36]

Later retreat notes and correspondence do not reflect whether this discussion actually occurred, but this incident, along with the previous tension raised by Oliver's correspondence, alludes to issues of decline for other black feminist organizations. In particular, the intensity of black women's relationships and the psychosocial impact of attempting to sort out issues of race and gender for themselves as individuals, while struggling around the same issues on behalf of black women collectively took their toll.

Despite these tensions, the network, spearheaded by Combahee, took seriously working through conflicts to arrive at a place of group strength and determination. In a memo to network members, Linda Powell acknowledged the numerous group dynamics to work through, but she demonstrated faith that the group could persevere: "I was especially heartened by what I consider our increasing ability to disagree with each other. . . . The Collective/Network/Retreat Group seems to be ready for a 'task'[.] It appears to me that we have worked through some very *basic* 'relationship' issues, and are better prepared to move to some of the more thorny 'political' ones."[37]

Records detailing retreat and network activities conclude with a fifth retreat in July 1979 and a seventh retreat in February 1980. A few changes are notable between the first retreats and the last few. Based on their agendas, the retreats appeared to take a turn more into what might be deemed womanist practice. On the one hand, current debates over womanism argue that womanism is the same as black feminism, according to the first definition offered by Alice Walker in her collection of essays *In Search of Our Mothers' Gardens*.[38] On the other hand, black feminist theologians and spiritualists have adopted womanism as a particular ideology concerned

with the spiritual and ethical aspects of gender, race, and class as integral to social justice movements, mainly as they concern black women.

The network retreats, in their last few incarnations, included opening and closing rituals meant to offer a healing space for black feminists activists. Rather than a complete turn to cultural feminist perspectives that valued the goddess or claims to female superiority based on their reproductive capabilities, the network's rituals seemed designed to supplement black feminist activism. Retreat participants shared significant life events that had happened between the last and current retreats, a ritual that spoke to the interconnectedness the network wanted to maintain as its members lived life as black feminists

Also evident from organizational records are the seeds of the edited volume *Home Girls: A Black Feminist Anthology*. Several retreat participants commented on their excitement over the possibility of reaching more black women with their ideas on feminism. Their main challenge was how to reach black women who were most in need of their views and analysis. The network members wanted to create a publication that could serve as an accessible workbook for black women's study groups. Ideas ranged from a quarterly magazine to a resource guide similar to the *Whole Earth Catalog*, which had become a manual of sorts for alternative living among the counterculture in the late 1960s.

Organizational records indicate that at least one mainstream publisher approached Barbara Smith about editing a volume on black feminism. Records also indicate that the retreats ended and Combahee disbanded before the group published the volume. But in the early 1980s, retreat participants Audre Lorde and Barbara Smith carried out the group's dream of self-publishing by cofounding (along with writer Cherríe Moraga) Kitchen Table Women of Color Press. In addition, several members of Combahee and the participants in the retreats contributed their prose, poetry, and fiction to *Home Girls*, thus in this way carrying out their wishes of sharing their black feminist views with black women who needed them most. *Home Girls*, in the 2001 revised edition, continues the important work of enhancing black feminist visibility through service as a blueprint for identifying and creating black feminist theory and praxis.[39]

* * *

Black feminists undertook activities that injected a race analysis into the feminist movement. However, it was not simply a matter of adding race to the recipe and stirring. At the same time as they were defining black

feminism for themselves, black feminists also were putting a public face on their views through activities directed at recruitment both to their organizations and to drawing more people to black feminist ideology. Their collective identity, which encompassed race, gender, and class concerns, needed to come through in their publications, conferences, and retreats, and through alternative education they hoped to reach black women and black communities with their message of ending sexism. Critically, many of these activities, though they were open to the public, had the potential to reach only those already convinced of the need for a black feminist movement.

5 ☆ BLACK FEMINIST IDENTITIES

IN CONTESTATION

Black feminists' collective identity and the process that led them to this identity helped define the structure of black feminist organizations. Certainly the social and political conditions from which black feminists emerged were necessary to this identity, but these conditions do not sufficiently explain the emergence of black feminist organizations. The very articulation of a collective identity for movement members was just as important to the emergence of these organizations because such an articulation signaled the start of the *cognitive liberation* process. The cognitive liberation process is the critical juncture in the translation of individual grievances into collective action.[1] Black women could have followed the path forged by foremothers in the black women's club movement, prioritizing racial uplift over gender oppression. Instead, a number of black women in the early 1970s defined a black feminist collective identity that was "interactionally constituted," or shaped by interactions with other movement participants and external forces.[2]

Miriam Harris's study of the involvement of black women in President Kennedy's Commission on the Status of Women (PCWS), the NBFO, and Combahee works through sociologist Rose Brewer's theory of *polyvocality* to argue that black feminists developed the race, class, gender, and sexual orientation paradigm in a linear fashion from the 1960s to the 1980s.[3] According to Harris, race issues were the primary concern of black PCWS members, and only later, in 1973, did the NBFO argue that race *and* gender impacted black women's lives. She then asserts that Combahee moved black feminism from the race/gender intersection to a polyvocal assessment of class and sexual orientation as factors of black women's identity.

Harris thus proposes a linear evolution of black feminist theory and organizing: race → race and gender → race, gender, class, and sexual orientation. Such a model presumes, as have other studies of African American women's activism, that predecessors to contemporary black feminism were solely concerned with race work. The addition of the TWWA, NABF, and BWOA as significant contributors to black feminists' collective identity disrupts a linear assessment of the evolution of black feminist identity. The development of a black feminist collective identity was, in fact, non-linear and subject to constant redefinition by black feminists based on their interactions with one another and the social movement community. Such an assertion creates a more complex picture of the black feminist movement and its organizations. Black feminist collective identity from 1968 to 1980 was polyvocal from the start. The black feminist identity of organizations changed according to whether organization members and constituents perceived their economic, educational, sexual orientation, or skin color privileges vis-à-vis other black women. Black women were consistently concerned with race *and* gender oppression, but they strategically prioritized race over gender depending on available openings in the social movement and political opportunity structures.[4]

Organizational position statements of purpose (see appendix C) illustrate the emergence of collective feminist identity for black women and their organizations.[5] Black feminist collective identity was dynamic and, in fact, was open to redefinition by organizations within the movement. However, as table 2 shows, the individuals who created the organizations placed varying emphases on these aspects of identity, and these emphases are reflected in their statements of purpose and activities.

For the movement, it was important to have a vision of social change distinct from the civil rights and women's movements that addressed black women's multiple jeopardy;[6] the black feminist movement's analysis of race and gender effectively did so when no other movement could or would. The civil rights movement and agitation on the part of women's movement activists provided opportunities for black women's growing cognitive liberation. Simply put, black women took the negative implications of racism and sexism and turned them into positive fuel for their organizing. Although they could not count on previous movements' success as a predictor for their organizations, black feminists tuned into cues that signaled political elites' vulnerability to race and gender demands.[7]

Black feminist organizations, as individual units in the movement,

Table 2. Placement of Emphasis on Identity Aspects:
Comparison among Black Feminist Organizations

	Black feminist movement	TWWA	NBFO	NABF	Combahee	BWOA
Race	X	X	X	X	X	X
Gender	X	X	X	X	X	X
Class	X	X	x	x	X	x
Sexual orientation	X	X	x	—	X	—

Note: The large Xs denote those aspects of black women's identities that were articulated in organizations' mission statements and acted on through activities, such as rallies, political forums, and committee work. The smaller xs denote those identity aspects that were articulated in organizations' statements, but marginalized in their activities. Last, the dashes denote those aspects of black women's identities that specific organizations did not explicitly address, either in statements or activities.

varied in the degree to which they effectively incorporated class and sexual orientation in their definitions of black feminism. Economic and educational privileges influenced the issues defined as part of their particular organizational agenda, so the organization members realized that all black women did not hold the same ideological principles. This became most obvious when organizations addressed, or did not address, issues such as sexual orientation or socioeconomic position. Some organizations effectively incorporated the plurality of black women's lives into their activities, but others did not and focused solely on race and gender demands.

For example, the two organizations that were similarly aligned in their members' collective identity and organizational vision were the Combahee River Collective and the Third World Women's Alliance. Both organizations articulated a position opposed to racism, sexism, classism, and heterosexism. Many of their members incorporated race and gender into their collective identity through their political activism as youths in the civil rights movement. Additionally, the TWWA and Combahee were both socialist organizations with a heightened awareness about class discrimination and the role of capitalism in oppression. Although both organizations in-

corporated antiheterosexist language into their mission statements at different points in their evolution, both organizations listened to the concerns of lesbian members and extended those concerns to their thinking about heterosexuality and the oppression of all women.

Black feminist organization founders uniformly recall their reluctance to join white feminist organizations as an impetus for black feminist organizing. Black women accused white feminists of narrowly defining the categories of sisterhood and women to include only those who were white and middle class. It was not merely race that was divisive for black women, but also white women's class privilege as it dictated the goals of the women's movement. In issues such as abortion or employment, black women detected white women's reluctance to look deeper into how race and class simultaneously impacted access to legal, *affordable* abortions and *better* employment for women already working outside the home.

Authored by SNCC and TWWA member Francis Beal, "Double Jeopardy: To Be Black and Female" was one of the earliest essays to connect black women's life experiences to sexism and modern-day feminism.[8] Beal challenged sexism within the black liberation movement, specifically the zealousness with which black men ascended to leadership positions at the expense of true libratory practice: "Where the black man is beginning to reject the values or mores of this horrendous system on most issues, when it comes to women, he seems to take his guidelines from the pages of *Ladies Home Journal.*"[9] Reasoning that a black nation could not be built without the energies and talents of black women, Beal concluded by questioning the logic of strong black men and weak black women as complementary in forging a strong, unified community.

Black feminist organizations echoed Beal's theory of double jeopardy in their mission statements.

THE THIRD WORLD WOMEN'S ALLIANCE

Our purpose is to make a meaningful and lasting contribution to the Third World community by working for the elimination of the oppression and exploitation from which we suffer. We further intend to take an active part in creating a socialist society where we can live as decent human beings, free from the pressures of racism, economic exploitation, and sexual oppression.[10]

THE NATIONAL BLACK FEMINIST ORGANIZATION

Black women have suffered cruelly in this society from living the phenomenon of being Black and female, in a country that is *both* racist and

sexist. There has been very little real examination of the damage it has caused on the lives and on the minds of Black women.[11]

BLACK WOMEN ORGANIZED FOR ACTION
We are *Black*, and therefore imbedded in our consciousness is commitment to the struggle of Black people for identity and involvement in decisions that affect our lives and the lives of other generations of Black people who will follow. We are *Women*, and therefore aware of the sometimes blatant, waste of the talents and energies of Black women because this society has decreed a place for us.[12]

NATIONAL ALLIANCE OF BLACK FEMINISTS
Black feminism, then, is the belief that Black women have the *right* to full social, political, and economic equality. We do not accept the proposition that because we are born Black and female in a society which is both racist and sexist, that we should accept the role which society dictates to us. Instead, we seek to unshackle ourselves from our "place" as Blacks and women to become individuals free to live to the fullest of our potential.[13]

COMBAHEE RIVER COLLECTIVE
The most general statement of our politics at the present time would be that we are actively committed to struggling against racial, sexual, heterosexual, and class oppression, and see as our particular task the development of integrated analysis and practice based upon the fact that the major systems of oppression are interlocking.[14]

These organizations constituted the black feminist movement because of their common recognition that race, gender, and class were inextricably linked aspects of black women's identity. The articulation of black feminist identity as multiply situated in racist, sexist, and classist society laid the foundation for later theorizing on black feminist thought, such as Collins's assertion that black women espouse a both/and standpoint, taking into account their experiences as both blacks *and* women.[15]

Black feminist collective identity evolved through consciousness-raising —a popular tool across the spectrum of activists—that increased black women's personal efficacy. Four of the five black feminist organizations, the TWWA, NBFO, NABF, and Combahee, formally built consciousness raising into their programs by making completion of one session or more mandatory for membership.[16]

Consciousness-Raising in Black Feminist
Collective Identity Formation

SNCC's Black Women's Liberation Committee (BWLC), as a civil rights movement organization and progenitor of the Third World Women's Alliance, established a distinct bridge between the civil rights and women's movements. The BWLC's consciousness-raising process grounded black feminists' collective identity process in the ethos of the personal as political. Through these similar instances of "identity talk,"[17] black feminists in organizations reevaluated their place as racialized, gendered, and classed beings in a predominately white, male-dominated, allegedly classless society. Consciousness-raising set the cognitive liberation process in motion for black feminists to make connections between social structures, racism, sexism, and classism in their lives.

In her history of the radical feminist movement, Alice Echols contextualized consciousness-raising: "The proponents of consciousness-raising took their inspiration from the civil rights movement where the slogan was 'tell it is like it is,' the Chinese revolution when peasants were urged 'to speak pains to recall pains,' and from the revolutionary struggle in Guatemala where guerillas used similar techniques."[18] Black feminist organizations used this technique during the height of the contemporary women's movement, but black and white feminists alike were familiar with consciousness-raising based on their interactions with activists in the civil rights movement. Beal, of the TWWA, recalls her introduction to consciousness-raising in SNCC: "That term was very common. 'You have to get your consciousness raised, brother,' you know, 'sister.' It wasn't just in terms of women. That had to do with what it meant to be black and to fight for freedom and be an activist as opposed to accepting racism and being like that. That term of consciousness raising was not—I don't know if it came out of the black movement, but we sure used it. We sure used it there."[19]

Women's liberation organizations used consciousness-raising to analyze the political implications of sexism in society and New Left movements, while civil rights organizations used consciousness-raising to heighten black awareness of racism. Consciousness-raising had a gendered aspect that valued talk and prompted an analysis of racism, sexism, classism, and often heterosexism, in black women's subordinate position in society. Black feminist organizations found that consciousness-raising influenced personal efficacy because it alleviated members' sense of isolation

and feelings of "craziness," transforming individual grievances into group identification.[20]

The BWLC's consciousness-raising sessions are exemplary in charting the evolution of a black feminist collective identity that examined race, gender, and class. Beginning with the organization's emergence as the BWLC and through its evolution as the TWWA, the women in this organization educated themselves and other people of color about the interplay of racism, sexism, classism, and imperialism in their lives. In particular, black women's self-image was a recurring topic in BWLC consciousness-raising sessions.

Similar to white feminists in radical groups, the BWLC adopted consciousness raising to heighten members' awareness about sexism, but it also combined race and gender consciousness into an analysis that was more complex than collective identities offered by the civil rights and women's movements. Beal explains, "first it [their analysis of beauty standards] was in relationship to white women and then it was in relationship to . . . women's femaleness and physical kind of thing. . . . Some of our first meetings were about 'This is what the body is. This is where your ovaries are. This is where this happens.' Can you imagine? We felt women had a right to know."[21]

Thirty years ago, for most women, basic information about the female body was an important starting place for women's gender consciousness. For young women, their bodies were a mysterious terrain, which was not unusual during this decade because black women, like their white counterparts, came of age under shared 1950s sexual taboos. Granted, dominant society's patriarchal views of black and white women's bodies defined them in opposition to one another, but Beal's statement engaged the realities of women's corporeality. Learning about the physical female body, the primary site of gender and sexuality, was an obvious and necessary first step in deconstructing what it meant to embody womanhood.

Equally important to discussing women's relationship to their bodies, the BWLC dealt with the ramifications of being black women in a society where whiteness was the norm. The BWLC continually questioned the relationship between beauty and blackness. According to Beal, "We had sessions on well, what does it mean to be in a white society, to be defined by physical characteristics as your essence? And people forget that, irrespective of what white women were saying [about beauty standards], it did have an impact on us as black women."[22] Regardless of white feminists' theorizing on prescribed beauty standards, many black women still experi-

enced self-loathing. Mainstream black periodicals, while espousing black pride rhetoric, continued to carry advertisements for hair straighteners and skin bleaching creams. The BWLC, in its consciousness-raising, attempted to decipher the double messages of Eurocentric society and increasingly Afrocentric black communities.

One might assume that if black women managed to reject white beauty standards and accept black pride standards, there would be little more for black women to discuss in their consciousness-raising. Aesthetically, in the 1970s black Americans redefined what it meant to live as a person of African descent in a Eurocentric culture that degraded their heritage. Yet, the BWLC concluded that black pride ideology exerted a unique kind of tyranny in the lives of black women:

> So we said . . . it's very good to say, "Okay, we should wear Afros," which we all did, and we should honor our own physical characteristics, which we said was great. But there was something deeper here. There was something wrong with still accepting the male/female ideas and just saying now, well, beauty is now black and that's beauty and that's female. . . . Well, what about a lot of black women who are not built in these, like, svelte thing, you know, big busted, big behinds? And what does it mean to try to live up to this white image type of thing. We said, "Well, why should we live up to any female? Why should women be defined by physical characteristics at all?" . . . So, again, we went very deep, I think, in terms of these things and then we did it from an ethnic view.[23]

The BWLC, in members' discussions of the unforeseen negative effects of black pride, did not believe that changing beauty standards to meet an Afrocentric worldview would solve problems of self-esteem. Instead, members delved deeper into the actual constructions of femaleness and how that construction impacted women based on their racial identity.

The BWLC also theorized abortion in its consciousness-raising as an issue of race, gender, class, and sexuality. Abortion was a difficult topic to wrestle with due to the personal and, at that time, illegal aspects of the procedure. Beal and Margaret Sloan of the NBFO both claim that in New York State, Puerto Rican and black women had the highest incidence of death from illegal abortion.[24] To complicate matters, the black liberation movement labeled abortion and oral contraception genocidal acts by white supremacists. Black women's reproduction and socialization of children became the accepted mode of female production for the revolution. Bambara railed against black men and women who, under the guise of nationalism,

voiced more concern for heirs to the movement than for the revolutionary reproductive options and lives of black women.[25] The illegality of abortion and the rhetoric of the black liberation movement compelled Beal to ask, "What about *living* for the revolution, not just being prepared to die for the revolution?"[26]

While previous studies' emphases on black and white dating in SNCC are significant, this was not the only aspect of sexuality SNCC women critiqued. Abortion, forced sterilization, and women's basic health concerns were also a part of the dialogue of the BWLC. The emerging black feminist community was no doubt aware of, and to some degree mobilized by, the involuntary sterilization of black women and girls, such as the twelve- and fourteen-year-old Relf sisters in Montgomery, Alabama. The Relf sisters' case was an often-repeated scenario in the United States in the 1970s: women and girls' mothers who were receiving public assistance were told, at federally funded facilities, that unless they or their daughters underwent an undefined "procedure," they would be cut off.[27] Black women, particularly those working in the South and in major urban areas, learned of these cases and wondered how they fit into their growing awareness of the need for black women's self-determination over their bodies and lives. Consciousness-raising in the BWLC helped black feminists see the social forces and influences within and external to black communities that contributed to the control of black women's bodies by everyone but black women.

Beal mentions that the BWLC "didn't do much except talk," but she also immediately recognized the importance of open and honest talks between black women. Black women talked to one another in the midst of a revolution of social and political mores, and, in that context, talk was a revolutionary act. Talking openly with other women about issues that before had been considered private began the process of linking the symptoms of racism and sexism to systems and institutions, rather than attributing problems to personal failings, which is a typical response under Western individualist thought. Returning to the involuntary sterilization example, in discussing the denial of black women's reproductive rights, BWLC women could rethink this issue as not one of black women's inability to control their sexuality or a propensity for unplanned pregnancy, but as an issue of access to contraception, access to abortion (illegal at the time), access to prenatal care, ability to support children, and a host of other issues related to the decision whether or not to have children. Talk changed the way black women experienced their physicality, their relationships to white women, their relationships with black men, and their roles as leaders. Most significant, talk

led to action for the BWLC in its later development of a SNCC position paper on black women and the women's liberation movement.[28]

Class and Black Feminist Collective Identity

Although many black feminists sought to eradicate class-based oppression, they were not immune to the tensions raised when women of differing class backgrounds came together to form a cohesive identity. Black women saw the poverty of the black underclass as integral to the oppression of black women and a priority for any organization. Much like their foremothers in the black women's club movement, black feminists already middle-class or aspiring to that class believed that their economic and social destinies were tied to working-class and poor women's daily realities.

Sharon Harley, in her examination of the black middle class, observes that economic standing directly impacted how black women approached community activism.[29] She outlines three tiers within the black middle class and the roles that women adopted based on economic privilege, skin color, educational advantages, and family reputation. The *upper middle-class social elite* consisted of those women who were often light in complexion; descendants of free black ancestry; and from families of educational, professional, and financial means. Members of the *new professional middle class* were black women of a range of skin colors, who came from impoverished backgrounds but held a stronger sense of their value and commitment to black communities than the upper middle-class elite because of the ties the professional class had to the cultural values of everyday blacks. The *lower middle class* consisted of those women who worked as domestics and lacked financial, educational, and professional advantages.[30] Harley offers no assessment of the lower middle class' commitment, or lack thereof, to community.

Harley discerned that determinants of middle-class status in black communities were not always tied to income or job description; other indicators included decorum, respectability, and moral refinement. Incorporating these cultural norms, it was difficult for black feminists to theorize anew the parameters of the meanings of class because blacks' class status was marked by more than economic background. These distinctions are relevant to black feminist collective identity because they help explain the recurring class tensions most black women would face in their attempts to define their organizational visions.

Upwardly mobile African American parents had rising expectations

for their daughters and sons to pursue advanced degrees and better employment opportunities. Yet, often these same parents were barred from employment opportunities commensurate with their educational achievements.[31] Most black feminist organization members had gone to segregated schools and experienced a vital, self-reliant black community, but often later had the opportunity to attend desegregated colleges and universities.[32] They knew that black women suffered economically, relative to black men, white women, and white men, but many black feminists grew up in homes where one or both parents held degrees in higher education. True to sociological theories on relative deprivation, in defining an agenda, many black feminists were aware of the realities of racism their parents experienced, but they also envisioned better possibilities in a society free from discrimination based on their rising expectations. They brought these differing expectations into their activist work and, because of them, clashed with one another over the meaning of liberation for black women across class lines. Did liberation mean breaking through the glass ceiling or simply no longer cleaning the office floor?

Organizational records reveal that the TWWA and BWOA experienced the fewest class conflicts within their ranks because of the similarities in members' class identities and aspirations. The TWWA, as a socialist organization, managed to reconcile its articulated class critiques with its activist work through continuous involvement with working-class and poor men and women in the community. Taking a cue from its connection to SNCC, the TWWA let constituents decide the issues that concerned them and then served the community by gathering more information and organizing for direct action. In this way, the needs of women of disparate class backgrounds in the TWWA were met and third world identity was solidified in the community, as well as on the individual and organizational levels. The organization was not exclusively focused on upward mobility and did not neglect the initial steps to economic justice, such as fair wages and non-discriminatory employment opportunities. These factors could potentially allow more third world women into the upper echelons of the workplace, but they were necessary first steps to daily economic survival.

The BWOA, in comparison to the TWWA, purported to have members of all economic backgrounds. Although the organization had members who were part of the new professional class, some of its working-class members aspired to middle-class status. Membership in the BWOA allowed women of all economic backgrounds access to respectability in an organization consistently involved in local politics and connected to politicians of the

black upper-middle class. For the BWOA's members, their common aspirations for upward mobility connected them, so few tensions existed between members and this agenda.

The class tensions that did exist revolved around hierarchy versus collectivism. Valerie Bradley, a former BWOA member, links the few class tensions in the organization to recurring new professional middle-class members' demands to bureaucratize the organization:

> Well, a group of corporate buppies [black urban professionals] joined [laughter]—we didn't call them that then—one is a very close friend of mine now in corporate marketing and stuff like that. . . . She and her group of friends wanted—it seemed like more inclusion. But they weren't being excluded, yet, they weren't doing the work. But they were, like, newcomers. I think they were more accustomed, rather than to a community-based kind of initiative to a more corporate structure and maybe it was more alien to them. But we struggled with it, and the organization did not break up as a result, you know what I mean? We worked it out. They did get involved, those that wanted to be more involved, but they had to understand that with . . . leadership comes responsibility.[33]

The class tensions, arising from new professional middle-class women's desire for *more* hierarchy, was a reaction to the BWOA's divergence from traditional patterns of black women's organizations (e.g., sororities, church auxiliaries), which included elected officers.

The NBFO and NABF were less successful in navigating class conflicts. A persistent criticism of the NBFO is that the organization was too focused on middle-class black women's issues.[34] The most damaging assertion, often repeated in secondary sources, is that the NBFO was akin to a "black NOW" and therefore out of touch with the needs of working-class and poor black women.[35] Critics' comparisons of the NBFO to NOW assumed that, even though the NBFO's members were black, the women's movement was white, therefore entirely middle class and thus as out of touch with the needs of lower-income black women as were white feminists in NOW. Critics of NBFO accused the organization of prioritizing upward mobility in white society—as if class mobility were not also of interest to integrationist leaders in the civil right movement.

Given the brief existence of the NBFO (1973–1975) and its struggle to define itself, these accusations appear unfounded. The NBFO's agenda included committees on employment and welfare, concerns of both middle-

class and poor women. Interviews with organization founders reveal that because of a lack of structure and volunteers, both committees experienced difficulties getting established within the organization.[36] Critiques about the alleged middle-class nature of the NBFO also conflated the existence of organizational hierarchy with adherence to middle-class values. Dealing with racism in institutions such as public housing, welfare offices, and schools, black women encountered institutional discrimination and were likely reluctant to join a hierarchical organization, even a feminist one. It would seem that the NBFO's potential constituents and members held the organization to a higher standard for class accountability because of their explicitly feminist stance and assumptions about feminist organizational principles.

In response to critiques of their organizations as too middle-class oriented, Margaret Sloan and Brenda Eichelberger defended the black middle class as historical catalysts of change in black communities. Sloan, in her defense of the NBFO's leadership, and Eichelberger, as the NABF's founder and executive director, both cited the importance of the middle class in mobilizing black communities. In an interview with Karla Jay for *The Lesbian Tide*, Sloan noted gender bias in the middle-class critique of black and white feminist organizations. She detected a sexist aspect to this critique and viewed it as a divisive tactic only deployed against women's organizations:

> I don't respond to the accusation that the Women's Movement is white and middle-class anymore than I respond to the accusation, that is nonexistent, that our [civil rights] movement is Black middle-class. Nobody criticized Dr. King for having a PhD or Stokely [Carmichael] for going to Howard University or Fred Hampton for coming from a suburb. People are able to get excited about the fact that these Black men were able to get up and out of their oppressive situations and bring about a movement. . . . In any movement, it's always the overeducated that get it together anyway. People who are so oppressed—rock bottom—don't even have time to shit. . . . It's so important for Black women to survive that we can't afford the luxury of saying "Well, you oppress me because your father is a minister or the chairman of IT&T [International Telephone & Telegraph]." We can't get involved in that . . . not saying that we shouldn't have sound arguments about class. But when feminists do that, here we are women who claim not to be male-identified but when we go into a class thing what we do is judge her by the man she's attached to, because most women who

do come from a privileged class got it from the dude they sleep with, the man that kept them, the father that had them. It's never because of their money. Very few women in this country really have power and money.[37]

Sloan extended the biographical availability theory when she noted that only black *women* were derided for any kind of middle-class achievements. The impetus behind this criticism of black women was that black women's main priority should have been hearth and home as their realm of social activism. These criticisms were based on theories of a black matriarchy and black women's so-called inability to conform to traditional ideals about womanhood. Sloan also, similar to Harley's argument, called for a racialized interrogation of middle-class status as bringing organizational momentum and energy to a movement where the constituency was mostly poor and disenfranchised. Still, in the end, Sloan reverted to an economic definition of class to diffuse accusations that the NBFO had only the interests of middle-class black women in mind, noting that most of the organization's members earned less than $10,000 per year.[38]

Brenda Eichelberger, as the central organizer of the NABF, claims a middle-class background that included a stay-at-home mother and a father who worked for the postal service, but held an advanced degree. When challenged about the class background of other women who were active in the organization, Nelson and Eichelberger duly credit the middle-class educators and clergy with maintaining civil rights movement organizations, holding up Dr. Martin Luther King Jr. as an example. Nelson and Eichelberger do not claim that middle-class blacks were the only people active in the civil rights movement and in their organizations. However, as Nelson explains, middle-class interests held sway in the NABF:

> One thing I noticed was that there was a class difference in the organization. . . . We had women who were, basically, blue collar who had jobs that were dead-end jobs. . . . They had maybe a high school education or maybe not even high school education. And then we had another segment of women that were very — had bachelor's degrees on up and still pushing. And I noticed that in some instances we — plus we were very verbal — and I noticed in some instances we [middle-class women] kind of overshadowed them [blue-collar women]. Not intentionally, but we could verbalize certain things that they couldn't verbalize and then they kind of felt, kind of like "Well, maybe this isn't the organization for me. It's not going to answer some of my needs."

The class issue came up—whether we should focus more on certain things that black women, in general, were having problems with. Like being on aid for health facilities. . . . And then there were those of us who, basically, were working, and what we were interested in was making more money in the field that we were in. How do we get up the corporate ladder? How do you progress in the field that you're in? How do you get into graduate school for the PHD?[39]

Within the organization, then, there was a split between those women who hoped the organization could focus on material concerns and women who, while not unconcerned with these issues, hoped for an organization that could serve as a resource for upward mobility. Nelson also recalls the class-based demands Eichelberger encountered as the NABF's executive director:

I remember we were having a meeting one time, and one of the members said, "Now, Brenda, which direction are you going to take this organization in? Are you going to try to answer and satisfy some of the needs and raise some of the issues that the ordinary black woman is faced with," which would be the blue-collar woman or the woman who's in a situation where she's being abused by her husband and all kind of stuff. (Remember this was in the '70s, and a lot of these things weren't really on the national agenda, but these things were happening.) "Or is this going to be a middle-class organization?" . . . And it was like, [women would] look at Brenda and say, "Now what you gonna—which way?" You know what I'm saying? And there was this other group that was saying if you take it in that direction you're gonna lose us, and if you take it in this direction you're going to lose us. . . . I think they wanted it on the table as dialogue and they wanted us to form an agenda that included, basically, the grassroots woman. I think a lot of people wanted to take it in that direction toward the grassroots, rather than us doing a lot of intellectualizing and a lot of talking about what we do.[40]

Nelson's recounting of the class dynamics in the NABF reflects a middle-class bias in the leadership, and this contingent succeeded in directing the focus of the organization. Again, it is important to reiterate that a middle-class bias in a black feminist organization is not necessarily one of economic privilege, but, as Nelson points out, middle-class women in the organization had more education and were able to better articulate their needs. Middle-class women were also biographically more available to assert their

needs within the NABF than working-class women with less discretionary time and income.

The final organization that fits into this context is the Combahee River Collective. Class conflicts among members of Combahee also played out through issues of education and upward mobility. The majority of Combahee's members came from working-class and lower-middle-class backgrounds. As children of these classes, and socialized during the Jim Crow era, several members pursued master's and doctoral degrees while active in Combahee. This disparity in educational and class aspirations created conflicts for those who worked in blue-collar jobs and desired more direct contact with working-class black communities. Mercedes Tompkins, a member of Combahee, recalls: "One of the things we did—the main activities that we did was we read books and we critiqued—and spent a lot of time thinking and talking about different issues that came out of the books that we would read and—you know, hey, I wanted to move outside of just talking about it. I wanted to do it."[41] In its statement, Combahee advocated a socialist revolution and the rights of workers, but this was a difficult position to maintain as, if not economically, upwardly mobile, highly educated black women. As it is reflected in the organization's writings, Combahee had to negotiate which actions counted as activism. Were writing, scholarship, and theorizing activist endeavors or did these activities fall solely under the category of "armchair activism?" For Combahee members pursuing advanced degrees, scholar/activist was a valid political identity, but it was not without its limits.

Barbara Smith, a Combahee cofounder and contemporary black feminist pioneer, recalls that Combahee's members recognized their educational privilege relative to many people in black communities, but Tompkins saw that privilege dominate the activities of the organization. For example, in debating whether to publish a black feminist newspaper or book, differing viewpoints emerged among the members. Tompkins cites conflicts over publishing as an example of how educational privilege could split the organization: "I think that . . . a lot of the women that were attracted to this group were women who had master's and beyond—PHDS and master's—they really bought into the system of, of course, being published. You know what I mean? Getting tenure and being a part of that whole established system—the educational, academic system. So, that was kind of the audience: women who were willing to read their stuff."[42]

Conversely, Smith recalls the disparagement she and other women in the organization faced when they pursued advanced degrees:

One of the things that used to bother me so much in Combahee—when I was a member of Combahee—was that people would make fun of the fact that I was pursuing a graduate degree and would trip me out about that. That was really difficult for me because I loved what I did. I loved the literature and I valued education and learning, and I found it ironic in later years that some of those who gave me a hard time about pursuing that level of education themselves went on and got their degrees, unlike myself. It really is ironic.[43]

Some Combahee members' acculturation into academic culture ran counter to other members' concepts of class struggle and grassroots activism. Although aware of the false assumption that working-class people do not read books, Tompkins's example illustrates how class differences created tensions over organizational strategies for achieving a socialist revolution. At the crux of Combahee's class conflicts were differences over how education aspirations fit into collective ideas of class struggle. More simply, book knowledge and street knowledge were set in false opposition to each other in defining Combahee members' black feminist collective identity.

To summarize, the NBFO, NABF, and BWOA did not espouse any particular political ideology as the solution to black women's oppression, claiming neither partisanship political affiliation, nor particular class allegiance. These three organizations were open to all women. As Eugenia Wilshire, of the NBFO, summarizes so succinctly, "Our politics was black women."[44] Sloan further explains: "I can't really speak for the group. I know that my philosophy has always been that feminism is inherently radical and so if you put adjectives onto it, it makes it seem as if feminism is not enough."[45]

While Sloan personally subscribed to a socialist philosophy of feminism, she summarizes the sentiment of all black feminist organizations that claimed a nonideological position as a recruitment strategy. Yet they were, by default, reformists in their political demands because, though these organizations accepted class as a given part of black women's identity, their activities focused mainly on articulating the racialized and gendered nature of black women's lives. Class was marginalized in the actual activities of the NBFO, NABF, and BWOA, but still became integral to the black feminist movement's vision.

Of the five organizations, only the TWWA and Combahee advocated socialist revolution as the solution to eradicating class exploitation in black and third world communities. While the black feminist movement espoused an abhorrence of class discrimination, few organizations were able

to effectively challenge classism internally in and externally to their organizations. Organizations that did not consistently articulate and act on class concerns faced frequent challenges from their membership about commitment to working-class and poor women. Sometimes these challenges were a ruse for antifeminist sentiment; at other times, though, accusations of classism were rooted in a desire for a truly inclusive black feminist identity and agenda.

Sexual Orientation and Black Feminist Collective Identity

Again, it is important to return to the distinctions among the black feminist movement, the separate organizations' visions of black feminism, and black feminist collective identity. While the black feminist *movement's* initial vision did not include sexual orientation as a defining aspect of black women's identity, individual organizations and members articulated lesbian-positive and/or antiheterosexist principles to the movement's vision. The NABF, NBFO, and BWOA included discussions of sexuality in their organizations, but they did not interrogate heterosexism as an oppressive force in black women's lives, regardless of sexual orientation.[46] However, the East Coast branch of the TWWA and Combahee both laid the foundations for challenging heterosexism and including lesbianism as an integral part of the black feminist movement.

Combahee was the only organization in this sample to mention "heterosexual oppression," but it did not thoroughly explain this form of oppression and its impact on black women's identities. The term *heterosexism*, the normativity of heterosexuality, was not yet in use among activists.[47] However, most readers of Combahee's statement may have deduced the implicit meaning of heterosexual oppression as heterosexism or homophobia. For other readers, the Combahee statement was possibly the first time they were forced to recognize *publicly* black lesbian existence, the daily oppression black lesbians face, and the considerable sexual diversity within black communities.

Combahee was on the front lines of black lesbian feminist struggle in the 1970s, yet the statement neglected to specify the ways black communities were complicit in perpetuating heterosexism. Barbara Smith explains this omission as the result of an intersection of the personal and political from the perspective of one of the statements' authors: "I think for the record, it's important to know that I was coming out in '74, '75. What's

important about that is that I declared myself—considered myself to be a black feminist before I came out. So for those who—who telescope or whatever that word is—black feminism and black lesbianism, I think it's important to know that one can be a black feminist. Some would say the reason we were black feminist is 'cause you were gonna be a lesbian and just didn't know it [laughter]."[48] The Combahee statement omitted an explicit challenge to heterosexism, due to the timing of organization members' individual coming-out processes and the desire to explain feminism on its own merit. Smith and other Combahee members strategically claimed a black and feminist identity *before* they claimed a lesbian one, though they claimed all three equally. For Combahee members, the separate emergence of feminist and lesbian consciousness undermined stereotypes of all feminists as lesbians and all lesbians as feminists. For people who relied on this analogy, feminist and lesbian were conflated identities and the sum total of a black feminist identity. The Combahee statement sought to disrupt this conflation. To a degree, an explication of black heterosexism was present, but underarticulated in the interest of establishing the foundational basis of solidarity between Combahee's black feminism and black communities. Still, lesbian visibility was a courageous and revolutionary move for Combahee to make, particularly in a social movement environment often divided by homophobia.

Predominately white feminist organizations experienced lesbian/straight splits that divided organizations and disrupted a unified definition of feminist identity. Of the five black feminist organizations, only the TWWA's members recall an expulsion of lesbians similar to the homophobia that gave rise to the "Lavender Menace" in NOW.[49] Homophobia erupted in both the East and West Coast branches of the TWWA and impacted the development of their feminist collective identities. How these two branches of the same organization handled issues of lesbian inclusion and homophobia differed dramatically.

It is unclear whether West Coast heterosexual members, succumbing to fears of lesbian baiting, expelled lesbian members or whether members who were lesbians, weary of homophobia, left the organization. Regardless of that distinction, the West Coast branch lost several members who were central to running the organization. The expulsion acted directly against the established principles of the TWWA, but there were no formal sanctions against the West Coast branch.

On the East Coast, Beal recalls, the organization was approached by out lesbians about membership. Unlike the schisms on the West Coast, the East

Coast TWWA eventually saw the inclusion of lesbians as an opportunity for growth in its organizational objectives:

> *Beal:* That was the other ideological fight that we had, which was important. We were approached by two lesbians . . . who said, "Listen, we want to be completely honest: we're lesbians. There's no organization for us." One was Puerto Rican, one was black . . . so we had a big discussion about that. Some people said, "Oh, my god. We have enough problems as it is! People are already calling us lesbians." That was another thing. We were lesbian-baited. . . . Two people said that they were lesbians, and we had this big discussion whether we should do this and some people said no, we shouldn't do it.
>
> *Interviewer:* Allow them to be in the group?
>
> *Beal:* Yeah. And finally, like I said, we had all this debate. People were very honest in terms of discussion and feelings and stuff, but finally people said, "In New York, how can we do this? I mean, we can't really turn sisters away. If they agree with the political orientation and purpose of the organization, there's no way that we can be prejudiced." So we came up with this, what I consider now—from what I understand about the gay and lesbian movement now—we came up with this very liberal position. Whether it's biological or social—you know, homosexuality—people should not be prejudiced and discriminated against. That was, basically, the position. . . . And a couple women left over that. They said, "no." They had enough problems as it was. They didn't want to be lesbian-baited. . . . It was a big question 'cause we said, "Oh, we're not lesbians." Oh, just because you talk about liberation, you're a lesbian? My god! Give us a break. "You hate men. That's your problem." It was all these ways of not dealing with the concrete question, you know, freedom, liberation, equality, equity—all of those things. If you could just call people names, then you didn't have to deal with the subject of the questions that were being raised. You could just call them names.[50]

Beal cogently deconstructed the intent of lesbian baiting: it split the organization interpersonally and ideologically. In response, the East Coast branch incorporated an antiheterosexist position into the TWWA's principles of struggle, recognizing the connections between patriarchy and homophobia: "Whereas behavior patterns based on rigid sex roles are oppressive to both men and women, role integration should be attempted. The true revolutionary should be concerned with human beings and not limit themselves to people as sex objects. *Furthermore, whether homosexu-*

ality is societal or genetic in origin, it exists in the third world community. The oppression and dehumanizing ostracism that homosexuals face must be rejected and their right to exist as dignified human beings must be defended."[51]

This statement, appearing in the 1972 issue of *Triple Jeopardy*, is not only politically progressive for the early 1970s, but is chronologically well in advance of Combahee's later assertion of the existence of lesbians and gay men in black communities. Hence, when Combahee is cited for its pioneering efforts to expand the black feminist agenda to include antiheterosexism, the work of the East Coast TWWA should also be recalled.

Not all black feminists or organizations openly opposed homophobia, and some were restrictive in their definitions of sexual freedom. Some members of the NABF, for example, did not want to discuss lesbianism in their consciousness-raising groups, committees, or Alternative School workshops on sexuality. The intricacies of black sexual diversity were decidedly marginal to some NABF members' definitions of black female sexuality.[52] Eichelberger recounts an incident in which she revealed that someone attending the NABF's monthly meetings was transgendered:[53]

> *Eichelberger:* We even had one time, and I don't remember the person's name—in retrospect, I should have said nothing, but I'm the one that brought it up—I brought up the fact that there was a man at our meetings. That this was a man in drag. This was a—I won't say, "drag." This was a man who was dressed like a woman. And actually what made him come . . . was a professor at U of I [Illinois]. . . . She was a black woman. She had me speak to her class, and this guy was there at the time—dressed like a woman all the time.
>
> *Interviewer:* In class?
>
> *Eichelberger:* Yeah, in the class and then he joined our organization. Now, I shouldn't have—well, of course, coulda,' shoulda,' woulda'—I can't change the past. But anyway, I know at one time I mentioned—because he was coming to the meetings—and I mentioned—I said, "You know we have someone here who was a man." And, um, I think some women knew who it was, and others were saying "Who? Who? Who? Who?" And, so, a number of women got very upset, and they wanted to confront him and they did confront the guy.
>
> *Interviewer:* Why did you feel the need to bring it up? Just so people would know?
>
> *Eichelberger:* Well, I didn't know they were gonna have the reaction that they had. I really didn't. I guess the reason I brought it up was because

it was supposed to be for black women. The way the Alliance was set up is that anyone could be affiliated. White men could be affiliated. We had white men affiliated. We had white men coming in and doing volunteer work. But to be an officer or anything like that you had to be a black female because that was our concentration, our focus. And, so, this person was black, but he wasn't female. And so somehow I felt, well, you know this is someone who is a man here.

Nelson: This was actually a man who had had a sex operation and was now a female. And we were real concerned about that. I remember Brenda calling up the members saying "What should we do? What should we do?" Because if we put him out, he could sue us [because of the NABF's nonprofit status] . . . and luckily, things petered out. He just disappeared. He didn't come back.

Interviewer: After being confronted he didn't come back?

Nelson: The person didn't come back anymore. I think he felt rather uncomfortable. I felt that he was testing us to see what our reaction was going to be. If I remember correctly, he had had a sexual operation . . . but we found out that he was a male and, I mean, that really gave us a loop.[54]

Rather than attempt to understand gender identity and how this particular female/male conceptualized existence as a woman in the organization, some members of the NABF pushed her/him out of the organization with their limited knowledge of transgender identity and homophobia.[55]

This incident within the NABF highlights a number of issues that occurred in black and white feminist organizations in the 1970s. It is too simple to conclude that black feminists were conservative and counter to the sexual revolution ethos of "anything goes." Despite the NABF's claims to legal concerns, all feminist organizations, irrespective of race, faced a lack of language to describe the diversity within biological sex and gender, homophobia, and fear of difference.

Some lesbian NABF members felt other members were homophobic and that the organization's activities did not reflect black feminist collective identity in its entirety. Looking for affirmation and advice, Chicago NBFO chapter members such as Sharon Page Ritchie asked other black feminist organizations for guidance. Upon learning of Combahee's plans for a black feminist retreat in Boston, she wrote this in reply to Combahee's 1977 preretreat survey: "The small NBFO chapter we have exhausted itself in trying to counter [a local black feminist leader]. We never got much past

C-R [consciousness raising], and eventually we stopped meeting for that. How have other women dealt with women who claim to be feminist, yet behave in very anti-woman, anti-lesbian ways."[56] Ritchie's query and the aforementioned incident with the NABF's transgendered recruit connect two issues: black women's divergent definitions of black feminist identity and the homophobia of heterosexual black women. In response to accusations of homophobia in the NABF, Eichelberger resolves the issue as one of members' differing expectations:

> *Eichelberger:* Maybe it was as if they [lesbian members] felt that it should have more of a lesbian agenda. But, you know, *lesbian* wasn't in the title. *Feminist* was in the title, which didn't mean that you're antilesbian. But you know, the thing is, the organization was trying to embrace all black women or any black woman that wanted to be a part of it. . . . But it wasn't an organization to have solely a lesbian focus, so there's nothing wrong with being a lesbian.
>
> *Nelson:* But they couldn't see it that way. Each one of the [factions] wanted to take the organization into the direction that they wanted to take it into. There were little factions like that.[57]

Eichelberger conceptualized the NABF as an umbrella organization. From her perspective, lesbians who wanted more of a focus on "a lesbian agenda" should have used the NABF as a resource to start independent organizations. Eichelberger and Nelson group lesbians with other groups of women they labeled as "factions," for example, socialists in the organization, but to frame lesbians as a special interest group ignores discrimination and the heterosexual privilege of straight black women. Members who agreed with Eichelberger saw *lesbian* as a category separate from *feminist*. Although they wanted to broaden the feminist agenda to include race, some heterosexual members of the NABF effectively excluded sexual orientation, and its implications for heterosexual women's sexuality, from the agenda of the NABF.

In other black feminist organizations, lesbians and straight women worked together to varying degrees of success. Generally, those organizations (e.g., the NBFO and Combahee) were founded by lesbians and included opposition to homophobia by integrating an antiheterosexist position into black feminist collective identity. Eichelberger and Sloan note that most NBFO members knew that Sloan was a lesbian and respected her role in starting the organization.[58] Still, there were some members, lesbian and heterosexual, who had problems with her prominent role in the orga-

nization. One concern was that Sloan's lesbianism would deter potential constituents and allies from supporting the NBFO. Similar to the TWWA's struggles concerning homophobia, Sloan, Eichelberger, and Singletary recall debates about lesbianism and heterosexual women's concomitant fear that they would be seen as lesbians by association.[59] Sloan did not see external homophobia as a concern of the NBFO, but she believed that internal homophobia slowed down the organization's momentum:

> It [the ideological dispute] was just stuff about race, and there was ideological stuff about whether we were going to—the group was multisexual. I mean, there were straight women and bisexuals and lesbians. And I think that there was a fear that people would think that we were a lesbian organization—God forbid—so they didn't want us to—those of us who were lesbians—I think that they wanted to sort of keep that—it was sort of like NOW in the early days. You know, "We know you're running this. We know you're the best, but let's just keep that down." . . . So stuff like that, you know, any time a group of women gather people assume you're lesbian, so that was what they said about a lot of the organizations during that time. It wasn't a big concern—it wasn't a big, big issue, but it was a concern. It was a concern.[60]

Similarly, Jane Galvin-Lewis and Deborah Singletary, in noting the role of lesbians in starting the NBFO, remark on the reverberations of homophobia from within and without the organization:

> *Galvin-Lewis:* And even though that is the case people have this notion, "Oh yeah, well, you know, if they had a man they wouldn't be pro-woman." And it's much like the race thing. You know, if you're pro-black it doesn't mean you have to be antiwhite. And to be profemale does not mean you have to be antimale. But because we were going with the feminist notion and people had their own ideas about what that meant, . . . one of the constant ongoing debates was about it being a gay organization, which it never was, was never intended to be, and that was not the point. But that kept raising its head. . . . Then, on the other hand, we had those people when we just—as women—we would want to take a stand on a position that had to do with gay women—we got the overwhelming groundswell of people that felt, "Oh, no! Don't touch that. That's not what we want to be about. . . ." I'm just saying that had raised its head several times, as I recall, and we never gave into because it was not our point. That's not what we wanted to be about. We

wanted to be about women—not any gay women, straight women—we
wanted to be about *women.*

Singletary: We did have a committee called "Triple Oppression: Being
Black, Female, and Lesbian," and they formed to deal with some of the
gay issues.

Wilshire: But I think it's to the credit of the organization that that [a gay/
straight split] was not what split it—ever.

Galvin-Lewis: No. It wasn't. . . . It never took hold, but it was raised on
several occasions. And on the other side it was raised on several occasions.[61]

The NBFO, despite outside criticism, was one of the few black feminist organizations besides Combahee to have a committee dedicated to connecting
the concerns of black lesbians to the organization's agenda. But the NBFO,
like the NABF, had contested definitions of black feminist identity at work
in the organization. Although a gay/straight split did not damage the organization, this ideological dispute was only the beginning of the struggle to
incorporate antiheterosexist principles into black feminist collective identity and the movement's vision more broadly.

The presence of lesbians or demands for inclusion did not disrupt
black feminist organizations. But, the homophobia of heterosexual women
stunted the growth of a cohesive black feminist collective identity. Although black lesbians were central to the formation of black feminist collective identity from the beginning, there were attempts to erase them from
these organizations' historical narratives.

* * *

Black feminists and their organizations provide a case study that links the
political process model of cognitive liberation and social constructionist
perspectives on collective identity formation. Black feminists engaged in
the simultaneous process of defining the vision of the movement, their
organizational objectives, and their own collective identity as black feminists. This was a daunting process because it involved convincing individuals that problems, such as poverty, were not personal shortcomings but the
result of structural systems—systems that could be altered through political action.

Black feminists' collective identity formation process involved not only
seeing the larger structural aspects of racism, sexism, classism, and heterosexism, but also recognizing pluralism in their organizations. A failure to

make visible differences in class and sexual orientation yielded a bifurcation between black feminists' visions of the movement and individual organizations' objectives. While the black feminist movement's vision was linked to struggles against simultaneous oppression based on race, class, sexual orientation, and gender, individual organizations grappled with these four aspects to differing degrees of success in their objectives.

All of the organizations used consciousness-raising groups as a tool to define members' collective identity around race and gender, but the successful incorporation of black women's class differences into their organizational activities eluded them. In general, the agenda of upwardly mobile members often overwhelmed the agenda of working-class and poor members, so much so that black feminist organizations, such as the NABF and NBFO, faced accusations of bourgeois tendencies.

Similarly, the black feminist movement was hard pressed to include sexual orientation as a salient issue in black women's lives, often leaving black lesbian feminists to figure out for themselves how sexual orientation intersected with racial, gender, and class discrimination. The other impact of the exclusion of sexual orientation was the undertheorizing that occurred regarding black heterosexual women's sexual agency as an integral part of black feminist identity. For both lesbians and straight women, homophobia and heterosexism were open secrets within black feminist organizations and black communities. As a result, black feminist organizations were susceptible to lesbian baiting and its negative effects on recruiting potential members.

Much like the larger women's movement, black feminists risked creating margins as they sought a place in the center of the movement. While critiquing predominately white feminist organizations for their racism and classism, black feminists simultaneously faced internal critiques of discrimination. As a result, it is fair to conclude that black feminists sought to create a black feminist identity when, in fact, the plurality of black women's lives indicated the need for black feminist *identities*.

Collectively, the black feminist organizations examined in this study spanned twelve years of activism. Black women engaged in consciousness-raising that clarified their position in relationship to mainstream feminism, boycotted corporations with discriminatory hiring policies, ran for public office, and educated segments of black communities about the exploitative nature of capitalism. Thus, black feminist identity and organizations enacted a belief system that reflected the intersectional politics of gender, race, class, and often sexual orientation. Yet, by 1981 the TWWA, the NBFO, the NABF, Combahee, and the BWOA were all defunct. Radford-Hill succinctly encapsulates the challenges black feminists faced in the 1970s: "History and enmity impaled black feminists on the horns of three impossible challenges. The first challenge was the need to prove to other black women that feminism was not for white women only. Confronting white feminists with the demand to share power and to affirm diversity was the second challenge. The third challenge involved fighting the misogynist tendencies of black nationalism."[1] Faced with this triple challenge, black feminist were, as NBFO member Jane Galvin-Lewis describes, "war weary warriors."[2]

And while those external challenges were significant, inter- and intra-organizational conflicts proved problematic for the long-term survival of black feminist organizations. Insufficient resources precipitated the decline. Directly related to insufficient resources was the burnout activists experienced as they attempted to capture the momentum of the civil rights and women's movement protest cycles by mobilizing large numbers of black women around feminist issues. Moreover, internal factionalism in

the form of ideological and leadership struggles hindered the organizations' viability. Strategies for maintaining movement momentum were consistently disputed within black feminist organizations, causing intra-organizational disputes between black feminist activists over power, privilege, and the future of black feminism. They may have forged an identity and organizations from between the cracks of the civil rights and women's movements, but they also experienced cracks in their own organizational structures and fissures that shifted the identity formation process.

Overview of Black Feminist Organizations' Decline

You know, the time really—the political climate really changed radically and the ability to sustain an organization, to have it all—kind of all on volunteer energy. You know, you do it in the cracks. There's no—nobody's even thought about funding much less—you know, in sort of the—what's considered the grassroots and progressive community now; it's all funding-based and funding-driven. We came out of kind of a "let's make a revolution" context and funding; the world of philanthropy was about the furthest thing from our mind. So, we were going on and motivated by politics and youthful energy. So, we conducted our politics in the cracks: we had part-time jobs that we didn't care very much about and we, basically, made this our life. So, that is not sustainable over an extended period of time [laughter]. You can operate like that for a while with twenty-year-olds and people in their early thirties, but after a while that doesn't work anymore. And then the political tide that threw up organizations like the Third World Women's Alliance receded and had not come back around again. And the Third World Women's Alliance and Alliance Against Women's Oppression are only two of numerous organizations that did not survive, essentially survive the Reagan/Bush years.

—Linda Burnham, interview by author, 12 February 1998

A black feminist organization is defunct if it no longer holds meetings, can no longer claim an active membership, or is no longer attempting to further its goals under the organizational banner. Table 3 summarizes the fundamental factors in the decline of black feminist organizations. The remainder of this chapter outlines the unique aspects of organizational decline, then focuses on the commonalties and differences in how the organizations declined. Specific examples from each of the five organizations

Table 3. Factors in Black Feminist Organizations' Decline

	TWWA	NBFO	NABF	Combahee	BWOA
Insufficient resources	Yes	Yes	Yes	Yes	No
Activist burnout	Yes	Yes	Yes	Yes	Yes
Ideological disputes	No	Yes	No	No	No
Leadership disputes	East : No West : Yes	Yes	Yes	Yes	No

illustrate how resource mobilization and collective identity theories merge to better explain organizational decline than could one theory alone.

Third World Women's Alliance

The East Coast Third World Women's Alliance (TWWA) stopped meeting in 1977. Archival records and interviews did not yield a precise date, but activists estimate that the West Coast chapter of the TWWA continued meeting until 1978 or 1979.[3] At that point, members decided that it was time to reach out to the broader women's movement community by building a new multiracial organization that included white feminists. Although a number of TWWA members left the organization over this decision, including the West Coast founder Cheryl Perry, the Alliance Against Women's Oppression pursued many of the TWWA's goals.[4]

National Black Feminist Organization

The organizers' inability to keep up with the rapid growth of the organization led the National Black Feminist Organization to close its national office in 1975. The organization received hundreds of letters per week from black women interested in membership and wanting to know more about black feminism. The NBFO's 1973 press conference and subsequent media coverage led potential recruits to believe that the national office and local chapters were already established, when, in fact, the national office lacked official guidelines and the financial means to implement them until just before the organizations' demise.[5]

The NBFO also faced the challenge of attempting to institutionalize the organization before it had a solid indigenous membership base. Conflicts between the leaderships' national aspirations and the New York City membership stalled the organization's development. Between power struggles with the New York City chapter and attempting to define the main organization's vision, NBFO founders succumbed to internal division after just two years in existence.

National Alliance of Black Feminists

Interviews and organizational calendars indicate that the National Alliance of Black Feminists ceased operations between 1980 and 1981. Leadership burnout and disagreements over the organization's objectives were the main contributors to the decline of the NABF. For example, the organization's executive director, Brenda Eichelberger, and the chairperson, Gayle Porter, moved on to other activities, such as graduate school. The departure of these two leaders, especially Eichelberger, left a void in the organization's leadership.[6]

Ideological splits over the role of sexual orientation and class also created conflicts within the NABF. Although Eichelberger voiced the desire for the NABF to serve as an umbrella organization for black feminists in Chicago and nearby Midwestern areas, this goal was made explicit in hindsight. This pluralistic outlook for the organization was not reflected in its leadership structure or organizational records, putting black feminists in conflict with one another over the goals of the NABF. Eichelberger asserts that the NABF's role as an umbrella organization was not inclusive of black lesbian feminists or black working-class women who sought a black feminist organizational affiliation and resources for organizing.

Combahee River Collective

The Combahee River Collective's organizers held their last Black Women's Network Retreat in February 1980, but organizational records do not indicate when the Boston-based collective ceased meeting. For an organization such as Combahee, it is difficult to determine a precise date of decline because many of its members came to the group through preexisting friendship and activist networks. Although Combahee may have stopped meeting as an organized body, members still encountered one another in the Boston women's community and in the black feminist movement

nationally. Yet, of all the possible reasons for Combahee's decline, leadership and interpersonal disputes stand out as decisive factors. As I demonstrate below, Combahee members' developing a collective identity as black, socialist, lesbian feminists collided with their individual ideas about organizational collectivity and interpersonal relationships.

Black Women Organized for Action

One of Black Women Organized for Action's founders, Aileen Hernandez, maintains that the BWOA never experienced a decline or cessation of operations. The organization officially ceased publication of its newsletter, *What It Is!*, and stopped meeting in December 1980 because, according to a final editorial, its members wanted to "take a breather" following seven years of continuous activism.[7] In the wake of Ronald Reagan's election to the U.S. presidency the BWOA predicted that the organization's members would need to "regroup, reassess, and re-direct" their energies in anticipation of a conservative backlash against minorities and women, particularly black women. As the BWOA's final editorial stated, "We must prepare ourselves to meet the challenge from the right. . . . We cannot necessarily depend upon the tools used over the past twenty years to help us now. . . . The Jimmy Carter presidency taught us to live with unkept promises. Reagan will force us to deal with promises kept."[8] Like many progressive organizations of the period, the BWOA planned to rethink its course of action in the face of new regressive policies rooted in conservatism and the rise of the religious Right.

Predicting this closure in the political opportunity structure, Hernandez later renegotiated the BWOA's organizational status and redefined its longevity in the black feminist movement's narrative. In 1996 the BWOA signed on as a supporting organization to a multipartisan "Contract with Women of the USA" full-page advertisement that appeared in the *New York Times*. The advertisement, initiated by the Women's Environment and Development Organization and the Center for Women Policy Studies, included women's organizations that concurred with twelve principles adapted from the Fourth World Conference on Women in Beijing's 1995 Platform for Action.[9]

The BWOA's support of the contract confirmed its members' prediction that the organization needed new strategies in the face of a conservative backlash that began during Reagan's presidency, gained momentum under George Bush Sr., and culminated with the Republican-dominated

Congress's "Contract with America." The BWOA's support of the "Contract with Women" came sixteen years after the organization ceased its monthly meetings. Hernandez explains how she currently views the question of the BWOA's organizational status:

> We did not close down the organization. In fact, it's still not closed down. I periodically send off letters on the stationery of Black Women Organized for Action. . . . So, we continue to be involved because some of our members are still around. We haven't gone out of business, but we just don't hold meetings, that's all. . . . It's much more informal at this stage. I think people got "meeting'd out. . . ." One of the positive things that happened with Black Women Organized for Action is that many of our women got involved in lots and lots and lots of things. . . . They're still out there doing work, and they do it in the name of the BWOA whenever that's convenient, but they also do it on their own behalf. So I think what we've done is we've spread the leadership, which was our purpose.[10]

Social movement organization scholars have looked at the strategies that organizations use when the political opportunity structure closes. Leila Rupp and Verta Taylor, for example, call this a period of "abeyance" in which the women's suffrage movement, having won enfranchisement for women, harnessed its resources until the rise of the second wave in the 1970s.[11] William Gamson called this state of organizational stasis *pattern maintenance*: "Pattern maintenance exists when members of a group carry around their membership in latent form even while not actively participating in collective action. When they convene, the individuals are ready to begin functioning immediately as group members again. In this sense, the group continues to exist even while individual members are scattered about and not in direct interaction with each other."[12] The BWOA does not meet the criteria I have outlined of a fully functioning organization, but it is mobilized in the work of its members who, according to the BWOA's 1998 membership roster, still claim affiliation with the organization. The BWOA is not physically mobilized, yet the organization is not defunct, providing an interesting opportunity for future research on social movement organizations, particularly in relation to the question of organizational legacy and long-term influence on members' lives, paid employment, and activism. For the purpose of this book, though, 1980 marks the end point of the formal organization, and this date complicates the issue of the BWOA's organizational decline.

Factors of Black Feminist Organizational Decline

INSUFFICIENT MONETARY RESOURCES

The TWWA, the NBFO, Combahee, the NABF, and the BWOA all relied on member contributions, whether in the form of dues or contributions. There is little corroborating evidence to show that black feminist organizations, other than the NBFO, appealed to traditional funding sources for grants. The TWWA, for instance, aimed to be a self-supporting organization without reliance on outside funding sources and, subsequently, without risking co-optation.

The TWWA—though it had chapters on the East and West Coasts—had few expenses as a local organization. The organization's greatest expense was the publication of its newspaper, *Triple Jeopardy*. The West Coast members contributed articles, but the East Coast members shouldered the burden of production and costs.[13] After five years of continuous publishing, the membership of the organization dwindled to about twenty women, and the dues they paid were not enough to sustain the newspaper.[14]

Depending on the scale of organizational aspirations, some black feminist organizations needed more income than others to continue their full range of programs. For example, the NABF, as an aspiring national organization, sent out a monthly newsletter detailing the organization's activities to members who lived in the Chicago area, but also to dues-paying members throughout the United States. Another expense the NABF incurred was the costs of operating its black women's center and the Alternative School, which included rent, utilities, and remuneration for the school's instructors. Members of the NABF executive board, particularly the executive director, Brenda Eichelberger, often paid the rent for the office space because they did not receive sufficient dues or volunteer hours from NABF members to sustain the organization.[15] This financial strain and overextension of certain members led to a leadership breakdown in the late 1970s.

For example, in September 1976, several board members resigned from the NABF's leadership because of the financial situation and frustration that out of 133 members, only about 20 actively worked in the office, on committees, or in orientation and consciousness-raising sessions. The remaining board members, hoping to provoke the general body into action, wrote a letter posing the question "Should this organization be financed by whites as many other Black-based organizations are?"[16] The implication of the letter was the untoward influence of a white organization on the NABF's black

feminist image and mission. The general membership decided that this was an unacceptable proposition and helped to sustain the organization through greater participation until 1980.

On the other end of the black feminist organizational spectrum, local organizations, such as the Combahee River Collective, incurred fewer expenses. In their work with the black feminist retreats, women would contribute as little as ten dollars for food and lodging. Combahee's organizers never rented space for the retreats, because they relied on in-kind donations from Boston's feminist community and other allies with large homes that could accommodate members. Combahee's members were also members of other local organizations, so they cosponsored projects in several areas of feminist and civil rights activism.

In essence, Combahee used its members' collective identity as currency in Boston's social justice community. As the only black lesbian, socialist, feminist organization in the Boston area, Combahee was at the vanguard of articulating the parameters of black feminism. In market economy terms, its brand of theorizing was in demand in the marketplace of leftist ideas. Mercedes Tompkins, a Boston member of Combahee, explains how Combahee's political analysis and collective identity garnered influence in Boston's feminist, leftist, and socialist communities: "Within Boston people looked to Combahee for anchoring around things—around the whole issue of race and culture. So that if you touch base with us or we were involved in giving support to a certain position, it almost gave them a rubber stamp . . . 'Combahee was involved in this.'"[17]

Combahee did not literally sell its name or position as black feminists, but signed on to events in line with its political agenda and ideology of an antiracist, antisexist, antiheterosexist, and socialist revolution. In effect, Combahee bartered for a position on the political agenda of like-minded organizations. In addition, as with other black feminist organizations, Combahee's organizers remained vigilant to avoid being tokenized or used to give a seal of approval to other organizations that did not offer principled coalitions of social justice. Instead of dues, donations, or foundation grants, Combahee negotiated its unique political position as a valuable local resource.

The NBFO, on the other hand, hoped to use its position as a national organization with local chapters to secure a place in the national women's and black liberation movement communities. The rapid growth of the NBFO had significant implications for the leadership and daily operations of the organization. One of these implications was that the NBFO did not have the

financial standing of, say, NOW to run a national organization with local affiliates. An organization of this magnitude needed full-time, paid staff to manage the flow of information between the organization's leadership, its members, potential recruits nationwide, and the media.

The NBFO's sliding-scale dues system exacerbated its financial woes. The NBFO's national office could not formulate a realistic organizational budget, because it did not know how much members would contribute each year. Beverly Davis theorized that the NBFO could not sustain itself financially, because members did not pay the full amount of dues owed to the organization, not enough members paid dues at all, and not enough members paid at the high end of the dues scale.[18]

Another explanation for the NBFO membership's low dues participation lay in the organization's desire to gain support from women of all income brackets and class statuses. The sliding scale, while encouraging accessibility, worked against the organization's financial survival. In the NBFO's membership orientation packet, the following caveat was included with the suggested sliding scale: "This is not binding. Give as you feel is appropriate. Your card will be marked 'paid' only with no amount noted."[19] Thus any black woman could claim NBFO membership, but she could do so without a financial commitment or active participation. In the interest of representing a range of black women, this policy allowed poor women to join the organization and work to improve their economic standing. Yet, the policy also potentially allowed women who were better off financially to shirk their fiscal responsibility to the organization. True to Mancur Olson's free-rider concept, middle-class women could also claim membership without helping to sustain it.[20]

The BWOA is the only organization whose records do not reflect financial strain. The organization held fund-raisers such as yard sales, political forums, and theater benefits, and, like NBFO's, the BWOA's dues system was sliding scale, but I contend that enough members of the BWOA held white-collar jobs that they could effectively sustain the organization's activities. Expenses included political action events, donations to other organizations, dues to the Bay Area Feminist Federal Credit Union, and newsletter production. The group's treasurer's report, for example, stated that the BWOA had a surplus in its budget of $2,000 in 1976.[21] Unlike the records of the NABF or the NBFO, the BWOA's records never expressed concern that the organization would fold due to financial problems. Instead, activist burnout and, as mentioned previously, closing political opportunity structures factored into the organization's cessation of formal meetings.

Four out of the five black feminist organizations in this study lacked sufficient funds because, as John Lofland notes, "If the smo and its beneficiary constituency are poor, not to accept outside funding can be to condemn the smo to meager efforts focused mostly on simply surviving."[22] A cyclical dilemma ensnared black feminist organizations: they struggled for the economic survival of those situated on the lowest rung of the economic ladder in U.S. society, but these organizations' own viability depended on a population that had the least to give in terms of disposable income.

In the case of black feminist organizations' financial strain, they, again, enacted politics in the cracks. On one side were older civil rights organizations, such as the naacp and the National Council of Negro Women, who relied on black institutions, for example, black churches, sororities, and the bourgeois, middle class, to support their goals of racial uplift.[23] Organizations such as sncc and the Black Panther Party, while outside the realm of traditional funding sources, attracted the largesse of liberal whites and even, in the case of the Panthers, writers, artists, and celebrities. On the other side of black feminist organizations, both branches of the women's movement relied on members' dues, but they also summoned connections rooted in white privilege to garner in-kind support. Symptomatic of being at the forefront of a new movement that challenged racism, sexism, and classism simultaneously, black feminist organizations were trapped by the funding imperatives of the time that found black feminist politics too threatening or marginal to both race and gender privilege. Consequently, most black feminist organizations struggled for their organizations' daily survival, as well as for the survival of their personal investment in feminism.

ACTIVIST BURNOUT

Black feminist organizers found that regardless of personal commitment to their organizations, the social costs of activism were high. As organizations with little funding, they relied heavily on members to staff their offices, coordinate workshops, and facilitate events that promoted organizational growth. In the context of this and other social movement organizations, burnout, or activist fatigue, marked the growing awareness among activists that they committed more time to social movement organizations than to other aspects of their lives, such as work, school, children, or intimate partnerships. Burnout also signified a level of intense political activism that few political actors could sustain for a long period of time without

experiencing fatigue or, even, frustration that the achievement of move-ment objectives seemed distant, if not impossible.[24]

Few social movement theorists address the issue of activist burnout, and even fewer attend to the gendered nature of this phenomenon. Doug McAdam, in his analysis of biographical availability during SNCC's Free-dom Summer, notes that the student volunteers, as members of a privi-leged class, were not constrained by full-time employment obligations. Also, because of their age, students were often unmarried and free of family and marital commitments. White students from privileged back-grounds feasibly worked in the civil rights movement during the summer without disrupting their educational plans and were not obligated to sup-port spouses and children, in contrast to the grassroots communities they sought to help.[25]

Sex and sexual orientation, as categories of analysis, extend McAdam's analysis of biographical availability. These identities, though central to mo-bilization, were also central factors in black feminist organizers' fatigue. Neither femaleness nor lesbianism meant that black feminists were weak or less dedicated to social change and, therefore, unable to maintain their commitment to the black feminist movement. Keeping in mind that most of the activists in this study were in their early to mid-twenties, as females, some lesbian and heterosexual black feminists chose to have children at a particular point in their social movement careers. As single mothers, some black feminists supported their families without the assistance of their male partners. In other cases, for black feminists in heterosexual mar-riages, their families needed two incomes to survive in an economic sys-tem based on racial and gender discrimination. Depending on the sexual division of labor in their homes, these black feminists may have carried the double burden of household maintenance and employment outside the home. Black lesbian feminists faced biographical availability issues, as well, in their relationships with partners. Undoubtedly, black feminist partners, in the home and in the same social movement organizations, experienced the benefits and strains of their joint involvement in the same movement circles on a daily basis.

Paradoxically, though black women joined feminist organizations to al-leviate the financial, economic, and psychological burdens of black woman-hood, these same organizations added to their work. Black feminist orga-nizers, particularly those who founded the organizations, carried a triple burden. Black women who endured the intensity of black feminist orga-

nizing in a short period, emerged stronger in their political convictions, yet exhausted from the struggle.

In hindsight, black feminist organizers repeatedly have observed that their organizations might have lasted longer had there been money to pay full-time staff.[26] For some organizations, such as the NABF, the lack of full-time, paid staff or volunteers puts undue stress and strain on its founders. For example, the archives of the NABF evidence the huge amounts of correspondence the organization received from women interested in learning more about black feminism in general.[27] Eichelberger personally answered hundreds of letters over the course of the NABF's existence without the help of technologies such as copy machines, facsimile machines, or electronic mail. The time spent answering correspondence and mailing out information about the NABF was time taken away from advancing the organization's goals, though Eichelberger did speak to a number of black women nationally about black feminism and its connections to black women's lives.

In a similar position, Margaret Sloan, who left the NBFO in 1974, is still dedicated to black feminism, but weary of the strains of running a national organization.[28] She and Galvin-Lewis were the NBFO's only staff at its founding in 1973, and both believe that had the organization had the funds, even one full-time, paid staff member would have served it well. The following exchange between the NBFO's Deborah Singletary, Eugenia Wilshire, and Jane Galvin-Lewis occurred at the beginning of an interview, signifying activist fatigue as a top decline factor in the minds of organization members. Still, the endurance of black feminist political convictions and identification with its politics was at the forefront of the informants' collective consciousness:

> *Singletary:* Are we black feminists now?
> *Galvin-Lewis:* I think I am, but well. . . .
> *Wilshire:* War-weary . . . been in the trenches.
> *Singletary:* We're what?
> *Galvin-Lewis:* War-weary.
> *Interviewer:* War-weary warriors?
> *Galvin-Lewis:* War-weary warriors—that's nice.[29]

The alliteration of "war-weary warriors" resonates for Galvin-Lewis and summarizes for her the sentiments among black feminists as their organizations folded. They were warriors in the sense that they constantly struggled against racism, sexism, classism, and heterosexism in the dominant society and black communities. Yet, as the women of the NBFO found out,

they were also pioneers in a struggle to define black feminism and ensure the black feminist movement's growth.

IDEOLOGICAL DISPUTES

The ideological disputes black feminists encountered were rooted in an initial assumption about the homogeneity of black women's lives. Although black feminist organizations based their objectives in race and gender commonalties, black women had their own individual identities based in class, sexual orientation, and color differences. These differences affected their definitions of feminism and their visions of black feminist organizational objectives. In their attempts to reconcile the plurality of black feminist visions that emerged, black feminists encountered conflicts over funding sources and alliances with white feminists that contributed to organizational decline, but also enriched their organizations' legacy.

Black feminism, at the time these organizations came into being, was a new concept. As a theory and practice, it was vulnerable to the debate of whether black women should be involved in the feminist movement at all, but black feminists had already decided that it was a relevant political stance for their activism. Yet, black feminists did not expect to find dissension within their own ranks over the meaning and focus of a black feminist agenda. Ideological fissures within black feminist organizations address the inability of a singular black feminist collective identity to meet the expectations of all black women. Ideological splits within black feminist organizations hindered their mobilization of resources by limiting the number of benefactors (e.g., foundations, other organizations, etc.) some members deemed acceptable.

For example, Sloan recalls dissension within the NBFO over funding sources for its Eastern Regional Conference. Some women, Sloan claims, saw the influx of "white money" from *Ms.* and the Eastman Foundation into the organization as antithetical to an ethic of black self-reliance:

> And then we had a couple of nationalist women—I always figured, you know, if I'm invited to a party and I go to it and I don't like the music, if they don't change the music I have the option to leave. I never understood, but I mean, that's some people's agenda. We had some nationalist women who—we had free meeting space at the Women's Action Alliance. It was an organization that—actually Jane was in it and she was black and she was able to get the space. I think there were three women that worked there, two white and one black—they didn't want to meet there because it was in

a white women's office, you know. They didn't want to take the [Eastman] foundation money because it came from the white people. I said, "Well, you know, the barbecue place and all—they ain't giving us no money so we're taking this money. If they're going to give money for us to have a black feminist conference—yes." With no strings attached? I'd be a fool not to take it.[30]

A concern was that white organizations would co-opt the NBFO, thereby compromising its already precarious position with black communities as black-identified. The implication of Sloan's reply speaks to the lack of support the NBFO received from local and national black institutions (e.g., churches, sororities, local businesses). Walker, for example, noted in her 1974 letter to the editors at *Ms.* that the black press failed to send reporters to cover the conference, though they were invited. In highlighting the absence of overwhelming black support, Sloan countered nationalist admonishments with the reality that the NBFO's formative black feminist agenda was counter to the prevailing, patriarchal ideology of the black community and society at large.

Black feminist organizations complicate the interconnections between resources and collective identity, particularly the revolutionary stance of black feminism vis-à-vis black communities. The NBFO, Combahee, and the TWWA stood by principles that were antiracist and antisexist, thereby alienating the majority of funding sources on which other civil rights organizations could rely. The NBFO hoped to form committees to work with women in prison and women addicted to illegal drugs, but because of these populations' marginality the NBFO alienated upper-middle-class and middle-class blacks who contributed to racial uplift organizations such as the National Council of Negro Women.[31] Additionally, the TWWA and Combahee's anticapitalist, anti-imperialist, and antiheterosexist principles did not endear them to a black bourgeoisie that viewed these particular women as a threat to the status quo into which some middle-class blacks attempted to integrate. Black churches, sororities, and other institutions that favored integration would not fund revolutionary organizations that advocated the radical transformation of sexist institutions. Moreover, the TWWA's avocation of an antiheterosexist politic and Combahee's openly lesbian membership put them in opposition to the dominant moral position of the black church, which held, and still holds, an enormous amount of sway in dictating heterocentric sexual politics among African Americans.

Whether they liked it or not, black feminist organizations were part of the larger U.S. women's movement. They transformed the theoretical grounding of the movement from gender as the primary oppression to an examination of race, class, and gender as intersecting systems of oppression in the lives of all women. Black feminists proudly made this theoretical contribution to the women's movement, but they reacted differently to working with white feminists' organizations on a practical, direct action level.

Some black feminist organizations did work with white feminists when an issue addressed the intersection of race, class, and gender. They recognized commonalties with white feminists across racial categories, even if they encountered racism in the process of coalition building. Combahee and the NBFO, for example, held antiracism awareness workshops for white feminist organizations.[32] Black feminists issued white women a challenge to educate themselves about racism and the complexity of other cultures, but they were also adamant that it was not black feminists' *responsibility* to educate them. Educating whites about racism was not the primary goal of black feminist organizations; building black women's self-image and destroying internalized racism were the priorities.[33]

The BWOA saw building black women's self-image and promoting antiracism among white feminists as related projects. A major enactment of this work was the organization's participation in the Bay Area Feminist Federal Credit Union. The BWOA members served on the credit union board along with white feminist members from the Daughters of Bilitis, the San Francisco Women's Center, and the Golden Gate chapter of NOW. The BWOA also worked with white feminists in filing public interest class action suits and in increasing the number of women employed in law enforcement. Since the BWOA was organized for action, it opted to work in coalition with white feminists, rather than hold workshops that would theorize about racism. Workshops were an effective means of antiracist organizing, but the BWOA's activities illustrate the principle of theory in action. Constituents' work connected them with white feminists and illustrates the links between different groups of women working in the financial and political interests of all women.

Interactions with white feminists were a contested terrain for the TWWA and the NABF. I have noted the early interactions of East Coast TWWA members with white feminists, such as their participation in NOW's August 1969

women's "Liberation Day" parade, that further decreased their trust in the possibilities of coalition building. Beal critiques the women's movement for narrow definitions of women's issues and interrogated the meaning of liberation. In doing so, she highlights the ways that the socialist and racialized aspects of the TWWA's collective identity put members in opposition to mainstream white feminists, whom the TWWA saw as merely attempting to appropriate the power of white males. This incident did not rule out alliances with socialist, antiracist white feminists, but the TWWA avoided those alliances that reflected little understanding of liberation as an issue of an antiracist, antisexist, anti-imperialist, anticapitalist position.

On the West Coast, the debate over working in solidarity with white feminists took on a form that contributed to the decline of the TWWA, but fostered the growth of a new organization. Archival records and informants were unclear on the dates of the transition, but between approximately 1979 and 1980 members of the TWWA's West Coast branch debated whether to expand the organization to include white women.[34] Sensing, as the BWOA did, a rise in conservatism nationwide, some TWWA members felt that it was time to form one organization that joined women of color and white women. The political ideology of the TWWA directly influenced the new organization, the Alliance Against Women's Oppression (AAWO), but not all TWWA members agreed with this transition. As Cheryl Perry explains, some members felt that the organization had finally reached a comfortable working relationship across their differences as women of color and that allowing white women to join their organization would be detrimental to the growing collectivity of women of color: "I mean, it was like—you know, it's like any other organization. You really get a good comfort zone. Just to overcome Asian and Black and Hispanic women coming together, you know what I mean? And even though there wasn't that much ideological difference—but culturally we were very different, but we overcame that through years and years of working together. So the notion of bringing white women into the group really caused a lot of ideological issues. And so some of us went on [with the new organization], and others went and did other things."[35] Linda Burnham, a TWWA member who took on a larger leadership role in the new organization notes, "That change came about as part of a complicated attempt to develop a more consistent class analysis in the organization."[36] Through an even stronger class-based approach than the TWWA's, Burnham and others involved with the AAWO thought that it was time for the organization to expand to include the needs and concerns of working-class and poor white women. West Coast TWWA members de-

veloped an analysis that maintained an antiracist agenda, but joined white feminists in integrating that agenda into a larger anti-imperialist movement. Although it meant the demise of the TWWA, the formation of the AAWO ensured the longevity of the TWWA legacy into the late 1980s.

The NABF did not experience a transition in the organization's structure, but there were disagreements over affiliation with white feminists. Gayle Porter, chairperson of the organization cites one particular example that highlighted concerns about affiliation with white feminists beyond interpersonal racism:

> Probably there were [ideological debates] that had to do with how much affiliation would there be with white feminist groups. How much affiliation would there be with lesbian groups? How many events would we have where we would bring our male partners or friends or husbands or brothers or sons? But I would say the most intense discussions were I think at times with the level of affiliation with white feminist groups. . . . I don't remember all of the organizations involved—was that there was going to be a big voters' registration push and I can recall, at one of our meetings, where one of the white groups volunteered to go into black churches to help register black people. And I said, "I mean this, to me, would be a poor use of your time since you haven't even been able to persuade enough white women to pressure a presidential candidate into selecting a white woman to be a vice-president. And you're the largest group in the country." So there could be that kind of, I mean for me, just an arrogance, but at the same time there were definite areas of such strong agreement and support, you know, for both causes. For making change in the white community, as well as making change in the black community. But I think some members were more or less comfortable with that.[37]

This incident illustrates an enduring trait of early feminist organizing: identity politics as a strategy of organizing in black communities. Black feminists felt the need to organize around their own oppression, but they did not carry this practice to the extent of separatism. In their coalitions with white feminists, black feminist organizations actively sought ways to support coalitions without reinscribing racial dominance.

LEADERSHIP DISPUTES

Resource mobilization and social constructionist theories overlap in their view of the role leadership disputes play in the decline of social movement organizations. With reference to black feminist organizations, re-

source mobilization issues at the organizational level combined with collective identity conflicts to manifest challenges to the authority of black feminist organization founders as feminist leaders. These factors took their toll on black feminist leaders and the membership, often creating an impasse in charting the future direction of organizations and the movement.

The BWOA and the East Coast TWWA both decided to stop meeting because they felt it was time to devise new strategies of organizing. These organizations sensed a rise in conservatism, and both membership bodies determined that 1960s strategies would not be effective in the predicted backlash against women of color, the working poor, and people of color communities. Founders of the BWOA, for example, sensed conservatism rising internally because some new professional members wanted to bureaucratize the organization, contrary to the BWOA's nonhierarchical structure:

> One of the positive things that happened with Black Women Organized for Action is that many of our women got involved in lots and lots and lots of things . . . I think what we've done is we've spread the leadership, which was our purpose. One of the reasons we structured it the way we did was that we did not want it identified as anybody's organization. So that it would be in my name and everyone would say, "Oh, that's Aileen's group." We didn't want that to happen. We wanted us to really create new leadership and we did that. I think we have significantly done that. There are so many Black Women Organized for Action members who are into many, many things, not only here in California, but around the world.[38]

Many skilled organizers emerged from the BWOA's and East Coast TWWA's collective leadership process and used their resources in the broader movement community. By making decisions collectively, these two organizations managed to circumvent strain on preexisting networks. Being leaderless from their inceptions made the collective decision to disband an investment in future activism, rather than causing one person to bear the responsibility for the organizations' demise.

A leadership dispute highlighted the personal consequences of leadership development, and collectivity precipitated the decline of the West Coast branch of the TWWA. Cheryl Perry, as the founder of the West Coast branch, admits feeling betrayed when, during the decline of the TWWA and the emergence of a new organization, other members made it clear that she would no longer have a leadership role:

Keep in mind—I'm not advocating that I should have been in leadership. But, simply, I was maintaining probably old methods of organizing. You know, I had not made the transition around what the new requirements were for political work. . . . So—and keep in mind I'm coming from a very grassroots sort of experience and I had not developed the oral and writ-ten—I had the oral skills, but I had not the ideological or written skills to participate that way. And so I think it was just a recognition that I'm a hel-luva' an organizer, but I wasn't someone who could lead political debates or sit in a room with five or six other organizations who all had different opinions about women's oppression and me to generate my ideas.[39]

Perry, while in her mid-twenties, amassed a high level of sophistication in the area of grassroots organizing, but she later realized that her skills did not fit the new organization's agenda for the struggle against women's op-pression across race and gender boundaries. She did remain in the new organization for a while, but she still grappled with being deposed as the leader:

Even though I carried on with people [in the organization], my leader-ship changed in the organization and I was more, let's call it, not neces-sarily periphery, but between the leadership and the periphery. What had happened is I had—you know, Third World Women's Alliance is my baby [laughter]. And so as it started to make the transition, I was having a hard time letting go—this is more personal than political—and as a result of that, people felt that I could not lead in the new organization. . . . I'm still fairly young, you know, not really—not able to . . . objectify my feelings about not being in the leadership. So, pretty much I pulled back, even though I still stayed active. . . . I was not in the leadership, so I attended the meetings, I did different things, but it wasn't like my heart was in it in the same way as with the Third World Women's Alliance. . . . You know, it's one of those things. I started the organization. Women, who are politically active now, I remember bringing them in. So it was all that stuff. I was un-able to objectify—in other words, I wasn't at the point where I could accept the fact that I wasn't leading the organization. I had done it for so long.[40]

Perry's position within the organization had to change for the organiza-tion to grow. The transition also allowed her to move on to other organizing, particularly among black professionals. But, Perry's characterization of her dissatisfaction as youthful inexperience and as personal rather than politi-cal is accurate but insufficient in explaining the social-psychological pro-

cesses of leadership decline. Although she was young, Perry's role in bringing the TWWA from the East to the West Coast was critical in the emergence of other women of color organizations with a socialist, feminist viewpoint. Age mattered little when Perry was unpaid for time and resources she put into the organization. She, in fact, donated dedicated labor with significant political implications for the development of black feminist organizing.

Also embedded in Perry's comments is an illuminating analysis of the paradoxes of feminist leadership. Like many other black feminist founders, Perry wanted to develop leadership skills in other women of color, but she did not anticipate a role reversal in which she became a follower of women she had trained as they tried different leadership roles. This shift in power dynamics was not an easy transition for Perry to make, especially since she saw herself as the "mother" of the West Coast TWWA branch. Undoubtedly, her hard work in transplanting an organization from one coast to another and building a successful grassroots organization was a testament to her ability as an organizer and, therefore, difficult to step away from. An unspoken pitfall of the equitable distribution of leadership roles for founders is that, eventually, founders are challenged to share the leadership according to the egalitarian terms they initially espoused.

Eichelberger experienced this type of challenge to her leadership position, but rather than a new organization emerging, the NABF folded under the pressure. Nelson, who was a member of the NABF and remained friends with Eichelberger, recalls Eichelberger's precarious position:

> Some of us . . . really did everything we could to protect Brenda from a lot of things that were going on in the organization. We did everything we could 'cause we could see things that were going down. We always used to suggest to Brenda that she should surround herself with people who were personally loyal to her. And Brenda was good-hearted, good-natured, and all that kind of stuff and the snakes—basically, the snakes got at her. . . . She was just too—her house was open to everybody. She tried to be a lot of everything to everybody—a lot of things to everybody. And we who were sitting back knew that this wasn't going to work.
>
> And Brenda was—the organization was, like, it was her life. She just put everything into the organization and we always felt that she was not appreciated as much as she should [be]. She spent her own money. She did all kinds of things for the organization and she wasn't getting the kind of cooperation that she should have been getting. Financially or—I remember Brenda used to—the newsletter would have to go out or something

like that and you [turning to Brenda] would be sitting there doing it your-self, when actually she was supposed to have input or somebody come in. In other words, if the committee didn't do what they were supposed to do, Brenda Eichelberger ended up spending her weekends or her evenings doing it. . . . I felt that they knew that Brenda was going to get it done. She was going to do whatever she could to keep it afloat.[41]

Eichelberger did not see the relationship between herself and the mem-bers of the NABF as exploitative, but she does admit that at the time, she felt some members wanted to criticize her efforts without contributing any-thing to the organization. Eichelberger found herself, during the NABF's decline, assuming the majority of responsibility for the organization out of her passion for black feminism and a formalized organization.

Demonstrating how power is interpreted differently from leader and fol-lower positions, Eichelberger disagreed with members who felt she had at-tempted to have exclusive control over the organization's agenda. Yet, some members felt that Eichelberger did not take seriously suggestions for other facets of the NABF's organizing efforts, for example, the creation of a black women artist collective.[42] In countering these claims, Eichelberger reiter-ated that the NABF was an umbrella organization that facilitated the growth of other black feminist enterprises.

Some members of the NABF felt that Eichelberger designated herself the prime crafter of black feminism and, therefore, the only person who could speak on behalf of the organization. This accusation created a split among members between those who appreciated Eichelberger's dedication to the organization and those who felt that her leadership style was autocratic. What both sides failed to realize was the symbiosis between Eichelberger's style of leadership and the media's tendency to create spokespersons or stars within social movements.[43] It is difficult to discern whether Eichel-berger wanted to, or could have, declined the role of spokesperson in favor of a more egalitarian mode of communication with the media. Might a col-lective, such as Combahee, have better success in negotiating the issue of leaders and the star system?

The Combahee River Collective suffered from similar internal leader-ship conflicts. As a published writer, Barbara Smith stood out from the other collective members as a highly visible representative. Smith contends that the group collectively made decisions, but other members had a dif-ferent perspective on the star system that evolved within Combahee. Mer-cedes Tompkins, for example, observes that Smith became the person other

organizations approached when they wanted input or participation from Combahee in activities. Consequently, Tompkins perceives Smith's prominence as a filter for the type of information that eventually reached the group. Although the collective structure was an effort to avoid hierarchy, Combahee encountered internal and external difficulties in devising a leaderless strategy that was truly egalitarian. Eventually, Combahee's historic statement on black feminism and Smith's published work with Kitchen Table Women of Color Press defined Combahee's lasting legacy.

As Okazawa-Rey pinpoints, it is difficult to ascertain where a leader's asserted dominance ends and members' acquiescence begins. In the cases of the NABF and Combahee, founders and rank-and-file members raised valid issues about the dangers of organizational leadership and the tyranny of structurelessness in masking power where there was thought to be none. Determining when a person crosses the boundary from dedicated leader to exerting inordinate power is a dilemma organizations must remain vigilant for from their inceptions.

Availability issues also played a role in complicating the leadership conflicts of black feminist organizations. It is possible that for Smith, Eichelberger, and Perry, black feminist organizing, compared to other personal obligations, held a higher priority than it did for other members. They all initiated the formation of their respective organizations. In light of this founder/organization connection, regardless of hierarchical or collective structure, it is possible that new members initially accepted the existing leadership structure. By the time new members gained organizing skills and wanted a chance to use them, the founders were firmly installed in their leadership positions. For an organization based on preexisting friendship networks, these leadership conflicts were even more damaging to the continuance of the organization because the political and personal were so thoroughly intertwined.

It is worth noting that for Combahee, these preexisting networks included friendships and romantic relationships, adding an additional layer to leadership conflicts. Barbara Smith's archived notes from the third retreat refer to a personal conflict that impacted the collective's political process. Recalling Smith's powerful position in Combahee, an individual personal conflict meant disruption for the entire collective. As an organization consisting of activists who were also friends, political discussions on lesbianism and the politics of being out overlapped with the joys and perils of intimate relationships. Intimate involvement is not uncommon in social movement organizations, but there is little research on the consequences

of this involvement for organization's functioning. How do the emotional aspects of political engagement interact with the political practice of leadership?[44] For Combahee, it meant that the person in conflict with Smith was asked to leave the organization or felt uncomfortable remaining, as was her friend who felt implicated in the conflict by association. This example provides an illustration of the difficulty of organizing black women, lesbian and heterosexual, who might assume political unity around their mutual identities without attending to interpersonal dynamics.

The NBFO encountered interpersonal difficulties in its organization, but its case shows that these relationships impact bureaucratic organizations, as well as collectives such as Combahee. The realization that all black women were not politically aligned or held the same interests came too late for the NBFO's leadership core. Organizational documents and informant interviews indicate that the NBFO's interpersonal conflicts were rooted in competition for control of the organization's agenda and ideological foundation. Interpersonal conflicts resulted in struggles over the leadership's bureaucratic structure, and, despite later cooperative efforts, the organization's failing infrastructure did little to give the organization ideological focus.

From the start, though the NBFO had a statement of purpose, the organization's strategy for building a nationwide black feminist movement was ill defined. Wallace complains, "after a while, it became an embarrassment to try and answer the question, 'what does NBFO do?'"[45] Sloan, as the first and only chair of the NBFO, felt extreme pressure to unite disparate views of black feminism under one organizational umbrella. Nationalists, socialists, mainstream liberals, and women who were politically undecided all wanted input in the organization's direction, but their lack of participation in the daily operation of the organization precluded that input and made it appear that Sloan was autocratic. Some members sporadically volunteered in the NBFO office, but the burden fell to Sloan and to Galvin-Lewis, who served as vice-chair. In Galvin-Lewis's opinion, their later attempts at egalitarianism were too flexible and this accelerated the organization's decline:

> In our desire for egalitarianism, we didn't put down our foot early enough on the ideology and politics of NBFO. And by the time we did that there had been two groups, in particular, that had taken hold and created *what we allowed to be* an argument. We had no business even allowing it to be a debate, but we were so busy saying "Oh, we're not going to be like other organizations. We're not going to say that we're running stuff." And the

irony—the *irony* in it was that that's what they accused us of *anyway*. I will never forget the "founding mother's conversation."[46]

The founding mother's conversation most clearly signaled the beginning of the NBFO's decline. After Sloan's resignation, several women formed a policy committee in August 1974 to establish guidelines for a new, coordinating council structure and workable guidelines for chapter formation. Although established as a short-term body, this committee remained in place until a coordinating council was elected in October of that same year.

The interim leadership, and the subsequent coordinating council members, including Galvin-Lewis and Singletary, made progress toward bringing the national office and its chapters together through the establishment of the NBFO newsletter. The leaders also organized the NBFO's first national convention, held in Detroit in the spring of 1975. The purpose of the convention was to solidify guidelines for chapter formation; come to agreement on the organization's purpose, philosophy, and goals; and establish a dues structure that would allow the organization to budget its resources. Fifty NBFO members attended and agreed to plan for a constitutional convention, but there were also initial challenges to the national, New York–based leadership.

The women who challenged the leadership also lived in New York, but they felt that the city should have a chapter independent of the national office because, in their opinion, the national office leadership held too much power. As an initial act of dissention, the contenders formed a New York City chapter in August 1975. Galvin-Lewis and Singletary characterize the dissenters as overzealous socialists or communists who deliberately attempted to disrupt the organization.[47]

Black feminist respondents, interviewed separately and on different occasions, mention Brenda Verner's antiblack feminist activism, in particular, as disruptive. She not only published the negative, homophobic review of the NBFO's Eastern Regional Conference discussed in chapter 4, but she also, in Smith's opinion, sought to disrupt the formation of the NBFO's Boston chapter.[48] Singletary and Galvin-Lewis, of the New York NBFO, recall the disruptive tactics of other possible provocateurs:

> *Singletary:* I remember being at one meeting. We had a conference on racism and sexism in the women's movement and—I'll go out on a limb here—but I remember someone getting up and saying "What about socialism?!?" And then there was a woman maybe down the way who stood up and said, "And what about such-and-such?!?" And what—I

saw us stop what we were doing and answer those questions. And later I thought, "Oh, we missed the boat there." We were on our way towards the end. But, I really do feel and I do not have any—I'm speaking on intuition. . . . I'm working on intuition here, but it seems to me that those interruptions were too strategic to be just the rantings of some women who did not respect the structure. And because we were not— I feel that we were so naive we never considered that any government body would pay us enough attention to send—what are they called?

Interviewer: Agent provocateurs?

Singletary: Is that what they're called? It never occurred to us—it never occurred to me anyway—that they would.

Galvin-Lewis: Yeah. But it did occur to me later.

Singletary: And I'm sure. Now I feel very strongly that that's what happened and we fell for it.[49]

The problem this type of disruptive behavior raises for a social movement organization is how to distinguish between agent provocateurs' intentional disruption and contenders' legitimate claims. Were these women FBI plants, or were they simply so against black feminism that they would take the time to attend conferences and meetings in an attempt to derail the proceedings? Were these women perhaps simply trying to convince other black women that another path, say that of emerging Africana womanism, was a more valid choice for black women interested in gender issues?[50]

In hindsight, social movement organizational theorists can only hypothesize on the role of a dissenting group by examining the outcome of the group's actions. For example, did the NBFO's anticapitalist contenders make legitimate claims for and participate in the daily building of a stronger class-based foundation, or did they intentionally derail the organizing process? In both cases—that of movement building or movement sabotage— the ideological dissension within the organization over leadership structure signaled the official end of the NBFO.

The growing confrontation between the NBFO's coordinating council and its opponents came to full fruition during the organization's Fall 1975 Constitutional Convention. Initially, the convention's organizers intended to develop bylaws and rules of governance for the national organization and its chapters. Instead of completing these tasks, members of the New York City chapter reignited the challenge issued to the coordinating council at the spring meeting in Detroit, but this time the challenge was more forceful and contentious. Galvin-Lewis recounts the details of the event:

By the time we [the coordinating council] finally said, "Look, if you wanna do it that way. Form your own," they [the socialist dissenters] had already gotten their foot—they had wedged the door so open that when we got to the floor at one of our conventions, they had organized a movement against the founders. . . . And the D.C. group [one of the NBFO's active chapters] for some reason was just hostile. They did not want—they just did not want peace and I never found—I never really knew whether it was because they were in with that socialist stuff—'cause some of them were—whether they were just the young Turks, you know, were feeling their oats and wanting to take over. I didn't know what, but for some reasons—there was nothing we could do. They said, "We wanna meet." "Okay let's meet. What time? Four o'clock?" "No, seven." "Okay, seven." "No, eight." "Okay, eight." "No, Sunday." "Okay, Sunday." I mean, they just jerked us around and we were so anxious, and I was very frightened because I saw the organization dissolving. I was so anxious *not* to let that happen that I fell for the old ploy. It's like driving a car in the snow. When you go into a skid, you turn into the skid. That's what straightens you out. But your immediate response is to pull away from the skid.

And that's what I was—did was [sounding anxious] to say, "Let's do everything we can to see that they feel that we're with 'em because we really are. We don't have anything against them. We're really with them." I saw them tearing the thing apart, and instead of just pulling back and saying "Lemme tell you something. You want it on Sunday at two? Then go meet with your goddamn self! You said you wanted it Saturday at four and we went along with you!" . . . Instead of that, we changed to Sunday and nothing would satisfy them. And when we finally got to the convention floor, they voted some Constitutional changes to the Constitution—and I tell you very honestly . . . it's probably because I just don't want to remember, but whatever those changes were—were endemic to destruction.

And I was almost in tears because I knew the vote was messed up because I had seen a bunch of them meeting by a car, and they [were making shushing noises]. And I said, "Awww, boy." And we then said, "Alright. You want to see this differently. Then how do you see it?" And after they made these changes they said, "We want the records. We want the books. We're going to call a meeting as soon as we get back to New York." And we [the coordinating council] called and called and *called*, "Come get the books. Come get the books. Don't you want to have a meeting?" And they then, literally, let the organization die. They destroyed the old structure and I think that was deliberate. And they just never called a meeting.[51]

These details are important because they highlight the emotional intensity involved in sustaining a new organization and movement among black women who previously were thought to be unified by race and gender. Black women were not unified in their orientation toward feminism. From the NBFO's example, it is clear that some women were dedicated to feminist ideals of egalitarianism and collective action but that others pushed alternative agendas that included socialism as a priority over feminism. Still others may have sought the intentional destruction of the organization, be it motivated by personal ideological differences or by government instigation.

Based on the outcome of the NBFO's Constitutional Convention and the failure of the contenders to call further meetings, it appears that this was a situation of adversarial intervention meant to destroy the organization. Had the bid for power been legitimate, further meetings would have been called and the organization restructured to open leadership opportunities to all members. Instead, as Singletary contends, the NBFO committed a form of organizational suicide: "I say suicide because we acted on what they were doing and, I feel, neglected to ask the question 'Why are they doing this?' and if we had asked the 'why' question, then we would have gotten to who we are as black women."[52]

* * *

Black feminist organizations complicate resource mobilization theory by inserting the question of collective identity into the process of resource attainment. The organizations offer valuable comparisons and contrasts for examining financial and human resources, ideological disputes, and leadership strain as they impact organizational decline. Contrary to previous women's movement histories that categorize difference and schisms as disruptive and divisive, these conflicts allow us to rethink the category *black woman*. Black feminist organizations' members discovered that black feminists spoke in a range of voices, displaying a heterogeneity that pushed the boundaries of black feminist organizing beyond their initial perceptions of feminist transformation.

In their efforts to mobilize resources, black feminist organizations encountered issues of black self-determination and racial authenticity, as well as co-optation dilemmas. Four out of five black feminist organizations, all except the BWOA, experienced financial strain that decreased their ability to publish newsletters, run small-scale activities (e.g., consciousness-raising) and large-scale events (e.g., workshops and alternative school programs),

or pay full- or part-time staff. The records of only one of the black feminist organizations, the NBFO, document disputes over whether to accept funding from white feminist and white liberal organizations. The organization's alignment with *Ms.* allowed the NBFO access to funding sources that other black feminist organizations may have alienated because of a more vocal nationalist, anti-integration stance that challenged the status quo.

All five black feminist organizations' memberships struggled to keep their organization functioning on a daily basis despite their lack of resources. The demands of black feminist organizing meant that often the same members completed a myriad of tasks, such as facilitating meetings, organizing rallies, writing and publishing newsletters, and giving speeches. Black feminist organizations and their members, in keeping up with the momentum of feminist mobilization, experienced activist burnout.

Although they were committed to organizing, black feminists found that their race, class, and gender limited how much of their time and effort was available to their organizations. Black feminists' availability issues did not stop at a lack of class privilege that prohibited their full-time activism. These organizations faced the reality that their constituency and beneficiaries lacked the resources to sustain organizations, particularly those that were national in scope. The black, woman, and often working-class aspects yielded an untenable identity matrix in respect to black feminists' biographical availability; were black feminists free from racial, economic, and gender discrimination they might have offered more resources to their organizations, but such freedom would effectively negate the purpose of their organizations. Instead, black feminists constantly struggled to maintain organizations that held their interests as primary and to reach consensus on what defined a black feminist agenda.

Lack of ideological cohesiveness led to disputes over the leadership of black feminist organizations. Organizational leadership structures ranged from the NBFO and the NABF's hierarchical structure to Combahee and the TWWA's collectives to the BWOA's rotating coordinators. The NABF and NBFO leaders were overextended because their leadership was centralized and they were ultimately responsible for all organizational maintenance; nevertheless, rank-and-file members felt excluded from the decision-making process. For the NBFO, though its members later attempted a collective structure, initial leadership tensions and later attempts at egalitarianism lead to direct challenges to the founders and eventually destroyed the organization.

Collective structures worked for a while in the TWWA and Combahee, but they, too, faced leadership disputes. For both organizations, decision making was too unstructured and permitted certain members to take on dominant roles as primary leaders. The West Coast TWWA evolved into a mixed-race women's organization, requiring the establishment of a new leadership structure according to the principles of its new members. In Combahee, the meaning of a collective was assumed and not explicated. Thus, members with certain oral and written strengths emerged as leaders, resulting in the resentment by other members who held different understandings of collectivity and the emerging black feminist movement.

Resource deficiencies partially explain the reasons for the decline of black feminist organizations, but are insufficient in describing fully their decline. Ultimately, a singular black feminist collective identity could not sustain organizations because it was, in its early stages, largely in reaction to the racism of some white feminists and initial universalizing conceptualizations of sisterhood and women. Also, a black feminist collective identity did not deal effectively with class differences among black women, which were crucial to the recruitment of new members. Moreover, black feminist collective identity was limited in its theorizing on interpersonal relationships between black women, platonic and intimate.

The decline of black feminist organizations resulted in the end of formal organizations, but the narrative of black feminist *organizing* does not end with the formal organizations. Jo Reger offers the hope that issues of decline, like factionalism, can result not in the end of social movement organizations but in the diversification of those organizations.[53] Thus, while these five black feminist organizations did not continue, diverse modes of thinking about and pursuing black feminist goals lived on past the decline of formal organizations. Black feminists involved with these organizations inspired future black feminists through their work and writing, but they also continue as activists in social justice causes. Black feminist organizations produced outcomes that radically change how we can define the success and failure of organizations and movements.

CONCLUSION

Unfortunately, too often our standards for evaluating social movement pivot around whether or not they "succeeded" in realizing their visions rather than on the merits or powers of the visions themselves. By such a measure, virtually every radical movement failed because the basic power relations they sought to change remain pretty much intact. And yet it is precisely these alternative visions and dreams that inspire new generations to continue to struggle for change.

—Robin D. B. Kelley, *Freedom Dreams*, 2002

This book aimed to dispel myths that black women were not, or are not, interested in feminism as a potentially libratory practice. The evidence shows that despite racism and sexism in other social movements, black women simultaneously struggled for their rights as both blacks *and* women. Black women in the Third World Women's Alliance, the National Black Feminist Organization, the National Alliance of Black Feminists, the Combahee River Collective, and Black Women Organized for Action were among the first to articulate identity where race, class, and gender intersect. These organizations add an organizational analysis to our knowledge that black women did this work independently of white feminists and black men, but in conjunction with one another and with the goal of building a movement.

Theoretically, the analysis of black feminist organizations' identity formation, organizational resources, activities, and decline construct a bridge between political opportunity and collective identity theories. Much like Collins's conceptualization of black women's both/and standpoint, I bring

that same standpoint to bear on these two seemingly oppositional branches of social movement theory. I conclude that while it is entirely possible to speak only of the organizational aspects of a movement or solely of the identity aspects of a movement's participants, a more holistic approach allows us to examine how they influence one another.

Bringing marginalized communities' social change efforts to the forefront also challenges assumptions about movement success and failure. The common query about whether black feminist organizations are still in operation suggests that because they are not, the organizations were unsuccessful or failed in their objectives. It is in this area that I seek to challenge traditional notions of success or organizational outcome. Gamson poses the question "Is a group a failure if it [the organization] collapses with no legacy save inspiration to a generation that will soon take up the same cause with more tangible results?"[1] In response to his own question, Gamson proposed thinking of "success as a set of outcomes," specifically, determining what became of the challenging group as an organization and what to make of new advantages distributed to the group's beneficiaries.[2] To what degree can we say that black feminist organizations were successful or failed in their objectives? Did they succeed or fail in distributing new advantages to their beneficiaries?

In general, I found that black feminist organizations as a social movement community did not succeed in achieving their main objectives: the eradication of racism and sexism. These persistent forms of discrimination, along with classism, heterosexism, and ableism, are still with us today. However, the black feminist movement was successful in initiating a process for thousands of black women who see the totality of their lives and resist white supremacy's ills. Black feminist theory would not exist without the organizing of black women around their unique position in U.S. society, and that theorizing has spread throughout the academy and into grassroots organizing.

The black feminist organizations in this study experienced a mixture of success and failure in their specific objectives. The BWOA, for example, was successful in raising its members' awareness of political issues affecting their community. The organization's intensive polling of political candidates on race and gender issues resulted in candidates' courting the organization and reevaluating the power of black women to influence local elections. The BWOA also achieved its goal of empowering black women in leadership positions through a rotating coordinator structure that allowed

numerous women, over the seven-year course of the organization's existence, to gain skills in facilitating meetings, fund-raising, serving as media spokespersons, and coordinating direct action events.

Similarly, the NABF, the TWWA, and Combahee raised black feminist awareness in Chicago, New York, and Boston, respectively, through consciousness-raising and activities directed toward investing in the well-being of black and third world communities. The NABF's open political forums and its Alternative School classes were open to women and men of all races, serving to promote the NABF's view of feminism as an aspect of humanism. The TWWA did not have a school established, but its continuous publication of *Triple Jeopardy* served a similar educational awareness function and reified its commitment to the third world community's survival and revolutionary potential. The Alliance Against Women's Oppression and the Women of Color Resource Center in Berkeley, California, are the fruits of former TWWA activists' labor that bring forward black feminist activism and theorizing from the late 1960s to the present.

Combahee's lasting contribution to the black feminist movement was undoubtedly its organizing statement that explained black feminist thinking and proposed black feminist praxis rooted in social justice. This statement laid the foundation for the socialist, feminist revolution Combahee and its members desired. For Combahee's members, the liberation process was not a finite process and is evident in everything from writing the statement, to its Black Women's Network Retreats, to coalition work in Boston's black and women's communities, to the thriving work of its members today.

The NBFO is the only organization for which clear-cut successes are more difficult to discern. Organizationally, however, the NBFO failed to reach its fullest potential as a national force in the women's and civil rights movements. Its initial infrastructure was unstable, and the organization lacked an established objective to recruit members. Once members joined, they did not know the organization's direction or goals; nor did they have a clear idea about expectations of members. However, in its short existence, the organization definitely touched the lives of its members and showed them the potential for black women's collective power. It increased black women's self-image through consciousness-raising and, for several black women, legitimized the women's movement as less the province of privileged white women, as it was stereotypically thought to be. The NBFO also provided the initial impetus for the emergence of the NABF and Com-

bahee, successfully planting the seeds for black feminism in Boston and Chicago.

While sharing commonalties, black feminists were not alike in their organizational structures, or feminist philosophies. Women's studies and feminist historians are beginning to reconceptualize how we think about feminism given the diversity of experiences among women. Use of terms such as *social movement community*, *protest fields*, and *sisterhood* create a space for inserting black feminist organizations into women's movement history. Collective identity theories serve as a tool for critiquing African American women's history for its theorizing of black womanhood and the dualism between race work and the gender question.

Can we speak of a monolithic feminist worldview? No, we cannot. The scholarly and activist response to accusations of racism in attempting to speak of "all women," "sisterhood," or "feminism," has been to think of feminism in the plural: *feminisms*. We also need to rethink the idea of "black feminism" as monolithic. Its very complexity may be a possible reason for the seemingly underground nature of black feminist activism today. White feminists were not the only ones guilty of universalizing tendencies in defining the categories of *women* and *sisterhood*; African American women activists also underestimated the limits of defining the category *black womanhood* by ignoring the heterogeneity of black women and communities.

Black feminist organizations succeeded in some but not all of their goals. The set of outcomes they produced is impressive, if not well known or acknowledged in women's movement or social movement theory circles. Today, black feminists serve as elected officials and in human rights agencies; teach at the college level; write prose, poetry, and essays; and work as journalists, to name a few of their occupations. They are also members of black women's organizations that, while they do not claim a feminist identity, advocate on behalf of women and are engaged in feminist praxis. Those organizations include the National Black Women's Health Project, the Black Radical Congress, the Women of Color Resource Center, and countless local organizing initiatives. The women who founded and ran black feminist organizations still claim a black feminist identity, but they manifest that identity through different organizations and types of direct action. They continue to inspire generations of women, men, and people of many races to struggle for social justice by confronting the status quo, as well as grappling with their own privilege. For a generation to take up

the challenge of its ancestors, the foundation needed to be laid for simply talking about oppression and its manifestations. Black feminists laid this foundation, and now that we're beginning to hear their stories, we as activists can build upon that legacy by adding our own blood, sweat, tears, and laughter to living for the revolution.

EPILOGUE

So, there are still black feminists out there?

—Deborah Singletary, NBFO, interview by author, 1997

Every five years I talk to some women and we say, "Maybe we should start something," and we say, "Yeah, let's do it." We keep thinking that some young women are going to do it. . . . I don't know whether the country would be ripe for it or not, but I know there's a lot of black women out there who clearly identify as feminist and I think that they feel that they're by themselves and they're alone. And that hasn't changed since when we did it. We would get these letters from these women who would be in these places saying "My God, I thought I was crazy. Maybe they're right. I want to be white. Just because I want simple justice for black women." We'd get these comments all the time. "Thank you, NBFO, for being there." We even fantasized. Let's start a magazine so these women who can't come to New York every month for a meeting. . . .

We had all these dreams and we just didn't do them.

—Margaret Sloan, NBFO, interview by author

I hope this book has shown that contrary to Sloan's lament, black feminists in the 1970s did a lot to enable future generations of black feminists and black feminist activism. Now that I have addressed the question of what happened to formal black feminist organizations, the persistent question seems to be, Why is there no formal black feminist organization today? It is a question black feminists continue asking in the popular and academic presses.[1] Again, keeping in mind that there are national black *women's* orga-

nizations that may or may not identify as feminist or womanist in principle, it is not for lack of interest that a national organization explicitly advocating black feminist politics does not exist; witness the 1991 mobilization of African American Women in Defense of Ourselves, which raised $50,000 in a matter of weeks to place full-page newspaper ads in national and local African American newspapers protesting Anita Hill's treatment before the U.S. Congress in the Clarence Thomas confirmation hearings. Or the ad hoc committee that Kimberle Crenshaw, law professor and black feminist, gathered to make a statement about the masculinist message of the Million Man March in 1995.

Given what we know from this study about black feminist organizations, which way forward?

I propose we change the question from asking why there is no national black feminist organization to asking, *What would it take to form a national black feminist organization?* Better yet, *What do black feminists want that organization to look like, and what is its purpose?* As the NBFO and its better-organized descendant the NABF found out, these questions need to be asked from the start if a national organization expects to have any sort of longevity.

Another question, one that sounds more flippant than intended, is, *Do we even need a national black feminist organization and, if yes, why?* Part of that question is actually one of structure (national vs. regional, state, or local), rather than the necessity of such an organization. Simply noting that black women are still at the bottom of the economic wage ladder, still experiencing violence at home and in America's streets, the fastest-growing population entering the U.S. prison industrial complex as inmate/no-wage workers, entangled in the failed "War on Drugs" and its infringements on reproductive rights, and still shaking their asses on BET/MTV and "in da club" because it pays more than the ever-expanding service economy are but a few of the reasons we need a national black feminist organization. When a national news magazine such as *Newsweek* can choose an entertainer who sings about being "bootylicious" to feature as testament to black women's advancement in the new millennium, we most certainly need a national voice for black feminism.[2]

So, what is it that today's black feminists want from a national organization? I can hardly speak for all black feminists, but I will propose a few hypotheses. We appear to want the following:

to hold on to the idea of organizations built upon participatory democracy
  principles;

to remain leaderless, or without a movement "star";

to stop talking and start *doing*;

to remain connected to the black community;

to speak in accessible, concrete terms;

to move beyond the academy and remain connected to its grassroots
  legacy; and

to put theory into practice in functional ways.

This list is, by no means, comprehensive and is based on contemporary
articles and recollections from meeting with other black feminists. If this,
then, is a partial wish list, what lessons can we take from 1970s black feminist organizations, and what would it take to make this dream of a national
black feminist organization come true?

First, we need to abandon the idea that one organization is going to
speak to all black feminist perspectives. This includes refusing to be de-
railed by those who want to argue about labels (e.g., how much longer
do we need to argue a false dichotomy between black feminism and
womanism as if they do not both hold more than similar concerns?).
Clearly, the absence of the black feminist organizations that started in
the 1970s is proof enough that it is time black feminists stopped caring
what others think of our politics and started practicing them with an un-
relenting determination. Refusing to debate the label is not dismissing
another person's political position. If a woman who uses, for example, a
womanist label wants to join a black feminist organization, but detests
the feminist label then, as Brenda Eichelberger of the NABF stated, what
is to stop that woman from either finding communion around the politics of the organization or from forming her own organization that works
in alliances around issues we all have in common as black women—
whether those are organizations of womanists, black nationalist women,
Pan-African women, professional black women's organizations, or the increasing number of young black women turning to anarchism? The appeal of the protest fields concept is that while we might all be part of
separate organizations, we remain in the same boat with the ability to
come together when strategically necessary. And, yes, I understand that
the feminist label causes some black women to shut down and tune us
out, but is it not the point to convince these women of the necessity
of the politics? If one woman rejects us, what is to stop us from mov-

ing on to the next woman and the next, speaking louder until we are heard?

Ideally, black feminists would like a decentralized organization in which all members are active participants in decision making. Did this ideal work in the late 1960s and 1970s for black feminist organizations? Regionally, it worked to the degree that for the BWOA, different members were given free reign every quarter to direct the organization. There is no evidence with these organizations that a participatory decision-making process worked nationally. Could this structure work now? Although (as one who wishes she were born in the heyday of the civil rights, black power, and women's movements) I wish it could work, (as a cynical, post-Soul, civil rights movement beneficiary), I think it's time we accepted the realities of the political culture at hand. Why not survey the current protest field and note what works in *today's* political climate? It is time for hierarchical structures (be it one of officers or an elected steering committee) that determine a course of action. Those elected to power, either on their own or through polling the organizations' constituency, *act* upon that course of action, willing to accept triumph or defeat, and ready for the next battle that presents itself.

Connected to this structure is the need for a leader(s), dare I suggest movement star(s)?—mind you, not celebrities who merely bask in the limelight or the hard work put in by others behind the scenes, but personalities who can serve as the voice of the movement. The star system I propose unites the voices of this new black feminist organization into one cogent analysis that is ready to comment when CNN, the Web site Common Dreams, NBC, Altnernet.org, or any mainstream or progressive news agency asks for "the black woman's perspective." What they will get is a *black feminist* perspective. It may be admirable that some of our most well-known black feminist thinkers and activists have shunned the traditional trappings of prestige, but, through no fault of their own, very few in the general public know who to turn to for a black feminist perspective, much less know that such a perspective exists. Advocating a black feminist star/leader perhaps sounds mercenary, but for a national black feminist organization to succeed and be visible, it will require media savvy unlike anything we have experienced before. In the flood of information available on television, radio, the Internet, and in print, only a star that shines brilliantly on behalf of a black feminist organization will ever get noticed.

It is evident from black feminist organizations' decline that for a national black feminist organization to succeed, it will need money and *lots of it*. Whether that money comes from mainstream or progressive founda-

tions, community institutions, or from its members own pockets, without a sound financial infrastructure supporting paid staff, any new black feminist organization will merely follow the same path as its foremothers. Black feminists cannot barter for airtime on major networks to protest the latest heinous stereotype showing at the local multiplex cinema. We cannot count on using the office photocopier or fax machine after hours to conduct mass mailings to our representatives or senators who are being "lobbied" on the expense accounts of big business enterprises such as Corrections Corporation of America to bring prisons into our communities instead of schools. If anything, U.S. black feminists might be best served by interning with our sisters in the so-called third world and observing how, through the nongovernmental organization structure, they manage to secure funds and conduct projects that change women's lives for the better daily.

In the quest for a black feminism that does not only preach to the academic choir, I suggest we also remain vigilant for an anti-intellectualism that has the potential to shut down the growth of a vibrant national organization. Yes, absolutely, a national black feminist organization must focus on practical applications of black feminist principles with relevance to black women's daily lives. But to maintain that black women theorizing in the academy are of no use to black communities is shortsighted. We may have only twenty-four hours to a day, and limited energy as individuals, but social movement organizations need political thought as much as they need implementation of that thought in community activities. We need as many thinkers, writers, artists, and community organizers as we can gather to speak to the increasingly diverse body we might correctly start addressing as black *communities*.

Most important, black feminists will need to reckon with our interpersonal relationships. If we insist on challenging white feminists on tokenizing particular black women as if there are only a handful who can speak on black feminism, we should reckon with the tokenization we as black feminists enable among ourselves. This suggestion is in no way meant to deride the contributions of those black feminists who step up to the plate time and again to attempt to start an organization, but now might be a good time to recognize the cliquishness our isolation has wrought. If what we need is energy and new insights we may have overlooked in past attempts at organizing, it would behoove each of us to bring in women not typically within the black feminist radar.

In addition to making Audre Lorde's essay "Eye to Eye: Black Women Hatred, and Anger" required reading for all black feminist organization

members, black feminists must also deal with the ill behavior that prevents our coalescing as a national black feminist organization.[3] I quote extensively the NBFO's Deborah Singletary here because she offers an incisive analysis of the past that needs to be applied to the present:

> If you're dealing with a group of black women, you're dealing with a group of people who have had the least nurturing in terms of their esteem and their self-value. . . . We haven't been valued by the culture. And I feel that we had a lot of problems within our own emotional, psychological development that also made it difficult for us to get along with each other. . . . We needed a lot more work on ourselves and what I also remember—I remember being at meetings and realizing that I was with a group of very articulate women who were used to being "the only ones." They were used to going someplace and usually in a group of white folk or other black people who were not as expressive verbally as they and wowing the group and being the only one. And here there were a whole group of us and I think for many women that first time experience—they didn't adapt well. And so we were used to being "the one" that people listened to. I don't think we adapted very well to that.[4]

This characterization does not, of course, apply to all black women. Some of us are fortunate to have families and sistah-friends who nurture us and allow us to do the same for them. Yet, we pay little attention in our political organizations to our relationships as people trying to work together on many issues that cut close to the bone and that, for many of us, are a matter of (physical, mental, or spiritual) life or death. Ultimately, we are not "the only ones" and the more often we recognize that and strive to maintain relationships that are not about policing boundaries of an authentic black feminism, the stronger a national black feminist organization could be. In this sense, the star we create to represent black feminism would not be the only one, but one out of many who can rest assured that a supportive black feminist community has her back.

The task at hand is to establish a national, independent black feminist organization with clear goals, a solid infrastructure, leaders ready to truly lead, and black feminists who know that they are not alone in believing that the goal of eradicating racism, sexism, heterosexism, and all other forms of discrimination that impact black women's lives is not only possible, but imperative. Eugenia Wilshire, NBFO member, recalls of her group, "What we did have going for us is that we were dreamers. We really believed in what we were doing and that it was possible and that things could change

and would change. And there was really no doubt about that, and I think that's what's different between then and now. I don't think that there are dreamers anymore."[5] I respectfully disagree; black feminists in the 1970s were dreamers, but they also established an incredibly strong and dynamic foundation from which twenty-first-century national black feminist organizations can rise. These war-weary warriors did not give up the struggle. They have passed along a legacy that cannot, will not die.

National Black Feminist Organization

Kennedy, Florynce. Interview by author, July 1995.
Galvin-Lewis, Jane. Interview by author, 26 April 1997.
Singletary, Deborah. Interview by author, 26 April 1997.
Wilshire, Eugenia. Interview by author, 26 April 1997.
Norton, Eleanor Holmes. Interview by author, 6 August 1997.
Sloan-Hunter, Margaret. Interview by author, 8 August 1997.
King, Dorothy. Interview by author, 23 January 1998.

Chicago National Black Feminist Organization / National Alliance of Black Feminists

Eichelberger, Brenda. Interview by author. 13 February 1997.
Nelson, Janie. Interview by author, 13 February 1997.
Porter, Gayle. Interview by author, 18 June 1997.
Porter, Gayle. Interview by author, 6 May 1998.

Combahee River Collective

Okazawa-Rey, Margo. Interview by author, 20 October 1997.
Ritchie, Sharon Paige. Interview by author, 2 November 1997.
Tompkins, Mercedes. Interview by author, 6 May 1998.
Smith, Barbara. Interview by author, 19 June 1998.
Smith, Barbara. Interview by author, 15 July 1998.

Third World Women's Alliance

Beal, Francis. Interview by author, 15 August 1997.
Anonymous. Interview by author, 16 January 1998.
Burnham, Linda. Interview by author, 12 February 1998.
League, Cheryl (Perry). Interview by author, 17 June 1998.

Black Women Organized for Action

Hernandez, Aileen. Interview by author, 14 September 1997.
Bradley, Valerie Jo. Interview by author, 8 October 1997.
Dillenberger, Jean (Kresy). Interview by author, 28 October 1997.

APPENDIX B ☆ INTERVIEW QUESTIONS

Interviews with black feminist activists were conducted, when possible, in person. The following open-ended questions were posed to compliment archival documents.

1. Previous activism: Did you belong to any other organizations prior to your involvement with the organization?

2. How long did you participate in the organization?

3. How did you come to be involved with this organization?

4. How do you recall the organization being structured?

5. What role do you recall playing (activities, committees, leadership roles)?

6. Did you belong to any other organizations while you were a member of the organization (other black women's, Black Liberation, civil rights, or women's)?

7. What events stand out for you from your time with the organization?

8. Do you recall any ideological disputes?

9. How do you think the organization was viewed by other organizations?

10. Do you recall any coalition work? Do you recall the organization having any allies (government, feminist, black organizations)?

11. Were you aware of any other black women's organizations active around the same time period?

12. Do you recall any adversaries (government, feminist, black organizations)?

13. What do you think the organization accomplished?

14. Did you leave the organization or did it fold? If you left, why?

15. Why do you think the organization doesn't exist anymore?

16. Do you know the current whereabouts of other former members?

APPENDIX C ☆ STATEMENTS OF PURPOSE

Black feminists issued statements of purpose or mission statements articulating their position as blacks and women, as well as articulating a political ideology where race, gender, and class intersect. Statements are reproduced here in full with original punctuation and spelling. The Combahee River Collective Statement, a lengthier statement, is not reproduced here but is included as "A Black Feminist Statement" in Words of Fire: An Anthology of Black Feminist Thought, *Beverley Guy-Sheftall, ed. (New York: New Press, 1995), pp. 232–240.*

☆ *Third World Women's Alliance*

"Third World Women's Alliance at Work"
Triple Jeopardy 1:6 (September/December 1972):10–11

Our purpose is to make a meaningful and lasting contribution to the Third World community by working for the elimination of the oppression and exploitation from which we suffer. We further intend to take an active part in creating a socialist society where we can live as decent human beings, free from the pressures of racism, economic exploitation, and sexual oppression.

To create a sisterhood of women devoted to the task of developing solidarity among the peoples of the Third World.

To promote unity among Third World people within the United States in matters affecting the educational, economic, social and political life of our peoples.

To collect, interpret, and distribute information about the Third World, both at home and abroad, and particularly information affecting its women.

To build solid relationships with our men, destroying myths that have been created by our oppressor to divide us from each other, and to work together to appreciate human love and respect.

To train, develop, and organize Third World women to actively participate in the liberation struggles of our people.

★ *National Black Feminist Organization*

"To Seize the Moment: A Retrospective
on the National Black Feminist Organization"
Sage 5:2 (fall 1988): 46

The distorted male-dominated media image of the Women's Liberation movement has clouded the vital and revolutionary importance of this movement to Third World women, especially Black women. The Movement has been characterized as the exclusive property of so-called "white middle class" women, and any Black women seen involved in this movement have been seen as "selling out," "dividing the race," and an assortment of nonsensical epithets. Black Feminists resent these charges and have therefore established THE NATIONAL BLACK FEMINIST ORGANIZATION, in order to address ourselves to the particular and specific needs of the larger, but almost cast aside half of the Black race in Amerikkka, the Black Woman.

Black women have suffered cruelly in this society from living the phenomenon of being Black and female, in a country that is *both* racist and sexist. There has been very little real examination of the damage it has caused on the lives and on the minds of Black women. Because we live in a patriarchy, we have allowed a premium to be put on Black male suffering. None of us would minimize the pain or hardship or the cruel and inhumane treatment experienced by Black men. But history, past or present, rarely deals with the malicious abuse put upon the black woman. We were seen as breeders by the Master; despised and historically polarized from/by the Master's wife; and looked upon as castrators by our lovers and husbands. The Black Woman has had to be strong, yet we are persecuted for having survived. We have been called "matriarchs" by white racists and Black nationalists; we have virtually no positive self-images to validate our existence. Black women want to be proud, dignified, and free from all those

definitions of beauty and womanhood that are unrealistic and unnatural. *We*, not white women or Black men, must define our own self-image as Black Women and not fall into the mistake of being placed upon the pedestal which is even being rejected by white women. It has been hard for black women to emerge from the myriad of distorted images that have portrayed us as grinning Beulahs, castrating Sapphires, and pancake-box Jemimas. As Black Feminists we realized the need to establish ourselves as an independent Black Feminist organization. Our aboveground presence will lend enormous credibility to the current Women's Liberation Movement, which unfortunately is not seen as the serious political and economic revolutionary force that it is. We will strengthen the current efforts of the Black Liberation struggle in this country by encouraging *all* of the talents and creativities of Black Women to emerge, strong and beautiful, not to feel guilty or divisive, and assume positions of leadership and honor in the Black community. We will encourage the Black community to stop falling into the trap of the white male Left, utilizing women only in terms of domestic or servile needs. We will continue to remind the Black Liberation Movement that there can't be liberation for half the race. We must, together, as a people, work to eliminate racism, from without the Black community, which is trying to destroy us as an entire people; but we must remember that sexism is destroying and crippling us from within.

★ Black Women Organized for Action

Membership Brochure
Aileen Hernandez Papers

BLACK: We are *Black*, and therefore imbedded in our consciousness is commitment to the struggle of Black people for identity and involvement in decisions that affect our lives and the lives of other generations of Black people who will follow.

WOMEN: We are *Women*, and therefore aware of the sometimes blatant, waste of the talents and energies of Black women because this society has decreed a place for us.

ORGANIZED: We are *Organized*, because we recognize that only together, only by pooling our talents and resources, can we make major change in the institutions which have limited our opportunities and stifled our growth as human beings.

ACTION: We are for *Action*, because we believe that the time for rhetoric is past; that the skills of Black women can best be put to use in a variety of ways to change the society; that, in the political world in which we live, involvement for Black women must go beyond the traditional fundraising and into the full gamut of activities that make up the political process which affects our lives in so many ways.

★ *National Alliance of Black Feminists*

"Philosophy of NABF"
Brenda Eichelberger Collection, Chicago Historical Society

Year in and year out, statistics from the Labor Department, the Women's Bureau, and the Census Bureau indicate that Black women earn less income than white men, Black men, and white women. This economic disparity has been high-lighted by the fact that Black women, more often than whites and men, are disproportionately over represented on the public aid rolls. Yet, it is Black women who are most often the single heads of households. Thus, the people who need economic upgrading the most— not only for themselves but also for their offspring—are the people who get it the least!

As Black feminists, we just don't see this as fair. Black feminism, then, is the belief that Black women have the *right* to full social, political, and economic equality. We do not accept the proposition that because we are born Black and female in a society which is both racist and sexist, that we should accept the role which society dictates to us. Instead, we seek to unshackle ourselves from our "place" as Blacks and women to become individuals free to live to the fullest of our potential.

In order to reach this potential we realize that we must develop and grow as individuals, but since no Black woman lives in a vacuum, we realize that all of Black personkind, all colors of womankind, and the entire world community must *also* grow. As one great Black woman—Addle Wyatt—put it, "In order for the Black woman to get out of the bottom of the barrel, those on top of her must get out!" Thus, as Black feminists, we realize that once our consciousness has been raised sufficiently to politicize us, we must help to politicize others.

Therefore, the principle of self-help is the basic foundation on which our organization is built. We try to get in tune with our minds and bodies so that we may better understand ourselves, deepen and broaden our communica-

tion with others, and effectively learn to cope with everyday problems. We also try to heighten our awareness of the environment around us including those forces which prevent us from maximizing our human potential. It is in this spirit that we in THE NATIONAL ALLIANCE OF BLACK FEMINISTS offer various programs, including our Alternative School. These programs are designed to help foster our personal growth and development, thereby encouraging us to take "collective" action. In light of this philosophy, many of our programs, especially our Alternative School, are open to Black women in particular and the public at large.

NOTES

1. The Soul of Women's Lib

1 Toni Cade Bambara, *The Black Woman: An Anthology* (New York: Penguin, 1970); Barbara Smith, ed., *Home Girls: A Black Feminist Anthology* (New York: Kitchen Table Women of Color Press, 1983).

2 Patricia Hill Collins, *Black Feminist Thought* (Boston: Unwin Hyman, 1990).

3 Linda Burnham, interview by author, 12 February 1998.

4 For more extensive analysis of black women's activism in these movements, see Bernice McNair Barnett, "Invisible Southern Black Women Leaders in the Civil Rights Movement," *Signs: A Journal of Women in Culture and Society* 7:2 (1991): 162–182; Angela Davis, *Women, Race, and Class* (New York: Vintage Press, 1981); Paula Giddings, *When and Where I Enter: The Impact of Black Women on Race and Sex in America* (New York: William Morrow, 1984); Beverly Guy-Sheftall, *Words of Fire: An Anthology of African American Feminist Thought* (New York: New Press, 1995); and Belinda Robnett, *How Long? How Long?: African American Women in the Struggle for Civil Rights* (New York: Oxford University Press, 1997).

5 These women's movement histories include Maren Carden, *The New Feminist Movement* (New York: Russell Sage Foundation, 1974); Flora Davis, *Moving the Mountain: The Women's Movement in America since 1960* (New York: Simon and Schuster, 1991); Alice Echols, *Daring to Be Bad: Radical Feminism in America, 1967–1975* (Minneapolis: University of Minnesota, 1989); Sara Evans, *Personal Politics* (New York: Vintage Books, 1979); and Jo Freeman, *The Politics of Women's Liberation* (New York: David McKay, 1977).

6 These texts include Steven Buechler, *Women's Movements in the United States* (New Brunswick, N.J.: Rutgers University Press, 1990); F. Davis, *Moving the Mountain*; Alice Echols, *Daring to Be Bad*; Giddings, *When and Where I Enter*; and bell hooks, *Ain't I a Woman: Black Women and Feminism* (Boston: South End Press, 1981).

7 Chela Sandoval, "U.S. Third World Feminism: The Theory and Method of Oppositional Consciousness in the Postmodern World," *Genders* 10 (spring 1991): 15; Becky Thompson, "Multiracial Feminism: Recasting the Chronology of Second Wave Feminism," *Feminist Studies* 28:2 (2002): 337.

8 Thompson, "Multiracial Feminism," 359.

9 Texts that adopt the parallel development model to women's movement history include Guy-Sheftall's introduction to *Words of Fire*; Benita Roth, *On Their Own and for Their Own: African American, Chicana, and White Feminist Movements in the 1960 and 1970s* (New York: Cambridge University Press, 2003); and Deborah Gray White, *Too Heavy a Load: Black Women in Defense of Themselves, 1894–1994* (New York: W. W. Norton, 1999).

10 Wini Breines, "What's Love Got to Do with It? White Women, Black Women, and Feminism in the Movement Years," *Signs: A Journal of Women in Culture and Society* 27:4 (2002): 1113–1114.

11 Collins defines the matrix of domination as an interlocking system that demands attention to the interlocking and simultaneous nature of oppression (i.e., intersections of race, gender, class, sexual orientation, and physical ability). Collins, *Black Feminist Thought*, 225–226.

12 David S. Meyer, "Social Movements: Creating Communities of Change," in *Conscious Acts and the Politics of Social Change*, ed. Robin L. Teske and Mary Ann Trétreault (Columbia: University of South Carolina Press, 2002), 39–40.

13 The organizations included in this book were not the only organizations active in the 1970s and early 1980s on behalf of black women, but as I explain in the methodology section, I chose organizations that explicitly defined themselves as feminist.

14 Margo V. Perkins, *Autobiography as Activism: Three Black Women of the Sixties* (Jackson: University of Mississippi Press, 2000), 41.

15 Kathleen M. Blee and Verta Taylor, "Semistructured Interviewing in Social Movement Research," in *Methods of Social Movement Research*, ed. Bert Klandermans and Suzanne Staggenborg (Minneapolis: University of Minnesota Press, 2002): 93.

16 Buechler, *Women's Movements in the United States*; Nancy Cott, *The Grounding of Modern Feminism* (New Haven, Conn.: Yale University Press, 1987); F. Davis, *Moving the Mountain*; Leila Rupp and Verta Taylor, *Survival in the Doldrums: The American Women's Rights Movement, 1945 to the 1960s* (New York: Oxford University Press, 1987); and Barbara Ryan, *Feminism and the Women's Movement: Dynamics of Change in Social Movement, Ideology and Activism* (New York: Routledge, 1992).

17 Guy-Sheftall, *Words of Fire*; Robnett, *How Long? How Long?*; Deborah Gray White, *Ar'n't I a Woman* (New York: W. W. Norton, 1985).

18 Giddings, *When and Where I Enter*; Guy-Sheftall, *Words of Fire*; and Dorothy Roberts, *Killing the Black Body: Race, Reproduction, and the Meaning of Liberty* (New York: Vintage Books, [1997] 1999).

19 Sharon Berger Gluck, "Whose Feminism? Whose History?" in *Community Activism and Feminist Politics: Organizing Across Race, Class, and Gender,* ed. Nancy Naples (New York: Routledge, 1998), 35.

20 For further discussion of events and people that disrupt the normative wave analogy, see Thompson, "Multiracial Feminism"; and Kimberly Springer, "Third Wave Feminism?" *Signs: A Journal of Women in Culture and Society* 27:4 (2002): 1059–1081.

21 Some of these works include Jo Freeman, "The Origins of the Women's Liberation Movement," *American Journal of Sociology* 78:4 (1973): 792–811; William Gamson, *The Strategy of Social Protest* (Belmont, Calif.: Wadsworth Publications, [1975] 1990); Doug McAdam, *Political Process and the Development of Black Insurgency, 1930–1970* (Chicago: University of Chicago Press, 1982); John D. McCarthy and Mayer Zald, *Social Movements in an Organizational Society* (New Brunswick, N.J.: Transaction Publishers, [1987] 1994); and Anthony Oberschall, *Social Conflict and Social Movements* (Englewood Cliffs, N.J.: Prentice-Hall, 1973).

22 David S. Meyer, "Opportunities and Identities: Bridge-Building in the Study of Social Movements," in *Social Movements: Identity, Culture and the State,* ed. David S. Meyer, Nancy Whittier, and Belinda Robnett (New York: Oxford University Press, 2002), 3–21.

23 Raka Ray, *Fields of Protest: Women's Movements in India* (Minneapolis: University of Minnesota Press, 1999), 7–8.

24 Ibid., 7.

25 Sidney Tarrow, *Power in Movement: Social Movements, Collective Action and Politics* (Cambridge, England: Cambridge University Press, [1994] 1998), 86.

26 McAdam, *Freedom Summer* (New York: Oxford University Press, 1988), 51.

27 Robin D. G. Kelley, *Freedom Dreams: The Black Radical Imagination* (Boston: Beacon Press, 2002), 150.

28 Robnett, *How Long? How Long?*

29 David Snow, E. Burke Rochford Jr., Steven Worden, and Robert Benford, "Frame Alignment Processes, Micromobilization, and Movement Participation," *American Sociological Review* 51 (1986): 464–481.

30 Chela Sandoval, "U.S. Third World Feminism," 15.

31 Gloria Anzaldúa, *Borderlands / La Frontera* (San Francisco: Spinsters / Aunt Lute Book Company, 1987); Collins, *Black Feminist Thought*; and W. E. B. DuBois, *The Souls of Black Folks* (New York: Dover, [1903] 1994).

32 David A. Snow and Robert D. Benford, "Clarifying the Relationship between Framing and Ideology," *Mobilization: An International Journal* 5:1 (2000): 55–40.

33 Francesca Polletta, " 'It Was Like a Fever . . .' Narrative and Identity in Social Protest," *Social Problems* 45:2 (1998): 137–159.

34 Julia Sudbury, *Other Kinds of Dreams: Black Women's Organizations and the Politics of Transformation* (London: Routledge, 1998), 47–48.

35 Tera Hunter, "Domination and Resistance: The Politics of Wage Household Labor in New South Atlanta," *Labor History* 34 (1993): 207.

36 Angela Davis, "Reflections on the Black Women's Role in the Community of Slaves," *Black Scholar* 3 (1971): 2–15; Harriet A. Jacobs, *Incidents in the Life of a Slavegirl: Written by Herself*, ed. Jean Fagen Yellin (Cambridge: Harvard University Press, 1987).

37 White, *Too Heavy a Load*, 17.

38 Margaret Wilkerson, "Lorraine Hansberry (1930–1965)," in Guy-Sheftall, *Words of Fire*, 125–126.

39 The beloved community is the metaphorical space blacks and whites hoped to create through working and living together in the segregated South, as detailed in Wini Breines, *Community and Organization in the New Left, 1962–1968: The Great Refusal* (New Brunswick, N.J.: Rutgers University Press, 1982). In reflecting on the era, Breines further defines the beloved community as "a humanistic, universal, racially integrated sisterhood and brotherhood ideal where, hand in hand, we create a benign and just world." Breines, *What's Love Got to Do with It?*, 1096.

40 White, *Too Heavy a Load*, 110–141.

41 Vicki Crawford, Jacqueline Anne Rouse, and Barbara Woods, *Women in the Civil Rights Movement: Trailblazers and Torchbearers, 1941–1965* (Brooklyn, N.Y.: Carlson Publishing, 1990); Giddings, *When and Where I Enter*; hooks, *Ain't I a Woman*; JoAnn Gibson Robinson, *The Montgomery Bus Boycott and the Women Who Started It* (Knoxville: University of Tennessee Press, 1987); and Robnett, *How Long? How Long?*

42 Robinson, *The Montgomery Bus Boycott and the Women Who Started It.*

43 Giddings, *When and Where I Enter*, 268.

44 Breines, *Community and Organization in the New Left*; Clayborne Carson, *In Struggle: SNCC and the Black Awakening of the 1960s* (Cambridge, Mass.: Harvard University Press, 1981); Giddings, *When and Where I Enter*, 274–275; Aldon Morris, *The Origins of the Civil Rights Movement* (New York: Free Press, 1984); and Barbara Ransby, *Ella Baker and the Black Freedom Movement: A Radical Democratic Vision* (Chapel Hill: University of North Carolina Press, 2003).

45 Anne Standley, "The Role of Black Women in the Civil Rights Movement," in Crawford, Rouse, and Woods, *Women in the Civil Rights Movement*, 184.

46 Anna Arnold Hedgeman, *A Trumpet Sounds: A Memoir of Negro Leadership* (New York: Holt, Reinhart and Winston, 1964), 313.

47 Giddings, *When and Where I Enter*; Standley, "The Role of Black Women in the Civil Rights Movement."

48 White, *Too Heavy a Load*, 65.

49 E. Franklin Frazier, *The Negro Family in the United States* (Chicago: University of Chicago Press, [1939] 1966); Calvin Hernton, *Sex and Racism in America* (New York: Grove Press, 1965); William Grier and Price Cobbs, *Black Rage*

(New York: Bantam Books, 1968); and Daniel Patrick Moynihan, *The Negro Family: The Case for National Action* (Washington, D.C.: U.S. Government Printing Office, 1965).

50 Nick Kotz and Mary Lynn Kotz, *A Passion for Equality* (New York: W. W. Norton Company, 1977), 252.

51 Claude Lesselier, "No!: A Film in Gestation," interview with filmmaker Aishah Shahidah Simmons, *Lesbia Magazine*, January 2000 (version used for translators), 1.

52 Casey Hayden and Mary King, "A Kind of Memo from Casey Hayden and Mary King to a Number of Other Women in the Peaceland Freedom Movements," in *Feminism in Our Time: The Essential Writings, World War II to the Present*, ed. Miriam Schneir (New York: Vintage, 1994); Carson, *In Struggle*, 147; Evans, *Personal Politics*, 86.

53 Evans, *Personal Politics*; F. Davis, *Moving the Mountain*; Echols, *Daring to Be Bad*.

54 Hayden and King later assert that their first position paper was part of the effort to keep sNCC grounded in participatory democracy as the organization headed toward hierarchy and the expulsion of whites. Robnett, *How Long? How Long?*; Kristin Anderson-Bricker, " 'Triple Jeopardy': Black Women and the Growth of Feminist Consciousness, 1964–1975," in *Still Lifting, Still Climbing: Contemporary African American Women's Activism*, ed. Kimberly Springer (New York: New York University Press, 1999), 49–69.

55 Carson, *In Struggle*, 148; Evans, *Personal Politics*, 88.

56 Standley, "The Role of Black Women in the Civil Rights Movement," 1990.

57 Margaret Sloan, "Address Given by Gloria Steinem and Margaret Sloan on Women" (Northfield, Minn.: Carleton College Audio-Visual Department, 5 March 1973).

58 See Perkins, *Autobiography as Activism* for an exceptional look at gender and sexuality in the black nationalist movement.

59 Giddings, *When and Where I Enter*; Cheryl Lynn Greenberg, "sNCC Women and the Stirrings of Feminism," in *A Circle of Trust: Remembering sNCC* (New Brunswick, N.J.: Rutgers University Press, 1998), 127–151; and Standley, "The Role of Black Women in the Civil Rights Movement."

60 Deborah King, "Multiple Jeopardy, Multiple Consciousness: The Context of a Black Feminist Ideology," in Guy-Sheftall, *Words of Fire*, 294–317.

61 Bambara, *The Black Woman*; Patricia Hill Collins, *Fighting Words: Black Women and the Search for Justice* (Minneapolis: University of Minnesota Press, 1998); Giddings, *When and Where I Enter*; and Elaine Brown, *A Taste of Power: A Black Woman's Story* (New York: Pantheon Books, 1992).

62 Brown, *A Taste of Power*; Angela Davis, *Angela Davis: With Freedom on My Mind* (New York: Bantam Books, 1974); Traceye Matthews, " 'The Most Qualified Person to Handle the Job": Black Panther Party Women, 1966–1982," in *The Black Panther Party (Reconsidered)*, ed. Charles E. Jones (Baltimore: Black

Classic Press, 1998), 267–304; Assata Shakur, *Assata: An Autobiography* (Chicago: Lawrence Hill Books, 1987); and Fredi A. Smith, "Meet the Women of the Black Panthers," *Daily Defender*, 24 January 1970.

63 The FBI Counterintelligence Program (COINTELPRO) was J. Edgar Hoover's initiative to infiltrate and undermine organizations deemed extremist (e.g., communist, revolutionary, subversive) from 1956 to 1971.

64 "Black Panthers Sisters Talk about Women's Liberation," in *The Movement* (n.p.: New England Free Press, 1969), 2. Although women increased their public responsibilities in the party, did men also participate in the same role reversal when faced with tasks traditionally performed by women in the private sphere? In her examination of African American women in the Pan-African movement, M. Bahati Kuumba found that when a women's union emerged within the All-African People's Revolutionary Union, women expanded their roles into public speaking and strategizing, but they also remained solely responsible for child care and youth education. With this double burden, women in the Pan-African movement experienced burnout more quickly than men, adding another dimension to stereotypes about women as lesser revolutionaries than men. M. Bahati Kuumba, "Engendering the Pan-African Movement: Field Notes from the All-African Women's Revolutionary Union," in Springer, *Still Lifting, Still Climbing*, 167–188.

65 Buechler, *Women's Movements in the United States*; Echols, *Daring to Be Bad*; hooks, *Ain't I a Woman*; Jacqueline Jones, *Labor of Love, Labor of Sorrow: Black Women, Work, and the Family from Slavery to the Present* (New York: Vintage Books, 1985); Toni Morrison, "What the Black Woman Thinks about Women's Lib," *New York Times Magazine*, 22 August 1971, 14–15, 63–64, 66; Inez Smith Reid, *"Together" Black Women* (New York: Emerson-Hall, 1972); and Ryan, *Feminism and the Women's Movement*.

66 Ryan, *Feminism and the Women's Movement*.

67 Elizabeth Spelman, *Inessential Woman: Problems of Exclusion in Feminist Thought* (Boston: Beacon Press, 1988).

68 See Breines ("What's Love Got to Do with It?") and Thompson ("Multiracial Feminism") for two perspectives on whether, or to what degree, white feminists struggled against racism during the era. Breines maintains that 1970s white feminists are getting short shrift in the historical record and notes that, in particular, social feminist organizations such as the Boston-based Bread & Roses actively contested racism and work in coalition with groups such as the Black Panther Party. It is compelling to note, as Breines does, that this anti-racist work with black organizations often occurred through connections to men (publicly recognized leaders) in the organizations, not to black women.

69 The Louis Harris Polling Agency and the tobacco manufacturer Virginia Slims conducted a series of "American Women" polls that measured women's attitudes on political and social issues during peak years for the contemporary feminist movement: 1970, 1972, 1974, and 1980.

70 Madelyn Conley, "Do Black Women Need the Women's Lib?" *Essence*, August 1970, 29–33; Brenda Eichelberger, "Myths About Feminism," *Essence*, November 1978, 74–75, 92, 94, 96; Rose L. H. Finkenstaedt, "Women's Lib Has No Soul," *Encore*, March 1973, 38–40; Nikki Giovanni, "The Root of the Matter," *Encore*, January 1974, 22–25; Morrison, "What the Black Woman Thinks about Women's Lib"; and Smith Reid, *"Together" Black Women.*

71 "The War between the Sexes: Is It Manufactured or Real?" *Ebony*, June 1979, 33–39, 42; Helen K. King, "The Black Woman and Women's Lib," *Ebony*, March 1971, 68–71; and Morrison, "What the Black Woman Thinks about Women's Lib."

72 Morrison, "What the Black Woman Thinks about Women's Lib," 64.

73 H. King, "The Black Woman and Women's Lib," 70; emphasis mine.

74 Morrison, "What the Black Woman Thinks about Women's Lib," 70.

75 There were instances in which black women dated white men during this time period, but few memoirs or documents attest to this reality. Please see Alice Walker's *The Way Forward Is with a Broken Heart* (New York: Random House, 2000) for her autobiographical retelling of her interracial relationship during the late 1960s civil rights movement.

76 Sloan, "Address Given by Gloria Steinem and Margaret Sloan on Women."

77 "The War between the Sexes," *Ebony*, 70.

78 Secondary sources dispute whether Smith's addition was due to racism, paternalism, or both. Buechler, *Women's Movements in the United States*; F. Davis, *Moving the Mountain*, 39.

79 Tim Wise, "Is Sisterhood Conditional?" NWSA [National Women's Studies Association] *Journal* 10:3 (autumn 1998): 1–26; Shirley M. Geiger, "Employment of Black and White Women in State and Local Government," NWSA *Journal* 10:3 (autumn 1998):151–159.

80 Nell Irvin Painter, *Sojourner Truth: A Life, a Symbol* (New York: W. W. Norton, 1996).

81 A. Davis, *Women, Race, and Class*, 70–86; Buechler, *Women's Movements in the United States*, 135–136.

82 For more details on black women's involvement with this commission, see Miriam Harris, "From Kennedy to Combahee: Black Feminist Activism from 1960 to 1980," PhD dissertation, Department of Sociology (Minneapolis: University of Minnesota, 1997).

83 Susan M. Hartmann, "Pauli Murray and the 'Juncture of Women's Liberation and Black Liberation,'" *Journal of Women's History* 14:2 (2002): 74–77.

84 Cellestine Ware, *Woman Power: The Movement for Women's Liberation* (New York: Tower Publications, 1970); Florynce Kennedy and Diane Schulder, *Abortion Rap* (New York: McGraw Hill, 1971).

85 Smith Reid, *"Together" Black Women.*

86 Ibid., 50–51.

87 Echols, *Daring to Be Bad*, 369–377.

88 Ibid., 375.

89 Ibid., 104, 107, 376; F. Davis, *Moving the Mountain*, 79–80.

90 Breines, "What's Love Got to Do with It?," 1122.

91 Echols, *Daring to Be Bad*, 373, 377.

92 Ibid., 374.

93 Lorraine Bethel, "What Chou' Mean 'WE,' White Girl? Or, the Cullud Lesbian Feminist Declaration of Independence," *Conditions* 5 (1979): 88.

94 Breines, "What's Love Got to Do with It?" 1108.

95 Bethel, "What Chou' Mean 'WE,' White Girl?", 87.

96 P. Collins, *Fighting Words*, 280.

97 Frazier, *The Negro Family in the United States*. Sudbury helpfully notes a parallel situation for African women in the diaspora when she discusses African Caribbean women's economic and educational success as "evidence" that black women are contributing to black men's emasculation and white supremacy. *Other Kinds of Dreams*, 159.

98 Sheila Radford-Hill, *Further to Fly: Black Women and the Politics of Empowerment* (Minneapolis: University of Minnesota Press, 2000), xx.

99 P. Collins, *Fighting Words*, 75.

100 Ibid., 74.

101 K. Sue Jewell, *From Mammy to Miss America and Beyond: Cultural Images and the Shaping of U.S. Social Policy* (New York: Routledge, 1993).

102 Teresa Amott and Julie Matthei, "We Specialize in the Wholly Impossible: African American Women," *Race, Gender, and Work: A Multicultural Economic History of Women in the United States* (Boston: South End Press, 1991), 141–191.

103 Alice Kessler-Harris, "The Wage Conceived: Value and Needs as Measures of Woman's Worth," in *Feminist Frontiers IV*, ed. Laurel Richardson, Verta Taylor, and Nancy Whittier (New York: McGraw Hill Companies [1990] 1997), 201–214.

104 A. Davis, *Women, Race, and Class*; Carol Stack, *All Our Kin: Strategies for Survival in a Black Community* (New York: Harper and Row, 1974).

105 Demie Kurz, *For Richer, For Poorer: Mothers Confront Divorce* (New York: Routledge, 1995), 17–18.

106 Francis Beal, "Double Jeopardy: To Be Black and Female," in Bambara, *The Black Woman*, 90–100; Eichelberger, "Myths About Feminism"; Diane K. Lewis, "A Response to Inequality: Black Women, Racism and Sexism," *Signs: A Journal of Women in Culture and Society* 3:2 (1977): 339–361; and Pauli Murray, "The Liberation of Black Women," in Guy-Sheftall, *Words of Fire*, 186–197.

107 U.S. Bureau of the Census, 1988.

108 In 1975, for example, income by race and gender was as follows: white men earned $11,448; black men earned $7,541; white women earned $4,982; and

black women trailed behind them all, earning $4,732. U.S. Bureau of the Census, 1998.

109 In 1960, roughly 83.4 percent of black women worked in the manufacturing, domestic, service, and clerical industries, compared to 12.8 percent in the professional, technical, and managerial fields. Amott and Matthei, "We Specialize in the Wholly Impossible," 158.

110 Eichelberger, "Myths About Feminism," 94; Lewis, "A Response to Inequality," 349.

111 Jewell, *From Mammy to Miss America and Beyond*, 17.

112 Edward Mapp, "Black Women in Films," *Black Scholar* 4:6 (March–April 1973): 43.

113 Reportedly, Erika Huggins reminded Black Panther women that, like Vietnamese women in the revolutionary struggle, black women should consider their bodies as weapons. Brown, *A Taste of Power*, 136. See also Third World Women's Alliance, "History of the Organization and Ideological Platform," *Triple Jeopardy* 1:1 (September–October 1972): 8–9.

114 Donald Bogle, *Toms, Coons, Mulattos, Mammies, and Bucks* (New York: Continuum Publishing [1973] 1993), 236, 240; Mark A. Reid, *Redefining Black Film* (Berkeley: University of California Press, 1993), 77–82.

115 M. Reid, *Redefining Black Film*, 86–88.

116 Bogle, *Toms, Coons, Mulattos, Mammies, and Bucks*, 251; M. Reid, *Redefining Black Film*, 88.

117 M. Reid, *Redefining Black Film*, 86.

118 Ibid., 86. I must note Jennifer DeVere Brody's article that reexamines *Cleopatra Jones* and other films starring Pam Grier. She offers a perspective that asks how bringing a queer theory reading to cultural studies changes how we read *Cleopatra Jones* and issues of desire, thus "queering" the blaxploitation action heroine. Jennifer DeVere Brody, "The Returns of Cleopatra Jones," *Signs: A Journal of Women in Culture and Society* 25:1 (1999): 91–121.

119 The editors of *Ms.* magazine were most likely oblivious to these misogynistic overtones to blaxploitation films when they featured Pam Grier on their August 1975 cover as a model of black feminist, woman power.

120 Bill Montgomery, " 'That's My Mama': Black Women Assail TV Show as 'Demeaning,' " *Atlanta Journal*, 4 October 1974; NBFO Papers, University of Illinois at Chicago Special Collections Library; staff writer, "TV Sexism, Racism Hit by Feminists," *Atlanta Daily World*, 6 October 1974; and NBFO Papers, University of Illinois at Chicago Special Collections Library.

121 For a longer discussion of black feminist organizations and their interventions, see Kimberly Springer, "*Good Times* for Florida and Black Feminism," *Cercles: Revue pluridisciplinaire du monde Anglophone* 8 (2003), online journal, http://www.cercles/n8/springer.pdf.

122 For an extensive analysis of the race and gender implications of relevance pro-

gramming, alternately called social realism or quality television, see Kirsten Marthe Lentz, "Quality versus Relevance: Feminism, Race, and the Politics of the Sign in 1970s Television," *Camera Obscura: A Journal of Feminism and Film Theory* (2000): 44–93.

123 Ibid., 46.

124 Ibid., 74.

125 Aileen Hernandez, letter to Norman Lear, 9 October 1974, Aileen Hernandez, personal papers.

126 Ibid.

127 Valerie Jo Bradley, interview by author, 8 October 1997.

128 Geraldine Rickman, "A Natural Alliance: The New Role for Black Women," *Civil Rights Digest* 6:3 (1974): 57–65.

2. No Longer Divided against Ourselves

1 Beverly Davis, "The National Black Feminist Organization," *Sage* 5 (1988): 43.

2 David A. Snow and Robert D. Benford, "Clarifying the Relationship between Framing and Ideology," *Mobilization: An International Journal* 5:1 (2000): 55–40, here, 59.

3 Karen Kahn, "Rethinking Identity Politics: An Interview with Demita Frazier," *Sojourner*, September 1995, 12.

4 Francis Beal, interview by author, 15 August 1997.

5 According to COINTELPRO records, SNCC and the TWWA later experienced a rift in 1971, when the TWWA, the African-American Youth Movement, and specific ex-SNCC members were accused of being government infiltrators. In 1972, TWWA members called for their accusers to substantiate the claims, but there is no record as to how this conflict was resolved. Federal Bureau of Investigations, "Third World Women's Alliance: Extremist Matters," Field Office file no. 157–6167, 25 April 1973, 7–9.

6 Third World Women's Alliance, "History of the Organization and Ideological Platform," *Triple Jeopardy* 1:1 (September–October 1972): 8–9, here, 8.

7 Ibid.

8 Ibid.

9 Beal, interview by author, 15 August 1997.

10 Third World Women's Alliance, "History of the Organization and Ideological Platform," 8.

11 Lisa Albrecht and Rose Brewer offer a distinction important to this study between coalitions and alliances. Coalitions are temporary agreements to work together to achieve a specific goal, while alliances imply "a new level of commitment that is longer-standing, deeper, and built upon more trusting political relationships." Lisa Albrecht and Rose M. Brewer, *Bridges of Power: Women's Multicultural Alliances.*, B.C., Canada: New Society Publishers, 1990.

12 Beal, interview by author, 15 August 1997.

13 Ibid.

14 Sandy Pollack, "The Venceremos Brigade," *New World Review*, 1970, 24–33.

15 Contrary to interviews with TWWA members, FBI COINTELPRO records indicate that by 1974, the TWWA had chapters in Philadelphia, Seattle, and Elmhurst, New York. Federal Bureau of Investigations, Correspondence from Cincinnati to Washington, D.C., Field Office, 7 March 1974, 1.

16 Linda Burnham, Personal interview by author, 12 February 1998.

17 Cheryl (Perry) League, interview by author, 17 June 1998.

18 Federal Bureau of Investigations, "Third World Women's Alliance: Racial Matters," December 1970–March 1974 (503 of 509 documents available).

19 Margaret Sloan, "Address Given by Gloria Steinem and Margaret Sloan on Women" (Northfield, Minn.: Carleton College Audio-Visual Department, 5 March 1973), 98.

20 Michelle Wallace offered a more contentious version of the initial meeting, and the meeting to organize the press conference, in a 1975 account that depicts employees of *Ms.* magazine, members of Radical Lesbians, the Socialist Workers Party, and NOW as dominating the meeting's proceedings and rushing through the selection of Sloan as chair of the organization. Michelle Wallace, "On the National Black Feminist Organization," in *Feminist Revolution* (New York: Random House, 1978), 174–175.

21 Barbara Campbell, "Black Feminists Form Group Here," *New York Times*, 16 August 1973, 36.

22 Margaret Sloan, interview by author, 8 August 1997.

23 B. Davis, "The National Black Feminist Organization," 44.

24 Letters to the Editor, *Ms.*, August 1974, 4–6.

25 Deborah Singletary and Eugenia Wilshire, interview by author, 26 April 1997.

26 Bernette Golden, "Black Women's Liberation," *Essence*, February 1974, 36; B. Davis, "The National Black Feminist Organization," 44; and Sloan, "Address Given by Gloria Steinem and Margaret Sloan on Women," 99.

27 Chicago National Black Feminist Organization, NBFO, meeting minutes, July 1974, National Black Feminist Organization (Chicago chapter), Midwest Women's Historical Collection, University of Illinois at Chicago.

28 Ibid.

29 Chicago NBFO, meeting minutes, 3.

30 John Lofland, *Social Movement Organizations: Guide to Research on Insurgent Realities* (New York: Aldine deGruyter, 1996), 241.

31 NBFO, "Executive Board Letter to Membership," 23 September 1974, National Black Feminist Organization, Midwest Women's Historical Collection, University of Illinois at Chicago.

32 National Alliance of Black Feminists, "Philosophy of NABF," n.d., Brenda Eichelberger Collection, Chicago Historical Society.

33 Barbara Smith, interview by author, 15 July 1998.

34 One wonders if these same detractors would have said the same about black male leaders such as Dr. Martin Luther King, Muhammad Ali, or Huey P. Newton, who all opposed the Vietnam War.

35 Barbara Smith, interview by author, 1998.

36 Ibid.

37 Brenda Verner, "Brenda Verner Examines 'Liberated' Sisters," *Encore*, April 1974, 22–23. Verner's article is examined in more depth in chapter 4, "Black Women's Issues as Feminist Issues."

38 Barbara Smith, interview by author, 1998.

39 Breines, 1104; *We Raise Our Voices: Celebrating Activism for Equality and Pride in Boston's African American, Feminist, Gay and Lesbian, and Latino Communities*, the online exhibition of a Northeastern University Libraries exhibition, Boston, Northeastern University Libraries, 2003, http://www.lib.neu.edu/archives/voices.

40 Combahee River Collective, *The Combahee River Collective Statement: Black Feminist Organizing in the Seventies and Eighties* (New York: Kitchen Table Women of Color Press, [1977] 1986), 16; Breines, 1110.

41 Barbara Smith, interview by author, 15 July 1998.

42 Ibid.

43 Ibid.

44 Steven Buechler, *Women's Movements in the United States* (New Brunswick, N.J.: Rutgers University Press, 1990); Barbara Ryan, *Feminism and the Women's Movement: Dynamics of Change in Social Movement, Ideology, and Activism* (New York: Routledge, 1992); and Herbert Haines, "Black Radicalization and the Funding of Civil Rights: 1957–1970," *Social Problems* 32 (October 1994): 31–43.

45 Barbara Smith, interview by author, 15 July 1998.

46 Several other women spearheaded the emergence of the black feminist movement, challenging the dominance of white feminist leadership and concerns. They include Pauli Murray, Mary Ann Weathers, Cellestine Ware, and Doris Wright.

47 Marva Rudolph, "Aileen Hernandez," in *Epic Lives: One Hundred Black Women Who Made a Difference*, ed. Jessie Carney Smith (Detroit: Visible Ink, 1993), 276.

48 Liz Gant, "Black Women Organized for Action: They Collect Political IOUs," *Essence*, October [no year], 128.

49 Valerie Jo Bradley, interview by author, 8 October 1997.

50 Ibid.

51 Black Women Organized for Action, "Statement of Purpose and Activities," n.d., Aileen Hernandez, personal papers.

52 Gant, "Black Women Organized for Action," 46.

53 Ibid.

54 Patsy Fulcher, Aileen Hernandez, and Eleanor Spikes, "Sharing the Power, Sharing the Glory," *Contact Magazine*, fall 1974, 52.

3. Funding a Movement

1 Jo Freeman, "The Origins of the Women's Liberation Movement," *American Journal of Sociology* 78:4 (1973): 792–811.

2 Becky Thompson, "Multiracial Feminism: Recasting the Chronology of Second Wave Feminism," *Feminist Studies* 28:2 (2002): 346.

3 Beverly Davis, "The National Black Feminist Organization," *Sage* 5 (1988): 43; Jane Galvin-Lewis, interview by author, 26 April 1997; and Margaret Sloan-Hunter, interview by author, 8 August 1997.

4 Avyazian characterizes this phenomenon as "Founders' Disease." Cited in John Lofland, *Social Movement Organizations: Guide to Research on Insurgent Realities* (New York: Aldine de Gruyter, 1996), 173, n. 1.

5 The Women's Action Alliance (WAA), formed in New York in 1972, operated as an activist, social service agency. Active from 1971 to 1997, the WAA had considerable success in spreading feminism through professional referrals and offering services to help women free themselves from dependency. Marla R. Miller, "Tracking the Women's Movement through the Women's Action Alliance," *Journal of Women's History* 14:2 (2002): 154–156.

6 B. Davis, "The National Black Feminist Organization"; Jane Galvin-Lewis, interview by author, 26 April 1997; and Margaret Sloan-Hunter. Interview by author, 8 August 1997.

7 Ibid.

8 The members of the policy committee were Diane Lacey, Margaret Sloan, Doris Wright, Jane Galvin-Lewis, Carolyn Handy, Sylvia Vitale, Carolyn Reed, Lori Sharp, and Maxine Williams. Instead of recommending only two officers, the policy paper proposed delegating organizational responsibilities to a chair, a vice-chair, a recording secretary, a corresponding secretary, a treasurer, and an office coordinator. Each member elected to these positions would comprise the steering committee. NBFO, "Executive Board Letter to Membership," 23 September 1974, NBFO, Midwest Women's Historical Collection, University of Illinois at Chicago.

9 NBFO, policy paper, n.d., Brenda Eichelberger Collection, Chicago Historical Society, Chicago, 1.

10 NBFO "Executive Board Letter to Membership"; Margaret Sloan-Hunter, interview by author, 8 August 1997.

11 Jane Galvin-Lewis and Deborah Singletary, interview by author, 26 April 1997.

12 The NABF's structure was strikingly similar to the NBFO's proposed structure, suggesting cross-pollination between the two organizations despite their

later split. The NABF's officers included the executive director, chairperson, recording secretary, corresponding secretary, treasurer, financial secretary, social service director, and communications coordinator.

13 The NABF's first advisory board consisted of prominent women such as Carol Moseley Braun, a state representative at that time; Aileen Hernandez, former president of NOW and a cofounder of Black Women Organized for Action; poet and professor Sonia Sanchez; writer Vertamae Grosvenor; and former U.S. congresswoman Yvonne Braithwaite Burke.

14 Gayle Porter, interview by author, 18 June 1997.

15 Ibid.

16 Jo Freeman, *The Politics of Women's Liberation* (New York: David McKay, 1977), 204.

17 Sharon Page Ritchie, "Retreat Survey," folder 15, "Black Feminist Retreats: First Retreat," 1977, Barbara Smith Papers, Lesbian Herstory Archives, Brooklyn, N.Y.; Janie Nelson, interview by author, 13 February 1997; and Gayle Porter, interview by author, 6 May 1997.

18 Janie Nelson, interview by author, 13 February 1997.

19 Francis Beal, interview with author, 15 August 1997.

20 Honor Ford-Smith, "Ring Ding in a Tight Corner: Sistren, Collective, Democracy, and the Organizing of Cultural Production," in *Feminist Genealogies, Colonial Legacies, Democratic Futures,* ed. M. Jacqui Alexander and Chandra Talpade Mohanty (New York: Routledge, 1997), 213–258.

21 Freeman, *The Politics of Women's Liberation,* 203.

22 Barbara Smith, "Memorandum to Retreat Participants," folder 12, "Black Feminist Retreats: Fourth Retreat," 1975, Barbara Smith Papers.

23 Barbara Smith, interview by author, 19 June 1998.

24 Mercedes Tompkins, interview by author, 6 May 1998.

25 Ibid.

26 Margo Okazawa-Rey, interview by author, 20 October 1997.

27 Barbara Smith, interview by author, 19 June 1998.

28 Patsy Fulcher, Aileen Hernandez, and Eleanor Spikes, "Sharing the Power, Sharing the Glory," *Contact Magazine,* fall 1974, 52.

29 Ibid., 52.

30 Aileen Hernandez, interview by author, 14 September 1997.

31 In 1974 the BWOA fine-tuned its leadership structure by creating a steering committee to ease the transition from one coordinating team to the next. The steering committee consisted of the newly installed coordinators, the immediate past coordinators, and the facilitators of each meeting. The addition of a steering committee continued the BWOA's mission of sharing the leadership of the organization, ensuring that the organization did not collapse during the transition.

32 Aileen Hernandez, interview by author, 14 September 1997.

33 Valerie Jo Bradley, interview by author, 8 October 1997.

34 Third World Women's Alliance, "History of the Organization and Ideological Platform," *Triple Jeopardy* 1:1 (September–October 1972): 8–9, here, 8.

35 Karla Jay, "An Interview with Margaret Sloan," *Lesbian Tide*, 1974, 24.

36 "Black Women Organized for Action," membership brochure, 1977, Aileen Hernandez, personal papers.

37 NBFO, membership application, n.d., Black Women's Vertical File, Schlesinger Library, Radcliffe College, Cambridge, Mass.

38 National Black Feminist Organization (Chicago chapter), meeting minutes, June 1974, Midwest Women's Historical Collection, University of Illinois at Chicago.

39 John Lofland. *Social Movement Organizations: Guide to Research on Insurgent Realities* (New York: Aldine de Gruyter, 1996), 204.

40 See figure 2 ("Black Feminist Organizations: A Comparative Chart") at the beginning of this chapter. Black feminist organizations varied in detailing their explicit criteria for membership, but Lofland offers the following questions as useful indicators of membership: (1) How frequently does the person participate in SMO [social movement organization] activities? (2) How much money (or in-kind donations) does the person give to the SMO? (3) How well known is the person to people who are the most active SMO members, and how much power and influence does she or he appear to have? (4) What is the degree to which the person expresses disagreements or agreement with the beliefs of the SMO?

41 Lofland, *Social Movement Organizations*, 156.

42 Margaret Sloan-Hunter, interview by author, 8 August 1997.

43 Margaret Sloan, "Black Feminism: A New Mandate," *Ms.*, May 1974, 99.

44 Jane Galvin-Lewis, Deborah Singletary, and Eugenia Wilshire, interview by author, 26 April 1997.

45 "Black Women United: Sororities, Alliances, and Pressure Groups," *Ms.*, January 1979, 90; "Black Feminism," *off our backs* 3:10 (1973): 3; and Fran Pollner, Anne Williams, and Tacie Dejanikus, "Black Feminists Up Front," *off our backs* 4:2 (1974): 2–4.

46 David Snow, Louis Zurcher Jr., and Heldon Eckland-Olson, "Social Networks and Social Movements: A Microstructural Approach to Differential Recruitment," *American Sociological Review* 5:5 (1980): 787–801.

47 Cheryl (Perry) League, interview by author, 17 June 1998.

48 Letters to the National Alliance of Black Feminists, 1976–1980, Brenda Eichelberger Collection, Chicago Historical Society, Chicago; "The War between the Sexes: Is it Manufactured or Real?" *Ebony*, June 1979.

49 Black feminist organizations, reformist and radical, most often contributed to defense funds for political prisoners such as Angela Davis, the San Quentin Six, and Joanne Little.

50 The funds from *Ms.* came directly from the magazine because *Ms.* did not establish its formal granting foundation until 1979. The Eastman Founda-

tion, established in New York in 1946, was and still is a private family fund that provided seed grants and matching funds to organizations active in media, theater, aging, and women's issues.

51 Margaret Sloan-Hunter, interview by author, 8 August 1997.

52 Ibid.

4. Black Women's Issues and Feminism

1   CRISIS, "CRISIS! Wave of Violence on Black Women," pamphlet, n.d., Barbara Smith Papers, Lesbian Herstory Archives, Brooklyn, N.Y. For one account of this activism, see Jaime M. Grant, "Who's Killing Us?" in *Femicide: The Politics of Woman Killing*, ed. Jill Radford and Diane E. H. Russell (New York: Twayne Publishers, 1992), 145–160. In this account, Combahee members are credited with serving as a bridge between white feminist and local black activists. However, Okazawa-Rey, in an interview by the author (20 October 1997), disputes just how effective this bridge work was given homophobia on the part of some local black activists.

2   I obtained 500+ pages of COINTELPRO documents on the Third World Women's Alliance through the Freedom of Information Act (FOIA). The FOIA requests on the other four organizations yielded no other documents.

3   Charlayne Hunter, "Many Blacks Wary of 'Women's Liberation' Movement in U.S.," *New York Times*, 17 November 1970, 47, 60. Recent white feminist accounts maintain that radical socialist feminists, in fact, did support black political prisoners; see also Wini Breines, "What's Love Got to Do with It? White Women, Black Women, and Feminism in the Movement Years," *Signs: A Journal of Women in Culture and Society* 27:4 (2002): 1113–1114.

4   Barbara and Beverly Smith, "I Am Not Meant to Be Alone and without You Who Understand: Letters from Black Feminists, 1972–1978," *Conditions* 4 (1979): 62–77.

5   TWWA, "Now Attica!!!," "Murder at San Quentin," and "Kisha's Arrest," *Triple Jeopardy* 1:1 (1972): 2–4.

6   Francis Beal, "Feminine Stink Mystique," *Triple Jeopardy* 3:4 (1974): 7.

7   TWWA, "El Teatro Guerilla" and "Guerilla Theatre is Fun!," *Triple Jeopardy* 2:4 (1973): 13.

8   Ibid.

9   For extensive analysis of this interplay, see Kristin Anderson-Bricker, " 'Triple Jeopardy': Black Women and the Growth of Feminist Consciousness, 1964–1975," in *Still Lifting, Still Climbing: Contemporary African American Women's Activism*, ed. Kimberly Springer (New York: New York University Press, 1999), 49–69.

10 BWOA, "Still . . . Small Changes for Black Women," *What It Is!*, July 1980, 1.

11 "Black Feminism," *off our backs* 3:10 (1973): 3.

12 Karla Jay, "An Interview with Margaret Sloan," *Lesbian Tide*, 1974, 24.; Margaret Sloan, "Black Feminism: A New Mandate," *Ms.*, May 1974, 99; Life/Style, "Feminism: 'The Black Nuance,'" *Newsweek*, 17 December 1973; and "Uniting and Conquering," *off our backs*, December/January 1974, 1–4.

13 Beverly Davis, "The National Black Feminist Organization," *Sage* 5 (1988): 44.

14 "Uniting . . . and Conquering," 2.

15 Ibid.

16 Ibid.

17 Ibid.

18 "Letters," *Ms.*, August 1974, 4–7, 13.

19 Brenda Verner, "Brenda Verner Examines 'Liberated' Sisters," *Encore*, April 1974, 22–23.

20 There are no credits given for the illustrations, but often graphics or pull-quotes are an editorial decision, not that of the writer. Still, these illustrations —whether penned by a woman or a man—accurately reflect Verner's views.

21 "Uniting and Conquering," 4; Verner, 23.

22 For a closer examination of this point and the political life of Sojourner Truth, see Nell Irvin Painter, *Soujourner Truth: A Life, a Symbol* (New York: W. W. Norton, 1996).

23 Verner, "Brenda Verner Examines 'Liberated' Sisters," 22.

24 Ibid., 24.

25 Ibid.

26 Margo Jefferson and Margaret Sloan, "Equal Time: In Defense of Black Feminism," *Encore*, July 1974, 46.

27 Ibid.

28 NABF, calendar of events, 5 April 1978, Brenda Eichelberger Collection, Chicago Historical Society.

29 Gerda Lerner, *Black Women in White America* (New York: Oxford University Press, 1972).

30 Brenda Eichelberger, interview by author, 13 February 1997; Janie Nelson, interview by author, 13 February 1997.

31 Demita Frazier, Barbara Smith, and Beverly Smith, personal correspondence, 24 May 1977, Barbara Smith Papers, Lesbian Herstory Archives, Brooklyn, N.Y.

32 Ibid.

33 Linda Powell, personal correspondence, 9 January 1978, Barbara Smith Papers.

34 Pamela Oliver, personal correspondence, 10 January 1978, Barbara Smith Papers.

35 Cheryl Clarke, personal correspondence, 1978, Barbara Smith Papers.

36 Barbara Smith, personal correspondence, n.d., Barbara Smith Papers.

37 Linda Powell, personal correspondence, 9 January 1978, Barbara Smith Papers.

38 Alice Walker, *In Search of Our Mothers' Gardens* (New York: Harcourt Brace Jovanovich, 1983).

39 Barbara Smith, *Home Girls: A Black Feminist Anthology* (New Brunswick, N.J.: Rutgers University Press, 2000).

5. Black Feminist Identities

1 Doug McAdam, *Political Process and the Development of Black Insurgency, 1930–1970* (Chicago: University of Chicago Press, 1982).

2 Scott Hunt and Robert Benford, "Identity Talk in the Peace and Justice Movement," *Journal of Contemporary Ethnography* 22:4 (1994): 89.

3 Miriam Harris, "From Kennedy to Combahee: Black Feminist Activism from 1960 to 1980," PhD dissertation, Department of Sociology (Minneapolis, MN: University of Minnesota, 1997); Rose M. Brewer, "Theorizing Race, Class, and Gender," in *Theorizing Black Feminisms*, ed. Stanlie M. James and Abena P. A. Busia (London: Routledge, 1993), 13.

4 See also Deborah White, *Too Heavy a Load: Black Women in Defense of Themselves, 1894–1994* (New York: W. W. Norton, 1999).

5 The statements of purpose of the Third World Women's Alliance (TWWA), the National Black Feminist Organization (NBFO), and Black Women Organized for Action (BWOA)—reproduced in their entirety in appendix C—describe why black women chose to organize as black feminists, specifying racist and sexist discrimination in their lives. The National Alliance of Black Feminists (NABF) did not have a statement of purpose, but the document that most closely addresses the organization's purpose was a philosophy of the organization. This document is also reproduced in appendix C. The Combahee River Collective issued, as mentioned in the previous chapter (on the organization's emergence), a black feminist statement, the *Combahee River Collective Statement*, that encompassed a description of the beginnings of contemporary black feminism, a statement of members' beliefs, an analysis of problems they encountered in organizing black feminists, and a discussion of the issues and projects that members undertook.

6 Deborah King, in "Multiple Jeopardy, Multiple Consciousness: The Context of a Black Feminist Ideology," in *Words of Fire: An Anthology of African American Feminist Thought*, ed. Guy-Sheftall (New York: New Press, [1988] 1995), argues that black women managed their identity as multiplicative; they could not merely add race to the problem of sexism to arrive at a black, woman-centered analysis of discrimination. Oppression, King proposes, compounds, which makes it nearly impossible to ascertain which aspect of a black woman's identity accounted for discrimination in a given situation.

7 McAdam, *Political Process*.

8　I determined that Beal was either the sole author of or a major contributor to the earlier Black Women's Liberation Committee (BWLC) article "SNCC-Black Women's Liberation," due to significant parallels between it and her essay "Double Jeopardy." Other essays that performed a task similar to Beal's included Linda LaRue, "The Black Movement and Women's Liberation"; Pauli Murray, "The Liberation of Black Women"; and MaryAnn Weathers, "An Argument for Black Women's Liberation as a Revolutionary Force," all in *Words of Fire: An Anthology of African American Feminist Thought*, ed. Beverly Guy-Sheftall (New York: New Press, 1995).

9　Quote from Beal, "Double Jeopardy," 148. See also Student Non-violent Coordinating Committee, "Black Women's Liberation," n.d., Black Women's Vertical File, Schlesinger Library, Radcliffe College, Cambridge, Mass., 77.

10　Third World Women's Alliance, "Third World Women's Alliance at Work," *Triple Jeopardy* 1:6 (September/October 1972): 10–11.

11　National Black Feminist Organization, "Statement of Purpose," 1973, Midwest Women's Historical Collection, University of Illinois, Chicago.

12　Black Women Organized for Action," membership brochure, 1977, Aileen Hernandez, personal papers.

13　National Alliance of Black Feminists. "Philosophy of NABF," brochure, n.d., 32, Brenda Eichelberger Collection, Chicago Historical Society; Barbara Smith, interview by author, 15 July 1998.

14　Combahee River Collective, *The Combahee River Collective Statement: Black Feminist Organizing in the Seventies and Eighties* (New York: Kitchen Table Women of Color Press, [1977] 1986), 9.

15　Patricia Hill Collins, *Black Feminist Thought* (Boston: Unwin Hyman, 1990), 29, 225–226.

16　I define *formal consciousness-raising* as consciousness-raising that was mandatory for organizational membership.

17　Hunt and Benford, "Identity Talk in the Peace and Justice Movement," 489.

18　Alice Echols, *Daring to Be Bad: Radical Feminism in America, 1967–1975* (Minneapolis: University of Minnesota, 1989), 84.

19　Francis Beal, interview by author, 15 August 1997.

20　Combahee River Collective; National Alliance of Black Feminists, press release on the opening of the NABF Black Women's Center, 23 May 1976, Brenda Eichelberger Collection, Chicago Historical Society; and Margaret Sloan, "Black Feminism: A New Mandate," *Ms.*, May 1974, 97–100.

21　Beal, interview by author, 15 August 1997.

22　Ibid.

23　Ibid.

24　Ibid.; Margaret Sloan, "Address Given by Gloria Steinem and Margaret Sloan on Women" (Northfield, Minn.: Carleton College Audio-Visual Department, 5 March 1973). Dorothy Roberts confirms that "Half of the maternity-related

deaths among black women in New York City in the 1960s were attributed to illegal abortions," in Roberts, *Killing the Black Body: Race, Reproduction, and the Meaning of Liberty* (New York: Vintage Books, [1997] 1999), 101.

25 Toni Cade Bambara, *The Black Woman* (New York: Penguin, 1970), 162–179; Roberts, *Killing the Black Body*, 98–103.

26 Francis Beal, interview by author, 15 August 1997.

27 Richard F. Babcock Jr., "Sterilization: Coercing Consent," *Nation*, 12 January 1974, 51–53.

28 Francis Beal, interview by author, 15 August 1997; Black Women's Liberation Committee, "SNCC: Black Women's Liberation," *Women: A Journal of Liberation*, n.d.

29 Sharon Harley, "The Middle Class," in *Black Women in America: An Historical Encyclopedia*, ed. Darlene Clark Hine, Elsa Barkley Brown, and Rosalyn Terborg-Penn (Bloomington: University of Indiana Press, 1993), 786–789.

30 To clarify the distinctions between the upper-middle-class elite and the new professional middle class, Harley cites Mary Church Terrell as an example of the former and Anna Julia Cooper, Maggie Lena Walker, and Nannie Burroughs as examples of the latter. Terrell was the daughter of a millionaire, while Cooper, Walker, and Burroughs rose from humbler beginnings and ascended to prominent positions in education and business. Ibid.

31 Brenda Eichelberger, interview by author, 13 February 1997; Harley, "The Middle Class."

32 Francis Beal, interview by author, 15 August 1997; Barbara Smith, interview by author, 15 July 1998.

33 Valerie Jo Bradley, interview by author, 8 October 1997.

34 Beverly Davis, "The National Black Feminist Organization," *Sage* 5 (1988): 43; bell hooks, *Ain't I a Woman: Black Women and Feminism* (Boston: South End Press, 1981); and Gloria Joseph and Jill Lewis, *Common Differences: Conflicts in Black and White Feminist Perspectives* (Boston: South End Press, 1981).

35 Jacquelyn Jones, *Labor of Love, Labor of Sorrow* (New York: Vintage, 1986), 319.

36 Jane Galvin-Lewis, interview by author, 26 April 1997; Margaret Sloan-Hunter, interview by author, 8 August 1997.

37 Karla Jay, "An Interview with Margaret Sloan," *Lesbian Tide*, 1974, 3.

38 Ibid.

39 Janie Nelson, interview by author, 13 February 1997.

40 Ibid.

41 Mercedes Tompkins, interview by author, 6 May 1998.

42 Ibid.

43 Barbara Smith, interview by author, 15 July 1998.

44 Eugenia Wilshire, interview by author, 26 April 1997.

45 Margaret Sloan-Hunter, interview by author, 8 August 1997.

46 Wallace offers a compelling, if brief, perspective on the early NBFO that claims lesbians and their demands dominated the organization, which she saw as

counterproductive to attracting members. Michelle Wallace, "On the National Black Feminist Organization," in *Feminist Revolution* (New York: Random House, 1978).

47 The *Oxford English Dictionary* (2nd) cites 1979 as the first printed use of the word *heterosexism* in J. Penelope's *Articulation of Bias*. The OED also cites an article in the January 1979 issue of *Ms.* magazine as the first use of the word *heterosexist*.

48 Barbara Smith, interview by author, 15 July 1998.

49 Flora Davis, *Moving the Mountain: The Women's Movement in America since 1960* (New York: Simon and Schuster, 1991).

50 Francis Beal, interview by author, 15 August 1997.

51 Third World Women's Alliance, "Third World Women's Alliance at Work," 9; emphasis mine.

52 Brenda Eichelberger, interview by author, 13 February 1997; Janie Nelson, interview by author, 13 February 1997.

53 I use the word *transgendered* self-consciously, recognizing that this concept was not in popular usage at the time of this incident in the late 1970s. Transsexualism was a better-known identity at the time.

54 Brenda Eichelberger and Janie Nelson, interview by author, 13 February 1997.

55 This reaction was not unique for the time, and feminists still grapple with their internalized fear in such places as the annual Michigan Womyn's Music Festival. See, for example, Leslie Feinberg, *Transgender Warriors* (Boston: Beacon Press, 1996).

56 Sharon Page Ritchie, response to Black Women's Retreat Survey, Barbara Smith Papers, folder 15, Lesbian Herstory Archives, Brooklyn, N.Y.

57 Brenda Eichelberger and Janie Nelson, interview by author, 13 February 1997.

58 Brenda Eichelberger, interview by author, 13 February 1997; Margaret Sloan-Hunter, interview by author, 8 August 1997.

59 Jane Galvin-Lewis, interview by author, 26 April 1997; Janie Nelson, interview by author, 13 February, 1997; and Margaret Sloan-Hunter, interview by author, 1998.

60 Margaret Sloan-Hunter, interview by author, 8 August 1997.

61 Jane Galvin-Lewis, Deborah Singletary, and Eugenia Wilshire, interview by author, 26 April 1997.

6. War-Weary Warriors

1 Sheila Radford-Hill, *Further to Fly: Black Women and the Politics of Empowerment* (Minneapolis: University of Minnesota Press, 2000), 23.

2 Galvin-Lewis, Jane, interview by author, 26 April 1997.

3 Francis Beal, interview by author, 15 August 1997; Linda Burnham, interview by author, 12 February 1998; and Cheryl (Perry) League, interview by author, 17 June 1998.

4 Alliance Against Women's Oppression, organizational brochure, American Radicalism Collection Vertical File, Michigan State University, Lansing.

5 Secondary sources and informants claim that though the New York office closed, the Los Angeles chapter kept the NBFO name and continued to work toward Black feminist change in its geographic area well into the late 1970s. Beverly Davis, "The National Black Feminist Organization," *Sage* 5 (1988): 43; Deborah White, *Too Heavy a Load: Black Women in Defense of Themselves, 1894–1994* (New York: W. W. Norton, 1999).

6 Brenda Eichelberger, interview by author, 13 February 1997; Janie Nelson, interview by author, 13 February 1997; and Gayle Porter, interview by author, 6 May 1998.

7 Black Women Organized for Action, "Letter to BWOA Members and Newsletter Subscribers," *What It Is!* 8:9 (December 1980): 1.

8 Ibid.

9 The "Contract with Women of the USA" included the following principles of action: sharing family responsibility, an end to the feminization of poverty, accessible high-quality health care, sexual and reproductive rights, ending violence against women, educational equity, workplace rights, environmental protection, the inclusion of women in policy making to prevent war, U.S. Senate ratification of the UN Convention to Eliminate All Forms of Discrimination against Women (CEDAW), and the partnership of federal and state policy makers and women's groups to develop a long-range plan for women's equity and empowerment. Organizations supporting the contract included a long list of public and private institutions, diverse in their race, class, and physical ability identities (advertisement, "Contract with Women of the USA," *New York Times*, 29 September 1996, 16E).

10 Aileen Hernandez, interview by author, 14 September 1997.

11 Leila Rupp and Verta Taylor, *Survival in the Doldrums: The American Women's Rights Movement, 1945 to the 1960s* (New York: Oxford University Press, 1987).

12 William Gamson, *The Strategy of Social Protest* (Belmont, Calif.: Wadsworth Publications, [1975] 1990), 90.

13 Cheryl (Perry) League, interview by author, 17 June 1998.

14 Francis Beal, interview by author, 15 August 1997.

15 Janie Nelson, interview by author, 13 February 1997; Gayle Porter, interview by author, 18 June 1997.

16 National Alliance of Black Feminists, Steering Committee letter to membership, 23 September 1976, Brenda Eichelberger Collection, Chicago Historical Society.

17 Mercedes Tompkins. Interview by author, 6 May 1998.

18 B. Davis, "The National Black Feminist Organization," 45.

19 NBFO, membership application, n.d., Black Women's Vertical File, Schlesinger Library, Radcliffe College, Cambridge, Mass.

20 Mancur Olson, *The Logic of Collective Action* (Cambridge, Mass.: Harvard University Press, [1968] 1971).

21 Black Women Organized for Action, treasurer's report presented to the finance committee, 1 March 1977, Aileen Hernandez, personal papers.

22 Lofland, *Social Movement Organizations*, 171–172.

23 White, *Too Heavy a Load*.

24 John D. McCarthy and Mayer Zald, *Social Movements in an Organizational Society* (New Brunswick, N.J.: Transaction Publishers, [1987] 1994), 131. Herbert Freudenberger coined the term *burnout* for this context in his 1974 book *Burnout: The High Cost of High Achievement* (New York: Anchor). He defines it as "the extinction of motivation or incentive, especially where one's devotion to a cause or relationship fails to produce the desired results."

25 McAdam later addressed the impact of gender on the recruitment, experience, and subsequent activism of white women and men in Freedom Summer. He found that gender and sexuality represented a barrier to women's participation, but not men's. Women experienced a sexual double standard and the taboo of interracial dating in their application process to Freedom Summer. Doug McAdam, "The Biographical Consequences of Activism," *American Sociological Review* 97:5 ([1988] 1992): 1217–1224.

26 Brenda Eichelberger, interview by author, 13 February 1997; Dorothy King, interview by author, 23 January 1998; and Margaret Sloan-Hunter, interview by author, 8 August 1997.

27 Brenda Eichelberger Collection, Chicago Historical Society.

28 Margaret Sloan-Hunter, interview by author, 8 August, 1997.

29 Jane Galvin-Lewis, Deborah Singletary, and Eugenia Wilshire, interview by author, 26 April 1997.

30 Margaret Sloan-Hunter, interview by author, 8 August 1997.

31 Members of the NBFO were decidedly pioneers in adding the mass incarceration of black women and drug addiction to the black feminist agenda.

32 See Dorothy Allison, "Confrontation Black/White: Interview with Ginny Apuzzo and Betty Powell," in *Building Feminist Theory: The Best of Quest*, ed. Quest Staff (White Plains, N.Y.: Longman Publishing Group, 1981); Jaime M. Grant, "Who's Killing Us?" in *Femicide: The Politics of Woman Killing*, ed. Jill Radford and Diane E. H. Russell (New York: Twayne Publishers, 1992); Miriam Harris, "From Kennedy to Combahee: Black Feminist Activism from 1960 to 1980," PhD dissertation, Department of Sociology (Minneapolis: University of Minnesota, 1997); and Barbara Smith, "The Boston Murders," in *Life Notes: Personal Writings by Contemporary Black Women*, ed. Patricia Bell-Scott (New York: W.W. Norton: [1994] 1995), 315–320.

33 Margaret Sloan, "Black Feminism: A New Mandate," *Ms.*, May 1974, 99, 22.

34 Linda Burnham, interview by author, 12 February 1998; Cheryl (Perry) League, interview by author, 17 June 1998.

35 Cheryl (Perry) League, interview by author, 17 June 1998.

36 Linda Burnham, interview by author, 12 February 1998.

37 Gayle Porter, interview by author, 6 May 1998.

38 Aileen Hernandez, interview by author, 14 September 1997.

39 Cheryl (Perry) League, interview by author, 17 June 1998.

40 Ibid.

41 Janie Nelson, interview by author, 13 February 1997.

42 Sharon Paige Ritchie, interview by author, 2 November 1997.

43 See also Jo Freeman, *The Politics of Women's Liberation* (New York: David McKay, 1977); Todd Gitlin, *The Whole World Is Watching: Mass Media in the Making and Unmaking of the New Left* (Berkeley: University of California Press, 1980).

44 For an insightful look into the interaction of intimate relationships and leadership roles, see Margo V. Perkins, *Autobiography as Activism: Three Black Women of the Sixties* (Jackson: University of Mississippi Press, 2000).

45 Michelle Wallace, "On the National Black Feminist Organization," in *Feminist Revolution* (New York: Random House, 1978), 174.

46 Jane Galvin-Lewis, interview by author, 26 April 1997.

47 In the late 1950s through the 1970s, J. Edgar Hoover, then director of the Federal Bureau of Investigations (FBI), initiated a massive disinformation campaign against the civil rights, black nationalist, American Indian, Communist Party USA, Socialist Workers Party, and New Left movements. Under the aegis of the Counterintelligence Program (COINTELPRO), federal agents infiltrated these movements using extralegal tactics such as mail tampering, initiating disputes within movement communities through infiltration by agents or paid informers, unlawful search and seizure, and, some theorists believe, even murder. Ward Churchill and Jim Vanderwall, *The COINTELPRO Papers* (Cambridge, Mass.: South End Press, 1990).

Inquiries to the FBI and CIA under the Freedom of Information Act (FOIA), yielded a substantial file on the Third World Women's Alliance, but no information on the other organizations examined here. However, the NBFO did experience significant disruptions that black feminist respondents later hypothesized were orchestrated.

48 Barbara Smith, interview by author, 15 July 1998.

49 Jane Galvin-Lewis and Deborah Singletary, interview by author, 26 April 1997.

50 I am inclined to characterize Verner's position as the latter because of the number of speeches she has since given with titles such as "The Feminist Plot to Destroy the Afrikan Freedom Movement," Nubian Network, Global Consciousness: Lectures for International Thinkers, accessed 2 January 2004, http://www.blackconsciousness.com/sshop/buster.htm.

51 Jane Galvin-Lewis, interview by author, 26 April 1997.

52 Deborah Singletary, interview by author, 26 April 1997.

53 Jo Reger, "More than One Feminism: Organizational Structure and the Con-
struction of Collective Identity," in *Social Movements: Identity, Culture, and the
State*, ed. David S. Meyer, Nancy Whittier, and Belinda Robnett (New York:
Oxford University Press, 2002), 171–184.

Conclusion

1 William Gamson, *The Strategy of Social Protest* (Belmont, Calif.: Wadsworth
Publications, [1975] 1990), 28.
2 Ibid.

Epilogue

1 Kristal Brent Zook, "A Manifesto of Sorts for a Black Feminist Movement,"
New York Times Magazine, 12 November 1995, 86–89; Barbara Ransby, "Black
Feminism at Twenty-one: Reflections on the Evolution of a National Commu-
nity," *Signs: A Journal of Women in Culture and Society* 25:4 (2000): 1215–1221;
Lori S. Robinson, "A Feminist Vision," *Emerge*, March 1995, 20–23; Marilyn
Milloy, "The New Feminism," *Essence*, September 1997, 117–118, 120, 162,
164; and "Black Women Speak Out on Feminism, Black Men, Lesbianism,
Mothers, Daughters, and *That* Movie," *Village Voice*, 13 February 1996, 26–
44.
2 Ellis Cose, "From Schools to Jobs, Black Women are Rising Much Faster than
Black Men," *Newsweek*, 3 March 2003.
3 Audre Lorde, *Sister Outsider: Essays and Speeches* (Berkeley, Calif.: Crossing
Press, 1984), 124–133.
4 Deborah Singletary, interview by author, 26 April 1997.
5 Wilshire, Eugenia, interview by author, 26 April 1997.

INDEX

Numbers in italics indicate illustrative material.

and, 91–92; Student Nonviolent Coordinating Committee and, 50; Third World Women's Alliance and, 50; *Triple Jeopardy* and, 92

female sexuality: National Alliance of Black Feminists schools and, 104

feminism: heterogeneity of, 171; resistance distinguished from, 19–21; womanism and, 175–76

finances. *See* funding

Ford-Smith, Honor: Sistren and, 73

Foxy Brown (film), 41

frames and ideology, 15

Frazier, Demita: Black Women's Network Retreats and, 106; Boston National Black Feminist Organization and, 59; Combahee River Collective and, 73–74; on disjuncture, 45

Freeman, Jo: on organization styles, 65, 72, 73

Friedan, Betty: NOW and, 33

Fulcher, Patsy: Black Women Organized for Action and, 62

funding: alienation of sources of, 152; cessation of, 145–48; organizations, 83–86; sound financial infrastructure and, 176–77

Galvin-Lewis, Jane: on disruptions, 162–65; on internal homophobia in NBFO, 136–37; National Black Feminist Organization and, 68–69, 85; on NBFO coordinating council, 70; on NBFO leadership, 161–63; on war-weary warriors, 139, 150

Gamson, William: on pattern maintenance, 144; on success, 169

Garvey, Amy Jacques, 20

gender differences: in education and employment, 38–39

gender identity: and collective identity, 130–38

gender issues: in campaign organizations, 22–62; in nationalist movements, 26–28, 40–41; race issues and, 88–90

gender oppression: during slavery, 19

Gilford, Flora: Black Women Organized for Action and, 76

Gluck, Sharon Berger: on wave analogy, 8

Gone with the Wind (film), 40

Good Times (TV sitcom), 42–43

Hamer, Fannie Lou: bridge leadership and, 13; as Mother of the Movement, 22

Hansberry, Lorraine: as feminist, 20

Harley, Sharon: on black middle class, 122–23

Harris, Miriam: on polyvocality, 113–14

Hayden, Casey: Hayden-King Student Nonviolent Coordinating Committee position paper and, 24–25

Hernandez, Aileen: Black Women Organized for Action and, 62; on BWOA new strategies, 156; on BWOA organization, 75–76; on BWOA survival, 143–44; EEOC and, 33, 62; *Good Times* and, 43; NOW and, 34

heterosexism: and collective identity, 130–38. *See also* lesbian feminism

hierarchical organizations, 67–72

Hill, Anita: support for, 174

historical background, 19–21

Home Girls: A Black Feminist Anthology, 1; Combahee River Collective and, 111

homophobia: collective identity and, 131–33: National Black Feminist Organization and, 134–37. *See also* lesbian feminism

Hunter, Tera, *Domination and Resistance . . .* , 19
hypervisibility: stereotyping and, 88

identities, 113–38
identity formation: consciousness raising and, 118–22; in organizations, 14–15
ideology: disputes over, 151–52, 166
ideology/reality disjuncture, 45–46
imperialism: Black Women's Alliance and, 48–49
interstitial politics, 88: origins of, 1–4

Jackson, George: Third World Women's Alliance and, 91
Jacobs, Harriet A., *Incidents in the Life of a Slavegirl . . .* , 19, 194 n.36
Jefferson, Margo: response of, to Brenda Verner, 102
Jeffersons, The (TV sitcom), 42
Jet magazine: on women's movement, 29–30
Jewell, K. Sue: on stereotyping, 40
Johnston, Linda: and National Alliance of Black Feminists, 53–54
Jones, Clarey: on Eastern Regional Conference, 98–99
Jones, Claudia, 20

Kelley, Robin D. B., *Freedom Dreams*, 13, 168
Kennedy, Florynce: *Abortion Rap*, 33; National Black Feminist Organization and, 33–34; at NBFO Eastern Regional Conference, 95
King, Dr. Martin Luther Jr.: and Southern Christian Leadership Conference, 22
King, Mary: Hayden-King Student Nonviolent Coordinating Committee position paper and, 24–25

Lavender Menace, 131
leadership: bridge leadership, 13–14, 22; of civil rights movement, 21–26; disputes over, 155–65, 167; ideology incohesion and, 166; matriarchy and, 23–24; of National Black Feminist Organization, 66–70, 67; star systems and, 176
Lear, Norman: and "relevance programming," 42–43
Lebrón, Lolita: Third World Women's Alliance and, 92
Lentz, Martha: on *Maude* and feminism, 42
Lerner, Gerda, *Black Women in White America*, 103
lesbian feminism: collective identity and, 130–38; Combahee River Collective discussion of, 108; stereotyping and, 40–41
Liberation Schools: Third World Women's Alliance, 102
lifestyles: and activism, 2, 149
Lipsky, Suzanne: on Eastern Regional Conference, 97
Lofland, John, *Social Movement Organizations . . .* , 81
Lorde, Audre: Combahee River Collective and, 107; "Eye to Eye: Black Women, Hatred and Anger," 177–78

Macklin, Katherine: National Black Feminist Organization and, 59
Malcolm X College (Chicago), 105
mammy stereotype, 40
Mapp, Edward: on stereotyping, 40
March on Washington (1963), 23
matriarchy: women's leadership and, 23–24; myth of, and Black Women's Alliance, 47; social policy and, 37–44

Maude (TV sitcom) and feminism, 42

McAdam, Doug, 13; on biographical availability, 149

McDaniel, Hattie: in *Gone with the Wind* (film), 40

McNeil, Claudia: in *Raisin in the Sun* (film), 40

membership: criteria of, 78–79; numbers, 81–83

memory: collective, 6–7

men. *See* black men

Merritt, Theresa: in *That's My Mama*, 41

middle-classes: dominate organizations, 122–30

Militant Forum: National Alliance of Black Feminists and, 105

mission statements. *See* statements of purpose

mobilization: conferencing and, 93–102

monetary resources. *See* funding

Montgomery bus boycott, 22

Moore, Edwina: Chicago Black Feminists and, 55

Morrison, Toni, 5: on black men and women's movement, 29–30; *The Bluest Eye*, 108; *Sula*, 108

Mothers of the Movement, 22

Movement (newsletter), 28

Moynihan, Daniel Patrick: on black families, 37–39

Ms magazine: grant of, to National Black Feminist Organization, 84, 151; letters in, on Eastern Regional Conference, 97–99; NBFO coverage in, 52; organization listings in, 82; Margaret Sloan and, 33

Murray, Pauli: and NOW, 33

Nash, Diane: and Student Nonviolent Coordinating Committee, 24, 25

National Alliance of Black Feminists (NABF), 1; administrative burdens of, 150; Alternative Schools of, 102–6; calendar of events of, 90–91; Cassandra Peten Defense Committee and, 89; cessation of, 142; class conflicts and, 124, 125–28; cost burden of, 145–46; development of, 53–56; funding of, 83, 85; leadership of, 158–59, 160; lesbianism and, 134–35; membership criteria of, 80; National Black Feminist Organization and, 52; national conferences of, 106; organizational structure of, 66, 66, 67, 71–72; sexuality and transgender issues and, 130, 133–34; statement of purpose of, 117, 188–89; successes of, 170; white feminists and, 155

National Association for the Advancement of Colored People (NAACP): finance and, 148; Montgomery bus boycott and, 22

National Association of Coloured Women: on race and gender work, 20

National Black Feminist Organization (NBFO), 1, 25, 33–34: administrative burdens of, 150–51; cessation of, 141–44; Chicago chapter of, 53–55; class conflicts and, 124–25; development of, 50–53; disruptive forces within, 162–64; Eastern Regional Conference of, 56–57, 58–59, 93–102; Brenda Eichelberger and, 53–55; funding of, 83, 84–85, 147; *Good Times* and, 42–43; homophobia of, 135–37; leadership of, 66–70, 67, 161–65; membership criteria of, 79, 80; membership numbers of, 81, 82; national conferences of, 106; organizational structure of, 66, 66,

Kimberly Springer is a lecturer in the American
Studies Department of King's College London,
University of London. She edited *Still Lifting, Still
Climbing: Contemporary African American Women's
Activism* (1999).

Library of Congress Cataloging-in-Publication Data
Springer, Kimberly, 1970–
Living for the revolution : Black feminist
organizations, 1968–1980 / Kimberly Springer.
p. cm.
Includes bibliographical references and index.
ISBN 0-8223-3481-x (cloth : alk. paper) —
ISBN 0-8223-3493-3 (pbk. : alk. paper)
1. Feminism—United States—History—20th
century. 2. African American feminists—Societies,
etc.—History—20th century. 3. African American
women—Societies and clubs—History—20th
century. I. Title.
HQ1421.S68   2005
305.42′089′96073—dc22
2004019865